DONKEY
CONS

DONKEY CONS

Sex, Crime, and Corruption in the Democratic Party

Lynn Vincent
and
Robert Stacy McCain

NELSON CURRENT

A Subsidiary of Thomas Nelson, Inc.

Authors are represented by the literary agency Alive Communications, Inc., 7680 Goddard Street, Suite 200, Colorado Springs, CO 80920.

Published in Nashville, Tennessee, by Nelson Current, a division of a wholly owned subsidary (Nelson Communications, Inc.) of Thomas Nelson, Inc.

Nelson Current books may be purchased in bulk for educational, business, fundraising, or sales promotional use. For information, please e-mail SpecialMarkets@ThomasNelson.com.

Library of Congress Cataloging-in-Publication Data
Vincent, Lynn.
    Donkey cons : sex, crime, and corruption in the Democratic Party / Lynn Vincent and Robert Stacy McCain.
    p. cm.
    Includes bibliographical references and index.
ISBN 1-59555-024-0
    1. Democratic Party (U.S.)   2. Political corruption—United States.   I. McCain, Robert Stacy. II. Title.
JK2316.V56   2006
324.2736—dc22   2006002276

Printed in the United States of America
06 07 08 09 QW 5 4 3 2 1

To Danny, my heart

—Lynn Vincent

To Lou Ann, who always believed

—Robert Stacy McCain

Contents

Prologue: The Fugitive   ix

1 Modus Operandi: 1
   "Guilty as Hell, Free as a Bird"

2 Rap Sheet: 17
   Corrupt Democrats Serving Time—and in Public Office

3 Roots of the Rot: 45
   The Democratic Party's Criminal Legacy

4 The Gang's All Here: 61
   Democrats and the Mob

5 The Union Label: 73
   Labor Unions' Death-Grip on the Democrats

6 International Criminals: 91
   The Party of Treason and Subversion

7 Aiding and Abetting: 109
   Democrats' Pro-Criminal Policies

8 Scene of the Crime: 135
   Creating the Urban Nightmare

CONTENTS

9   Fat Cats and Democrats: 157
    The Real "Party of the Rich"

10 Presidential Predators: 181
    Fondling the Body Politic

11 Logical Legacy: 193
    The Clinton Years

12 Honor among Thieves: 217
    Hip-Deep in the "Culture of Corruption"

    Acknowledgments   227

    About the Authors   229

    Notes   231

    Index   265

PROLOGUE

THE FUGITIVE

DANGEROUS. THE WORD OCCURS MORE THAN ONCE IN DESCRIPTIONS written by those who knew the man. He was ambitious, brilliant, handsome, but also deceptive, secretive, and utterly ruthless. A lawyer, war hero, and once a promising New York politician, he had burned all his bridges behind him for a daring gamble, a "fanciful conspiracy" that he hoped might yet elevate him to new heights of glory. But, as with so many criminal schemes, the dangerous man's plan had been betrayed. One of his accomplices had gotten cold feet and ratted him out to the authorities, and now his only hope was to outrun the law.[1]

Wanted for murder in New Jersey and with a $5,000 bounty on his head in New Orleans, he had managed with the aid of a clever lawyer to avoid a federal indictment in Kentucky. But authorities from Ohio to Tennessee were hunting him. Now he'd jumped bail in Mississippi and was on the run, hoping to make his escape to Florida. The law caught up with him one storm-soaked February near a muddy little Alabama crossroads called Wakefield. It was nearly midnight, and he and another accomplice were searching for the home of a friend, a place where they could hide out for the night. Lost, they asked a stranger for directions.

The man told them the way, but the place they were looking for was a good ways off, the roads were bad, and the stranger suggested they check into a nearby inn and wait until daylight.

The two travelers rejected this advice and kept moving, and this aroused the suspicion of the stranger, who was in fact a federal agent named Nicholas Perkins. Why, Perkins wondered, were the two men traveling through the middle of nowhere in the middle of the night? Surely they were up to no good. And one of the men matched the description of a fugitive who'd jumped bail in Mississippi two weeks earlier. It was his eyes. Large, deep-set, and luminous, his hazel eyes "sparkled like diamonds." Perkins quickly summoned help from a nearby army installation, bringing along a lieutenant and a handful of enlisted men, and soon this ad hoc federal posse confronted the fugitive on the muddy road.

The lieutenant addressed the fugitive, the one with the glittering eyes: "I presume, sir, that I have the honor of addressing Colonel Burr?"

Indeed, he did. For this federal fugitive, this ruthless killer, was Aaron Burr, the same man who, less than two years earlier, had been vice president of the United States—and one of the most important founders of what was to become the Democratic Party.

Democrats have long proclaimed Thomas Jefferson the founder of their party, the nation's oldest. But it was Aaron Burr who captured New York for the party in the pivotal 1800 election, making Jefferson president and securing the vice presidency for himself. Burr built a political machine that would remain a powerful force in New York's Democratic Party for more than one hundred years after his death. The Burr-Jefferson alliance, formed as early as 1791, made the Democrats a national power.[2]

By the early twenty-first century, the terms "Democrat" and "Republican" had solidified in the public mind as representing two clear-cut political philosophies, appealing to two easily identifiable constituencies, a difference so clear as to be reducible to a simple map of Republican "red" states and Democratic "blue" states. But this was not true in the nation's beginning—the Constitution says nothing about political parties—and, indeed, history books now customarily refer to Jefferson's party during its early years as the "Democratic-Republican" party. (They actually called themselves Republicans; "democrat" was a slur their rivals used to suggest that Jefferson and his friends were a dangerous and radical bunch devoted to mob rule.)

As if the "Democratic-Republican" party label was not confusing enough, the Democrats of Jefferson's day were devoted to principles that are almost the exact opposite of what Democrats stand for today. The original Democrats stood for the interests of slave-owning Southerners and Indian-fighting frontiersmen, and passionately defended the Second Amendment's guarantee of the right of citizens "to keep and bear arms." They favored a conservative "strict construction" approach to the Constitution, and advocated "states' rights" up to and including the right to secede from the Union.[3] In matters of foreign policy, the original Democrats were hawks and imperialists, accused of fomenting wars of conquest to appease their land-hungry supporters.

The political aims and principles of Democrats have changed so much since their founding that, even as early as the 1930s, they began revising history to hide their origins. Any visitor to Washington today can see the evidence of this, carved in stone at the Jefferson Memorial. Built during the triumphant era of Franklin Delano Roosevelt, the memorial was intended to give Democrats some symbolic credit in the nation's capital, which boasted a monument to George Washington and another to the first Republican president, Abraham Lincoln. Seven decades after the Civil War, slavery was a disreputable cause and FDR's New Deal programs had gone a long way toward breaking African Americans of their old allegiance to Lincoln's GOP. So in memorializing Jefferson, the famous author of the Declaration's statement that "all men are created equal," Democrats sought to depict their founder as a prophet of emancipation by chiseling in marble his words: "Nothing is more certainly written in the book of fate that these people are to be free."

This is a partial quote, however, and the Democrats of the 1930s, burnishing a technique that would become a Party standard, were advancing a half-truth. Jefferson genuinely believed slavery wrong and harmful to both black and white. His ideal solution, however, involved a taxpayer-supported scheme that would transport the freed slaves back to Africa and compensate slave owners for the loss of their property. The full quote from Jefferson's famous words, written in 1821, was this: "Nothing is more certainly written in the book of fate than that these people are to be free. *Nor is it less certain that the two races, equally free, cannot live in the same government. Nature, habit, opinion has drawn indelible lines of distinction between them*" (emphasis added).[4]

The Democrats' effort to suppress inconvenient and impolitic historical facts continues today. Consider this statement from the "History" page at the Web site of the Democratic National Committee: "Thomas Jefferson founded the Democratic Party in 1792 as a congressional caucus to fight for the Bill of Rights and against the elitist Federalist Party."[5]

Not a word about Aaron Burr on the site, and as much as DNC officials may wish to think that Jefferson founded their party in 1792 "to fight for the Bill of Rights" in Congress, there's one problem: Congress passed the Bill of Rights in its very first session in 1789, and by 1791 the first ten amendments to the Constitution were ratified by the necessary three-quarters of the states. And the "elitist Federalist Party" that Jefferson fought against just happened to be the party of George Washington. Indeed, it was Burr's long-held grudge against Washington that helped make Burr such a natural ally of Jefferson in forming what would become the Democratic Party.[6]

While party officials promote such distortions of the past, the true history of the Democratic Party is a tale of dishonesty, crime, and corruption. This saga, full of juicy details and little-known scandals, will be a rollicking read for the partisan Right. And though there will be a few jokes at the Democrats' expense, there is a serious purpose: the unveiling of the tragic story of how the nation's oldest political party has inspired, then cruelly betrayed, the hopes of millions of Americans, including many of our friends and dear members of our own families—as well as sincere and honest officials within the party itself.

PROLOGUE

We intend this book as an antidote to the half-truths and voter amnesia on which the Democratic Party has come to depend. Like their fugitive founder fleeing justice, today's Democrats think they can outrun the truth. But as Aaron Burr learned on that stormy night in Alabama, the truth eventually catches up.

1

MODUS OPERANDI

"GUILTY AS HELL, FREE AS A BIRD"

"How long, O Catiline, will you abuse our patience? . . . Do you not know that your plans have been detected? Do you not see that your conspiracy is understood by us all?"
— MARCUS TULLIUS CICERO[1]

ON SEPTEMBER 11, 2001, THE *NEW YORK TIMES* PUBLISHED A FRONT-page feature about Billy Ayers and his wife, Bernardine Dohrn, two former leaders of the Weather Underground. A violent offshoot of Students for a Democratic Society (SDS), the Weathermen took their name from a Bob Dylan song, "Subterranean Homesick Blues," which included the lyrics, "You don't need a weatherman to know which way the wind blows." According to Dohrn, Ayers, and the other young radicals who formed the Weather Underground in 1969, the forecast was clear: student protests against the Vietnam War and other purported ills of "Amerikkka" were harbingers of violent Marxist revolution in the United States, and they intended to lead that revolution.[2]

In 1970, Ayers described what that revolution would mean: "Kill all the rich people. . . . Bring the revolution home, kill your parents, that's where it's really at."[3]

1

The Weather Underground claimed credit for a dozen bombings from San Francisco to New York. In 1971, they bombed the U.S. Capitol. A year later, they bombed the Pentagon. In December 1980, after living for years as fugitives, Dohrn and Ayers surrendered to the FBI. They were briefly jailed, but all charges against them were eventually dropped, prompting Ayers to brag later: "Guilty as hell. Free as a bird."[4]

The *New York Times* feature story in 2001 was headlined "No Regrets for a Love of Explosives" and was intended to hype Ayers's new book about his underground experience, *Fugitive Days*. Ayers was unapologetic: "I don't regret setting bombs. I feel we didn't do enough."[5]

Just hours after that issue of the *New York Times* hit the street, Islamic terrorists hijacked four airplanes and committed one of the greatest terrorist acts in history, killing nearly three thousand people and destroying New York's World Trade Center. Suddenly, warm and fuzzy features about unapologetic bombers weren't so cute. Ayers apparently realized this and wrote a letter to the *Times*, attempting to disown his defense of criminal violence as a means to achieve political ends, saying his book was actually "a condemnation of terrorism in all its forms."[6]

But terrorism is terrorism, whether committed by Islamic jihadists or affluent American college students (Ayers's father was chairman of a major utility corporation). What was telling about the *New York Times'* profile of Ayers was that it described him and his Weather Underground colleagues as "radicals" rather than terrorists. Editors of the *Times* understand that in media-speak, "terrorist" is a term that denotes bad guys: Bomb a clinic to protest abortion, and you're a terrorist. Bomb the Pentagon to protest a war, and you're a radical. *Times* editors could not bring themselves to apply the word "terrorist" to Marxist revolutionaries like Ayers and Dohrn, and adopted instead the euphemism favored by Ayers and his fellow travelers.

Ayers's subsequent disavowal notwithstanding, the *Times*'s celebration of an unapologetic terrorist was a perfect expression of one of the most important ideas of the '60s student Left. In 1965, Brandeis University

professor Herbert Marcuse expounded his doctrine of "progressive tolerance." Refuting traditional liberal ideas of tolerance elaborated by John
Stuart Mill and others, Marcuse said that progressive values required the
"suppression" of right-wing or "regressive" movements: "Liberating tolerance, then, would mean intolerance against movements from the Right,
and toleration of movements from the Left."[7] This ideology has had the
effect, observed by economist Thomas Sowell, of dividing the population
into "mascots" (minorities, women, labor unions, etc.) and "targets" (the
military, corporate executives, fundamentalist Christians, etc.).[8]

So it was that the most prestigious and influential newspaper in
America lent its pages to a scarcely disguised advertisement for a book by
a self-confessed bomber. Why? The Vietnam War is long over, Ayers is
not a celebrity, and it would be easy enough to ignore him as an obscure
criminal kook. (When was the last time you saw a major news story or
book about Charles Manson or the Unabomber?) The answer is that
Ayers represents an idea, an era, and a movement that profoundly shaped
the modern Democratic Party. To promote Ayers and celebrate the "radical" cause he represented is to promote and celebrate the Democrats who
shared that cause—and still share it today.

It's not just '60s radicals who get a pass. It seems almost any crime can
be excused or ignored if the perpetrator is a Democrat. A married
Democratic mayor can be caught smoking crack cocaine with a prostitute
and, even after he is convicted and sentenced to prison, manage to return
to public office. A married Democratic senator who leaves a party with a
single young woman and gets into a drunk-driving accident that kills her
does not merely avoid jail time, but retains his Senate seat and indeed
goes on to become one of the most powerful politicians in his party.
Wholesale corruption, election fraud, kickbacks, bribery, espionage, treason—if you're a Democrat, such acts apparently are never major scandals,
and certainly are never portrayed by the major media as evidence that you
or your party are untrustworthy.

At times, being a Democrat is like holding the "get out of jail free" card in a Monopoly game—almost. Plenty of Democrats do manage to find their way into prison. Yet no one seems to have noticed the pattern in this criminal behavior.

When we conceived the idea for this book, we researched the topic and were surprised to find that no book like it had ever been written. There were plenty of ideological attacks on this or that aspect of liberalism, and lots of books about this or that wrongdoing of the Clinton administration. But no one had ever tried to fit all the scandals of the Democratic Party into a single book. Once we started doing it, we quickly discovered why. The problem wasn't a shortage of Democratic cheats and crooks, but an astounding abundance of them—a veritable cornucopia of corruption, a direct line of scandal all the way back to the 1700s. After just a few days of digging up Democratic scoundrels, it began to appear that the main difference between the Democrats and the Gambino mob is that Democrats qualify for federal matching funds—and at least the Gambinos have never pretended to advance the cause of "social justice."

Here are a few of the amazing stories we discovered:

- The forgotten role of the killer and traitor Aaron Burr in founding the Democratic Party and turning a New York social club into the most powerful and enduring political machine in American history, Tammany Hall. (Chapter Three)

- How gangsters wielded influence over the Democratic Party for much of the twentieth century. Lucky Luciano bragged that his mob pals delivered the 1932 Democratic presidential nomination to Franklin Delano Roosevelt; Harry Truman was the protégé of the Mafia-backed political machine that made Kansas City "a seething cauldron of crime"; and Joseph Kennedy sought assistance from Chicago's Giancana mob to help his son John win the crucial state of Illinois in the 1960 presidential election. (Chapter Four)

- The astonishing corruption and criminality of some Big Labor bosses—including those with mob ties—who fleece their unions' rank-and-file and then deliver big bucks to Democrats' campaign coffers. (Chapter Five)

- Treason and espionage by top Democrats like Soviet spy Alger Hiss, a trusted FDR aide, and support given to America's enemies by Democrats like the congressman who went to Baghdad at the height of prewar tensions and declared that Saddam could be trusted, while asserting that the White House was likely lying. (Chapter Six)

- Democrats who ignore the suffering of victims and take the side of criminals, including rapists, robbers, and cop-killers, even going so far as pushing to allow convicted felons to vote—based on academic research showing that nearly 70 percent of the criminal class would vote for Democrats, if given the chance. (Chapter Seven)

- The brazen corruption of big-city Democrats—from Chicago to Atlanta to Philadelphia to New Orleans to Detroit—who preside over empires of graft and fraud while their policies bring nightmares of crime and squalor to the inner-city poor who are among the Democratic Party's most loyal supporters. (Chapter Eight)

- And, finally, the eight-year carnival of sleaze and unprecedented scandal that was the Clinton administration—arguably the logical culmination of every corrupt tendency of the Democratic Party. (Chapter Eleven)

Two Americas, Two Standards

If the Democratic Party is such a corrupt organization, one may ask, why does it endure? In a free country, why would this party be supported by a large percentage of Americans? The first and most obvious reason is that Democrats generally have the good fortune of running against Republicans (whom John Stuart Mill may or may not have had in mind when he referred to conservatives as "the stupid party"[9]). Republicans have committed their own share of criminal wrongdoing and political sleaze—the Whiskey Ring scandal during the Grant administration, Teapot Dome during the presidency of Warren Harding, and of course, Watergate during the Nixon years.

Some liberal author might want to write a book detailing every GOP scoundrel ever caught with his ethics down. But this is not that book. Besides, an accounting of crimes and corruption involving individual politicians of either party could go on forever—especially if we drilled down to the state and local level—and prove nothing. What is important here is a *pattern* of behavior by the Democratic Party. That pattern extends beyond the fact that the best available catalogs of corrupt U.S. politicians, though admittedly incomplete, show Democrats substantially outnumbering Republicans among those convicted of serious crimes (see Chapter Two).

Scandals generally have a devastating effect on the careers of Republicans, and partisan loyalty doesn't seem to prevent Republicans from sending their fellow Republicans to jail. Many Americans know Bob Barr as the former Georgia congressman who helped lead the team of House Republicans who impeached Bill Clinton in 1998. (Barr had actually called for Clinton's impeachment *before* the Monica Lewinsky affair.) But folks in Georgia remember Barr as the Reagan-era federal prosecutor responsible for sending to prison a fellow *Republican* (a Christian conservative congressman with the unfortunate-sounding name of Swindall) convicted of perjury.[10] When Rep. Randy "Duke" Cunningham was convicted in November 2005 of accepting $2.4 million in bribes from a defense contractor, there were no Republicans claiming that the California congressman was the victim of a "partisan witch hunt" since Cunningham was brought down by a team of federal prosecutors led by Bush-appointed U.S. Attorney Carol Chien-Hua Lam.[11]

Democrats seem to routinely survive scandals that might have a career-ending impact for Republicans. Many in the GOP defended Nixon during the Watergate scandal, but in the end it was Republican leaders, including conservative icon Barry Goldwater, who convinced Nixon to resign rather than put the country through an impeachment ordeal.[12] When it was revealed that House Speaker Bob Livingston had carried on an adulterous affair, he resigned in disgrace.[13] When South Dakota Rep. Bill Janklow was convicted of manslaughter in an auto accident, he resigned in disgrace.[14] Implicated in similar scandals, Democrats like Bill Clinton, Barney Frank, and Ted Kennedy were vigorously defended by their fellow Democrats and remained in office.

Why this double standard? We'll let former Sen. John Edwards explain. While campaigning for his party's 2004 presidential nomination, the North Carolina Democrat told an Iowa audience that the Bush administration had divided the nation into "two Americas":

One America that does the work, another America that reaps the reward. One America that pays the taxes, another America that gets the tax breaks. One America that will do anything to leave its children a better life, another America that never has to do a thing because its children are already set for life. One America—middle-class America—whose needs Washington has long forgotten, another America—narrow-interest America—whose every wish is Washington's command. One America that is struggling to get by, another America that can buy anything it wants, even a Congress and a President.[15]

Edwards was lying—in Chapter Nine we'll see which is the *real* "party of the rich"—but that's not the point. The point is that millions of Democratic voters evidently believe this kind of class-warfare rhetoric. They sincerely seem to think, as Al Gore proclaimed, that Democrats fight "for the people, not the powerful."[16]

It is tempting to dismiss Democrats like Gore and Edwards (both rather wealthy men, by the way) as cynical, dishonest demagogues. But consider a far more frightening possibility: *What if they really believe it?* What if Democrats really believe that they are protecting America from the depredations of those whom a *New York Times* columnist called "crony capitalists," "corporate insiders," and "malefactors of great wealth"?[17] Democrats' belief that they are fighting against such powerful evils—and if Democratic politicians don't really believe this, their millions of loyal voters obviously do—draws them into the Marcusean conceit of "progressive tolerance." The ends justify the means. What's a little graft, a little corruption, a drowned campaign worker, or a scandal that's "just about sex" to a party doing battle against the rapacious forces of greed and oppression?

So it is that sincere and idealistic Americans can support the Democrats and ignore even irrefutable evidence of corruption. And those who believe their cause is worth dying for will sometimes also think their cause is worth killing for.

"Such a Great Adventure"

When radicals like Ayers and Dohrn called for war against the "Establishment," their radicalism was echoed by many others, including one student who was recognized as a voice of her generation. In her 1969 Wellesley College commencement address, she touched on issues of peace and war, poverty, and civil rights. She blended philosophical ruminations with notes of narcissistic Baby Boomer self-celebration: "We're searching for a more immediate, ecstatic and penetrating mode of living," she said. But the Wellesley grad also talked about "a lot of New Left, collegiate protests" which she described as "a very unique American experience" and "such a great adventure." Employing the terminology then trendy among young campus radicals, she talked about liberation: "A liberation enabling each of us to fulfill our capacity so as to be free to create within and around ourselves."[18]

Gibberish? Of course, but just the sort of gibberish that was taken very seriously in 1969. She got a seven-minute ovation, and the Wellesley speech landed her in the pages of *Life* magazine.[19] She was thus something of a celebrity when she arrived in New Haven, Connecticut, as a

Yale University law student in the fall of 1969, and leapt into a controversy that forever linked campus radicals with one of the most violent criminal gangs in American history.

The Black Panthers are now venerated in media memory as merely a militant expression of the civil rights movement. They were in fact a conspiracy of murderous gangsters, founded on an explicit rejection of Martin Luther King's doctrine of nonviolence. Led chiefly by ex-convicts—thieves, rapists, and drug dealers—the Panthers spouted Marxist rhetoric while perpetrating crimes large and small. They murdered policemen. They made national headlines by kidnapping a federal judge and blowing his brains out with a shotgun. Wherever the Panthers went, violent crime followed—much of that crime committed against the black people whom they were supposed to be "liberating."[20]

On May 21, 1969, a Connecticut fisherman named John Mroczka made a grisly discovery in the Coginchaug River: the body of a twenty-four-year-old black man named Alex Rackley. His hands were bound, and he had been beaten, severely burned, and shot twice.[21]

Alex Rackley had been a Black Panther. It was perhaps coincidental that, two days before Rackley's body was found near Middlefield, Connecticut, the national chairman of the Black Panther Party, Bobby Seale, had given a speech at Yale University, twenty-five miles away in New Haven. It is certain that the Panthers tortured and killed Rackley, a member of the gang's Harlem chapter who had arrived in New Haven on May 17. The Panthers had become suspicious that police had infiltrated their ranks; in fact, as one lawyer in the case would later recall, the police "had everything wired and tapped" at the headquarters of the New Haven Panthers. But the Panthers wrongly suspected an informer was in their midst and, for reasons never fully explained, suspicion focused on Rackley. The young Panther was sadistically tortured, burned with cigarettes, and at one point doused with scalding water. Finally, he was taken to the river and shot dead.[22]

Police immediately arrested eight Panthers, while other suspects in Rackley's death fled New Haven. Eventually, as many as fifteen Black

Panthers were charged in connection with the murder of Alex Rackley, but the principal suspects became known as the "New Haven Nine" and were a *cause célèbre* of the radical Left.[23]

Three Panthers quickly pleaded guilty. George Sams Jr. had fled to Canada after Rackley's murder, but was apprehended within three months. Sams, who had led the interrogation and torture of Rackley, pleaded guilty to second-degree murder charges on December 1, 1969, telling police that the suspected informer had been murdered "on direct orders from Bobby Seale"—the national chairman of the Panthers. Sams named Warren Kimbro and Lonnie McLucas as Rackley's killers. When Sams pleaded guilty, another Panther defendant, Loretta Luckes, changed her plea to guilty on conspiracy charges. Kimbro, who admitted shooting Rackley in the head, pleaded guilty to second-degree murder on January 16, 1970.[24]

In March 1970, Seale was extradited to New Haven to stand trial on murder and conspiracy charges, and the campus at Yale University soon boiled over with protests in support of Seale and the other accused Panthers. Now a first-year Yale Law student, the Wellesley grad who had praised the "great adventure" of New Left protests was in the thick of it. Under the mentorship of left-wing professor Thomas "Tommie the Commie" Emerson, she took charge of a group of Yale Law students monitoring the Panthers' trial for civil rights violations. She worked closely with Panther lawyer Charles Garry, and her role involved visiting Black Panther headquarters "to obtain documentation and other information."[25]

In support of the Panthers, the Yale student government voted April 20 for a campus-wide strike. The next day, at a gathering of 4,500 students, a black assistant professor demanded that they "close down" the university. A campus group called the United Front for Black Panther Party Defense called for a "stoppage of all normal activities" at Yale. These actions effectively ended the school year at Yale—by April 22, about 80 percent of students had stopped attending class. The student strike was supported by the highest authorities at the university.[26]

The strike escalated to massive protests. For three days, May 1–3, 15,000 protesters gathered for campus demonstrations in support of the Panthers. To keep peace in New Haven, 4,000 federal troops were flown in to support local police and Connecticut state troopers. On the night of May 1, a group of about 1,500 student protesters poured onto the New Haven town green, where radical leader Jerry Rubin gave a speech declaring "to free Bobby Seale, we have to go to the only court left, the court of the streets." Responding to this expression of vigilantism, the protesters started throwing rocks and bottles at police, who responded with tear gas.[27]

While pro-Panther protests shut down the Yale campus, the Panther trials continued. In August 1970, after six days of jury deliberation, Lonnie McLucas was convicted of conspiracy to murder and sentenced to twelve to fifteen years in prison. In November, Bobby Seale went on trial along with Ericka Huggins, with Yale Law students assisting the defense. More than one thousand prospective jurors were interviewed in the jury selection process, which took four months, helping to make the six-month trial the longest in Connecticut history.[28]

The jury deadlocked. On May 25, 1971, Judge Harold H. Mulvey declared a mistrial and—saying that publicity about the case would make it impossible to get an unbiased jury for a second trial—dismissed the charges against Seale and Huggins. Huggins went free, while Seale was handed over to Illinois authorities for trial in the "Chicago 7" conspiracy case. None of the Panthers suffered meaningful consequences for the hideous torture and brutal murder of Alex Rackley. Huggins eventually was elected to a California school board. Kimbro served only four years, and upon his release received a graduate scholarship to Harvard University, eventually becoming a dean at a Connecticut state college. By 1977, only McLucas was still in prison.[29]

Many have credited the Yale campus protests—and the volunteer legal assistance provided by Yale Law students—for the fact that Alex Rackley's killers achieved the same "guilty as hell, free as a bird" status as the Weather Underground terrorists. The young Wellesley alumna who organized those student volunteers was Hillary Rodham. Her work with Charles Garry on behalf of the Panthers who murdered Rackley helped earn Hillary an internship in the offices of veteran Communist lawyer Robert Treuhaft.[30]

It might seem remarkable, perhaps even newsworthy, that a former first lady, U.S. senator, and perhaps future presidential candidate once would have been a defender of the Black Panthers, a murderous gang who styled themselves after Marxist revolutionaries. (Recall how, when three ex-convicts with ties to white supremacist prison gangs murdered a black man in Texas, media attention focused heavily on then Gov. George W. Bush.[31]) Yet in all her encounters with the media—interviews with Tim Russert, Diane Sawyer, Larry King, Barbara Walters, and others—it appears Hillary Rodham Clinton has never been asked about her role in the New Haven Panther trials. Amazingly, although the story of her participation in the Panthers' defense has been recounted in almost every major biography of Hillary, some persist in declaring that this is an "urban legend."[32]

As a Democrat, Hillary is judged by a standard that goes beyond Bill Ayers's maxim. She is guilty as hell, free as a bird. And no questions asked.

If this phenomenon involved only Hillary Clinton, it would scarcely be worth a magazine article, much less an entire book. But Hillary is just one of many Democrats who have benefited from the apparently widespread notion that Democratic scandals are never really scandals—they're the work of a "vast right-wing conspiracy," as Mrs. Clinton declared.

If that doesn't work, then there's always the "old news" tactic: how dare those mean-spirited Republicans bring up something that happened in the distant past? When it comes to Democratic wrongdoing, "distant past" can sometimes mean anything that occurred more than twenty-four hours ago. The rise of the 24/7 news cycle in the era of cable TV news, talk radio, and the Internet has been accompanied by a shrinking of the American attention span, a phenomenon the Clinton administration exploited to blunt the impact of scandals. In January 1998, when Americans first heard the name "Monica Lewinsky," the president's own pollster told him that, if it were proven that he had lied under oath, Americans would expect him to resign. "Well, we'll just have to win, then," Clinton replied.[33] The Clintons bought time—he with his finger-wagging denial, she with her talk of a conspiracy—while their aides and allies promoted the idea that Monica was just a love-struck fat girl, a "stalker" whose conversations with Linda Tripp were mere romantic fantasies.[34] The focus of the story shifted as the media's "Team Clinton" (almost 90 percent of the Washington press corps had voted for the Democrat in 1992[35]) ignored evidence of perjury and witness tampering, instead propagandizing the public with the White House spin: it's just about sex, and everybody lies about sex.[36]

By the time President Clinton testified to a federal grand jury in August 1998, Americans had spent seven months listening to the White House talking points. Then, and only then, did the administration admit the truth. It wasn't the GOP, but the DNA, that proved Clinton a liar. And yet the stain on Monica's blue dress—irrefutable proof of what most Americans had said in January would require a presidential resignation—might as well have been ranch dressing, for all the impact it had on Clinton's fate. Seven months is forever in modern politics, and Clinton wasn't about to resign because of "old news."

Just as Americans had forgotten their January outrage over *l'affaire* Lewinsky, so too were they expected to forget how Clinton's defenders had smeared Paula Jones, Gennifer Flowers, and other previous accusers. After the House voted to impeach him in December 1998, President Clinton declared: "It is something I have felt strongly all my life. We must stop the politics of personal destruction. We must get rid of the poisonous venom of excessive partisanship, obsessive animosity, and uncontrolled anger."[37] Democrats actually *applauded* this colossal lie—knowing that the president's supporters were even then aiming such destruction at the GOP, and any Republican in Congress who'd ever gotten a divorce or had an affair was a potential target. Newt Gingrich, Bob Livingston, Bob Barr, Dan Burton, Henry Hyde—none of them had ever lied under oath during a sexual-harassment case. None of those Republicans had solicited false affidavits or tried to hustle a potentially damaging witness out of town to a job arranged by a crony. And none of those Republicans had ever been accused of receiving sexual gratification from a government employee while discussing matters of national security with a congressman on the telephone. But while the sexual improprieties of these Republicans had no relevance to the charges against the president, after seven months of spin, Team Clinton had completely changed the subject: "It's about sex." Therefore, Dan Burton's illegitimate child was fair game, as were Bob Barr's divorce records and the ancient dalliances of Henry Hyde.[38]

It's hard to scandalize a party that is utterly immune to shame and that apparently thinks America is a nation of amnesiacs. Chappaquiddick? "Old news!" But Ted Kennedy's still in the Senate, and Mary Jo Kopechne is still dead.

Consider, for a moment, the possibility that the Lewinsky scandal actually saved Clinton's presidency. In the months before Monica became the world's most famous intern, Republicans in Congress had been investigating a crime of historic proportions. Evidence indicated that the Clinton-Gore 1996 reelection campaign had solicited and accepted millions of dollars in illegal contributions from foreign donors, including money connected to agents of the communist Chinese government. Overnight, and quite conveniently, the explosion of a lurid sex scandal pushed the illegal fund-raising story out of the headlines. And by the time the impeachment imbroglio ended, the Chinagate scandal was—can you guess?—old news (see Chapter Eleven).

Maybe Democrats think Americans are stupid. (They may be half right; 48 percent of voters apparently thought John Kerry would make a good president.) But just how stupid do they think we are? At this writing, Nancy Pelosi and her friends are talking about how Democrats will win control of Congress in 2006 by campaigning against a *Republican* "culture of corruption." This book was conceived more than two years ago, when no one outside Washington had heard of a lobbyist named Jack

Abramoff. (Democrats have reportedly pocketed something over $3 million from Abramoff's clients since 1997, as we'll see in Chapter Twelve.) If Democrats try to make "corruption" the central issue of their campaign, they'll surely lose—and we'll probably sell a lot more books.

Hey, Nancy: You go, girl!

2

RAP SHEET

CORRUPT DEMOCRATS SERVING TIME—AND IN PUBLIC OFFICE

"When the Constitution was framed no respectable person
called himself or herself a democrat."
—MARY R. BEARD, *AMERICA IN MIDPASSAGE,* 1939

WITH A FAT BRIBE, A PAIR OF THIEVES KNOWN AS "THE ROMANO brothers," and a parking-lot rendezvous with an undercover agent, the saga of Alcee Hastings reads like a Quentin Tarantino screenplay. Except that Tarantino's criminal characters don't usually wind up winning seats in Congress.[1]

In 1980, Hastings served as a U.S. District judge in Florida. The Romano brothers, Frank and Tom, had been convicted in his courtroom of stealing about $1 million from the Teamsters pension fund. As part of their penalty, Hastings in 1981 ordered the seizure of $1.2 million of the Romano's assets, including $845,000 in cash. By that time, William Borders Jr., a rising star in Washington legal circles, had become involved in the case, and the final judgment on the asset forfeiture was still pending. Hastings and Borders concocted a scheme: Frank Romano would pay Hastings $150,000 in cash. In return, Hastings would use his judicial power to ensure that most of the Romanos' assets were returned to them.[2]

17

At first, the bribery scheme unfolded as planned. Working through intermediaries to keep distance between himself and the Romanos, Borders secured from Frank Romano $25,000 in cash, a down payment that the lawyer then delivered to Hastings. But neither the lawyer nor the judge counted on William Dredge. Facing criminal charges himself, Dredge told federal prosecutors that a Washington lawyer named Borders had directed him to solicit a $150,000 bribe for a federal judge named Hastings. Suddenly, Dredge found himself working as a government informant. He arranged a face-to-face between Borders and Frank Romano, whom the lawyer had never met.[3]

But this "Romano" was actually a retired FBI agent working undercover. On October 9, 1981, the undercover agent met Borders in the parking lot of a Washington hotel, slipped into his car, and placed a bag on the seat containing $125,000 in cash. Borders didn't even make it out of the parking lot before FBI agents nailed him. U.S. attorneys indicted and tried both Borders and Alcee Hastings. Borders went to prison. Hastings, however, claimed Borders had used him as a dupe, and a jury in 1983 acquitted him. But a few years later, Judge Frank Johnson of the 11th Circuit Court of Appeals wrote in a decision upholding the Borders conviction that the jury also had sufficient evidence to find "beyond any reasonable doubt that Judge Hastings was a member of such a conspiracy."[4]

That led to a judicial ethics complaint against Hastings. A five-judge panel concluded in 1987 that, during his trial, Hastings had lied thirty-two times. After an investigation, the House Judiciary Committee, which holds sway over federal judges, recommended impeachment. But Hastings remained on the federal bench, drawing a full salary. In 1988, the House finally charged Hastings with seventeen acts of misconduct, including the bribery charge. The Senate found him guilty of eight impeachable charges and booted him off the federal bench in 1989. Undaunted, Hastings declared on the Capitol steps, "My momma had a *man*," and returned to Florida where he had become a celebrity victim railroaded by The Man.[5]

Hastings appealed. Then he ran for Congress. During his 1992 campaign, his opponent hammered on Hastings's impeachment and removal. But that same year, a U.S. district court, citing a technicality, overturned Hastings's judicial ouster. For Hastings, things seemed to be looking up. Voters even sent him to Congress. But just as he was being sworn in, the U.S. Supreme Court reversed the district court and upheld the Senate's decision to strip Hastings of his judicial robes. No matter, Hastings declared: impeachment law didn't affect his congressional seat (even though rules governing his judicial ouster prohibit booted judges from "hold[ing] . . . any office of honor, trust, or profit under the United States").[6]

Today, Hastings, a disgraced former federal judge whom the U.S. Senate declared guilty of accepting a six-figure bribe from two Italian thugs and then lying about it thirty-two times is in his seventh term representing Florida's 23rd District.

Alcee Hastings is a Democrat.

While Hastings's career includes an unusual dose of intrigue, in many ways it typifies the crime-pocked, consequence-dodging nature of the Democratic Party. Elected officials like Barney Frank (D-Massachusetts), Corrine Brown (D-Florida), and Ted Kennedy (D-Massachusetts) have proven that it is not only possible but routine for serious corruption and national-level public service to coexist within their party.

Are there Republican crooks? Absolutely. Our analysis of the Political Graveyard, a nonpartisan Web site that parses local, state, and federal politicians into numerous categories (nationality, awards won, religion practiced, and so forth), shows forty-nine Republicans born in the twentieth century who were convicted, pleaded guilty or no contest, or were censured or expelled by a government body. We didn't count members of third parties or people whose party we couldn't determine. We didn't count mere arrests—such as the two Democrats arrested while soliciting sex from policewomen posing as prostitutes. Neither did we tally two Democrats jailed after public demonstrations. We also cut Democratic Illinois state Sen. John Linebaugh Knuppel a break, judging that his refusal to wear a tie in court didn't rise to the level of corruption, even though he went to jail for it.[7]

Even with those concessions, Democratic double-dealers listed on the Political Graveyard far outnumbered GOP crooks: 88 to 49. It is interesting to note that Lawrence Kestenbaum, who owns and maintains the site, is an attorney, a member of the liberal activist group Amnesty International—and an elected Democrat in Washtenaw County, Michigan. Still, Kestenbaum notes that his list of corrupt politicians is "very incomplete," highlighting what we noted in Chapter One: that it would be nearly impossible to compile an exhaustive tally of crooked politicians. (As political humorist P. J. O'Rourke observed, "When buying and selling are controlled by legislation, the first things to be bought and sold are legislators."[8])

But as with the Political Graveyard, snapshots are available. Going back as far as 1975, we canvassed multiple sources, locating every member of Congress we could find who pleaded guilty; was convicted, expelled, censured, reprimanded, admonished, significantly fined, or received a disciplinary letter for serious misconduct; or, as in the case of Sen. Robert Torricelli, resigned under credible allegations of corruption or criminality.

Of sixty-one members, more than three quarters were Democrats. Two Republicans—John McCain of Arizona and Tom DeLay of Texas—still serve in Congress. In addition to Alcee Hastings, four other Democrats with histories of crime or corruption are still members. Here they are, in alphabetical order.

Corrine Brown

"She's a crook," activist Democrat Andy Brown said of the Florida congresswoman in a 2000 interview with the *Weekly Standard*. "There are 50 reasons why the woman should be in jail."[9] The bombastic Brown isn't in jail yet—she's still in the U.S. House of Representatives, hanging on to her seat despite a career shot through with scandal. In 1992, Brown ran for Congress, vying for a seat in a poor district. During and after her campaign, she misplaced, misappropriated, or misreported tens of thousands of campaign dollars, including $81,000 in preelection contributions. She also used money from a nonfederal campaign account, accepted donations from foreign citizens, and failed to report the use of a corporate plane.[10]

While in Congress, Brown sold a Tallahassee travel agency she owned, but failed to disclose the $40,000 deal in the annual financial report required by Congress. But she did disclose the sale of her Jacksonville travel agency for between $50,000 and $100,000 to Emilio F. Torres and partners in 1993. Subsequent financial reports claimed that the buyers owed her that much money. But state records show that Torres' group didn't buy the business—they only took over the lease when Brown fell more than $7,000 behind in rent. Meanwhile, the Airlines Reporting Corporation sued Brown in a U.S. District Court, claiming she owed $94,000 for unpaid transactions involving airline tickets sold through her travel agencies. Their claim was apparently on point: Brown paid the $94,000 and the suit was dismissed.[11]

Brown later narrowly escaped bribery charges in connection with her lobbying activities on behalf of Gambian businessman Foutanga Sissoko. After Sissoko was convicted of bribing U.S. Customs officials, Brown scribbled a letter to Attorney General Janet Reno requesting leniency. Three months later, the CEO of Sissoko's company sent Brown's daughter, Shantrel, a gift: a $50,000 Lexus. Brown has also been fined by the Federal Election Commission, dinged by the IRS for five-figure tax-filing omissions, and come under scrutiny for mysterious acquisitions of large sums of cash, bounced paychecks to employees, and a $10,000 check drawn on the secret money-laundering account of a Baptist minister under federal indictment.[12]

Barney Frank

The openly gay member of Congress never married the male gigolo who turned his Capitol Hill townhouse into a brothel. In fact, Barney Frank at first paid Steve Gobie $80 per visit—a crime in all fifty states. Frank met Gobie through a rather, well . . . frank personal ad in a gay newspaper, and later hired him as a driver and housekeeper. Sweet deal for Gobie, who lassoed not only a high-powered sugar daddy, but also a swanky trick pad where he could continue moonlighting as a hooker. Frank, who said he didn't know Gobie had turned their love nest into the Chicken Ranch east, was reprimanded by Congress in 1990 after he admitted preparing a memo containing misleading statements that could be "perceived as an attempt to use political influence" to fix his lover's parking tickets. Democratic voters don't care: Frank has since been reelected in a series of increasingly lopsided landslides.[13]

Jim Moran

This Virginia Democrat once told *Washingtonian* magazine that had he not pursued politics, he might have tried professional boxing. "I like to hit people," he explained.[14] While serving as mayor of Alexandria, he slammed a man against the bar in a pub near the Potomac River. But that wasn't his worst offense while holding local office. While serving as a city councilman, he was indicted on conflict-of-interest charges for casting a vote that helped a developer friend secure a lucrative land deal. Charged by state prosecutors with violating Virginia's conflict-of-interest law, Moran sobbed as he pleaded guilty to felony vote-peddling. He received a year's probation on a reduced misdemeanor charge and was forced to resign.

But that didn't stop Democratic voters from electing Moran to Congress, where he shored up his reputation for settling disagreements with his temper and his fists. Capitol police rushed to subdue him when he threw a punch at Rep. Randall "Duke" Cunningham in 1995. On another occasion, during a floor debate, the gentleman from Virginia screamed at Indiana Republican Dan Burton, "I'll break your nose!" In 2000, Moran reportedly put a chokehold on an eight-year-old kid whom he accused of trying to carjack him.[15]

Bobby Rush

In June 1969, the Federal Bureau of Investigation launched a series of raids on the offices of the Black Panthers, who styled themselves a community organization while spouting the slogan "Off the pigs." By then, Panther cells had also developed a rap sheet that included harboring fugitives, torturing and killing suspected informers—like Alex Rackley—and stockpiling illegal weapons. After a series of June raids and arrests in Chicago, Denver, and Salt Lake City, five Chicago policemen were wounded in a gun battle at the offices of the Illinois Panthers. Bobby Rush, the Illinois Panther's "deputy minister of defense," who had in 1968 gone AWOL from the Army, claimed the police "pulled up in front of the office, jumped out of the car and started shooting."[16] Police said the shooting started when a pair of patrolmen stopped two men, who appeared to be carrying sawed-off shotguns, in front of the Panther offices. When the officers left the patrol car to investigate, the two men fled into the Panther offices and opened fire on the police.

Just over four months later, on December 4, another shootout erupted in Chicago when police raided the apartment home of Illinois Panther chairman Fred Hampton. Police said they were acting on a warrant based on information that Hampton was stockpiling weapons there. Sergeant Daniel Groth pounded on the door with his pistol butt, announced that he had a warrant, and opened the door just as it exploded, blown to splinters by a shotgun blast. Black Panther Mark Clark, inside the apartment, had fired through the door from a range of fifteen inches, a grand jury later found. The grand jury also found that two policeman came through the front door shooting. More officers from the raiding party poured into the apartment through the back door, also shooting. In the ensuing gun battle, more than a hundred shots were fired, killing both Hampton and Clark. The Panthers said Hampton was "murdered in his bed."[17] The grand jury later found that only one round came from Panther weapons and that police who entered through the front door mistook shots from

23

fellow officers entering the rear of the apartment as return fire from the Panthers. Hampton, it turned out, had been killed in his bedroom by stray police bullets fired through the living room wall.

Four days later, Bobby Rush, the only prominent Illinois Panther not present at either raid, surrendered to police on charges of failing to register a weapon. But Illinois voters were apparently willing to forgive Rush's gangland résumé. They elected him a Chicago alderman in 1983. In 1992, they elected him to Congress. Rush, who still serves in the House, says that if he had it to do over again, he wouldn't advocate violence. But he notes that his Black Panther years "were an essential part of my development, and helped create the bedrock for my political career. Back then, I developed a commitment to making individual sacrifices for group advancement."[18]

Among those who made the crime and corruption list, but no longer serve in Congress:

- **Rep. Wayne L. Hays (D-Ohio), 1976:** Resigned before hearings could begin on charges of his retaining an "employee on public payroll for immoral purposes." For nearly two years, Hays, then sixty-four, paid twenty-seven-year-old Elizabeth Ray $14,000 a year, she told the *Washington Post*, to service him sexually for a few hours a week. Hays denied the charge: "Hell's fire! I'm a very happily married man," he said.

  Ray, however, was adamant: "I can't type, I can't file, I can't even answer the phone. . . . Supposedly, I'm on the oversight committee. But I call it the Out-of-Sight Committee."[19]

- **Rep. Charles C. Diggs Jr. (D-Michigan), 1978:** Convicted of obtaining kickbacks to help meet personal and business expenses by inflating salaries of staff members and hiring two others who did no government work. Voters reelected him after his conviction, but in 1980, he resigned after losing a criminal appeal, and reported to federal prison for a three-year sentence. In July 1983, Diggs won a two-year battle to obtain a mortician's license (it was initially denied him because he was a felon) and later that year opened a Maryland funeral home called "House of Diggs."[20]

- **Rep. Frederick W. Richmond (D-New York), 1982:** Resigned after pleading guilty to felony tax evasion, two misdemeanors involving a government contract, and misdemeanor marijuana possession. It was a bad year for Richmond: two months later, the nude body of an apparent suicide victim was found in his luxe New York apartment. A bottle of pills was found near the body of Gregory Bergeron, twenty-one, whose chest bore the words "I Will Always Love U," then—written backward in ballpoint pen as though he had been looking in a mirror—"XOXOX" and the words "Sin Angel."[21]

- **Rep. Mario Biaggi (D-New York), 1987:** Convicted of accepting illegal gratuities, triggering a House ethics investigation. The investigation was interrupted, however, when Biaggi was convicted in a separate case of racketeering, conspiracy, extortion, and bribery involving a defense contractor. He resigned the next day and was sentenced to eight years in prison.[22]

- **Rep. Gerald Kleczka (D-Wisconsin), 1987:** Convicted of driving under the influence in 1987, 1990, and 1995. He was ordered to spend a night in jail and serve eight days in a work release program, following the initial penalty of a $300 fine and a three-year suspension of his driver's license.[23]

- **Rep. Jim Wright (D-Texas), 1989:** The powerful speaker from Fort Worth, who flew with John F. Kennedy on Air Force One on the president's fatal trip to Texas, resigned from Congress in a plea bargain in which the House agreed to drop dozens of charges, including alleged improper receipt of $145,000 in gifts by Wright's wife from a Fort Worth developer and large profits from "sale" of Wright's speeches.[24]

- **Rep. Tony Coelho (D-California), 1989:** When you've been caught hiding high-dollar loans, soliciting corrupt savings and loan barons, and using an S&L crook's yacht to entertain Democratic contributors, what do you do next? Go on to run Al Gore's presidential campaign, of course. Coelho, embroiled in an ethics investigation over allegations he took money from a California S&L to buy junk bonds, resigned in 1989. Then he worked for ten years as a Democratic lobbyist before Al Gore called him up to the majors again to manage his White House run in 2000. That was a mistake. In June of that year, Gore was forced to jettison Coelho when charges surfaced that he had accepted more than $500,000 in loans and airline tickets while running the U.S. Pavillion at the 1998 World's Fair in Portugal. According to a State Department audit, Coelho also had rented a lavish apartment, hired friends and relatives, and used public funds to pay for a chauffeured Mercedes limo, even though he had a fleet of six vans at his disposal. The Gore campaign pushed the story that Coelho left because of illness.[25]

- **Rep. Austin J. Murphy (D-Pennsylvania), 1998:** There's something supremely ironic about electing a supervisor of elections by forging ballots with your candidate's name. That's the crime that earned Murphy six months probation for his role in a Fayette County voter fraud scheme. Murphy, who retired from the House in 1994, was indicted in 1997 for writing the name of his wife, Eileen, on absentee ballots forged with the names of patients at a Pittsburgh-area nursing home. Murphy denounced the indictments as "politically inspired," but was convicted nonetheless. Democratic County Elections Auditor Sean Cavanagh, who uncovered the scandal after detecting a suspicious spike in the number of absentee ballots, was so excoriated by his own party that he turned independent.[26]

- **Rep. Mel Reynolds (D-Illinois), 1995:** Democratic voters never seem to tire of nominating (and electing) convicted Democrats.

Former Congressman Mel Reynolds resigned from the U.S. House in 1995 amid boiling scandal. Convicted of campaign fraud and criminal sexual assault of a sixteen-year-old, Reynolds served five years in prison before Bill Clinton commuted his sentence in the orgy of indiscriminate forgiveness that preceded his Oval Office exit. Never mind all that: in 2002, 26,000 2nd Congressional District voters signed a petition that put Reynolds on the ballot to run for the same seat he left in criminal disgrace seven years before. Jesse Jackson Jr. had won Reynolds's seat in a 1995 special election. During the run-up to the 2004 primaries, Reynolds, the felon, decried the "negative press" triggered by his past. Why didn't reporters, he whined, pay more attention to the fact that his opponent, Jackson, had once helped a Nigerian heroin dealer purchase a car under a false name?[27]

- **Rep. Walter Tucker (D-California), 1995:** The Compton, California, congressman resigned four days after being convicted of extortion and tax evasion in a trash-hauling corruption case while he was mayor of Compton. Tucker remained defiant after the jury's verdict, saying, "I was not judged by a jury of my peers." He also painted his decision to resign from Congress as one of grace and decorum, although at least one member, Republican Jim Sensenbrenner of Wisconsin, had threatened to draw up a resolution to kick Tucker out if he refused to leave on his own.[28]

- **Rep. Jim Traficant (D-Ohio):** In 1990, Congressman James Traficant told reporters that it was his habit to sleep within arm's reach of a loaded shotgun. In 2002, the Ohio Democrat had to rethink that habit since federal prison guards don't allow inmates to sleep with weapons. In April of that year, Traficant, by then a nine-term congressman, was convicted on ten felony counts including filing false tax returns, and receiving gifts, cash kickbacks, and free labor in exchange for political favors.

There's a good chance Traficant learned his art from the mob. In

1983, Traficant, then a sheriff in Youngstown, Ohio, stood trial on federal bribery charges. U.S. attorneys prosecuting the case produced tapes of Traficant meeting with one Charles Carrabia, a Cleveland mob boss who, with Traficant's knowledge and consent, "raised" $103,000 for Traficant's campaign for sheriff—hedging the syndicate's bets in case Traficant won the election.

When the FBI confronted Traficant with the tapes, he signed a confession—yes, he had accepted bribes from organized crime. But the famously flamboyant Traficant defended himself at trial, telling jurors he had only taken the money from the Mafia so that he'd know whom to arrest once he was elected. They bought it and acquitted him. When, eleven years later, Traficant was again indicted for bribery, he claimed he was the victim of an FBI conspiracy, retribution for his having beaten the earlier rap.[29]

- **Sen. Robert Torricelli (D-New Jersey), 2002:** In a legal outcome patented by the Clinton administration and the Democratic National Committee, a donor went to prison for giving illegal contributions to Torricelli, who was never prosecuted for accepting the money. David Chang was sentenced to eighteen months in federal prison after pleading guilty to making $53,700 in illegal donations to Torricelli's 1996 Senate campaign. As part of his plea agreement, Chang cooperated with federal prosecutors, telling them that he'd given tens of thousands of dollars more in gifts—including a Rolex watch, Italian designer suits, and diamond earrings for one of the senator's girlfriends—in exchange for Torricelli's help with Korean business deals. Torricelli wrote to State Department officials asking them to help secure funds Chang said he was owed by the North Korean government, and the senator brought Chang with him on a trip to meet with South Korean government officials. But while federal investigators found documentary evidence that corroborated Chang's claims," Clinton-appointed U.S. Attorney Mary Jo White refused to prosecute Torricelli. Torricelli was reprimanded by the Senate in July 2002, in the middle of his reelection campaign, then resigned from office. That allowed New Jersey Democrats to retain the seat by substituting Frank Lautenberg as their candidate on the November ballot—in contradiction of state election law which states that candidates cannot be swapped out within fifty-one days of an election. The New Jersey Supreme Court allowed the Democrats to switch candidates anyway.[30]

Money Trouble

Here's a batch of Democratic congressfolk who were convicted or disciplined for money-grubbing:

- **Reps. John J. McFall and Edward J. Roybal (D-Both of California), 1978:** Disciplined for campaign finance violations in connection with the 1978 foreign influence scandal called Koreagate. Roybal was reprimanded. McFall resigned.[31]

- **Rep. Joshua Eilberg (D-Pennsylvania), 1978:** Pleaded guilty to conflict-of-interest charges in connection with money he received to obtain a federal grant for a Philadelphia hospital.[32]

- **Sen. Herman Talmadge (D-Georgia), 1979:** Punished after his ex-wife produced cash "gifts" from contributors, money Talmadge had hidden in an overcoat. Talmadge later wrote, "I wish I'd burned that damn overcoat and charged everything on American Express."[33]

- **Rep. Daniel J. Flood (D-Pennsylvania), 1980:** Resigned after pleading guilty to a misdemeanor count of conspiracy to defraud the government.[34]

- **Rep. Charles H. Wilson (D-California), 1980:** Censured by voice vote for accepting money from a person with direct interest in legislation and for maintaining a person on payroll performing duties not commensurate with pay.[35]

- **Rep. William H. Boner (D-Tennessee), 1987:** Resigned after violating House rules on gifts, improperly using campaign funds, conflict of interest, and improper use of official resources.[36]

- **Rep. Nick Mavroules (D-Massachusetts), 1991:** Pleaded guilty to charges of bribery and tax evasion.[37]

- **Rep. Larry Smith (D-Florida), 1993:** Convicted of campaign-reporting violations and income tax evasion.[38]

- **Rep. Carroll Hubbard Jr. (D-Kentucky), 1994:** Pleaded guilty to three felonies—conspiring to file false campaign reports, misusing government employees, and obstructing justice—and drew three years in prison. The judge said he might have drawn a lighter sentence had Hubbard not blabbed that he'd been working as an undercover informant—wearing a wire and going by the code name "Elmer Fudd."[39]

- **Rep. Walter Fauntroy (D-District of Columbia), 1995:** Pleaded guilty to a misdemeanor charge of falsifying a financial report to Congress. Fauntroy listed a $23,887 charitable donation to a church on his 1988 financial disclosure form, but did not give the money to the church until 1989. He was also later convicted in the House Bank scandal.[40]

- **Rep. Earl Hilliard (D-Alabama), 2001:** The five-term lawmaker earned a letter of reproval citing "serious official misconduct" after admitting to a "pattern and practice" of using campaign funds to pay for personal loans and the salaries of people working for companies run by Hilliard and his family.[41]

Grand Old Perpetrators

The House Ethics Committee disciplinary report lists several GOP members disciplined since 1975. **Rep. Newt Gingrich** appears eight times between 1994 and 1996 for alleged ethics violations ranging from improper use of volunteer services to an improper book partnership. Some charges were dismissed, but Gingrich took a serious whipping in 1997, when he was reprimanded for making two "materially misleading statements" in connection with a workshop and college course he was involved in.[42]

Newt had company. Here's our list of GOP congressmembers caught on the wrong side of ethics rules or the law:

- **Rep. Andrew J. Hinshaw (R-California), 1976:** Spent a year in the slammer after being convicted of accepting bribes when he served as county tax assessor.[43]

- **Rep. Jon Clifton Hinson (R-Mississippi), 1981:** Resigned from Congress after being arrested in a men's room and charged with oral sodomy. Hinson became a gay activist and died of AIDS in 1995.[44]

- **Rep. Pat Swindall (R-Georgia), 1988:** A two-term congressman in Georgia's 4th District, Swindall lost reelection after indictment on nine counts of lying to a federal grand jury that was investigating his dealings with an IRS agent who posed as a drug-money launderer. A court later reversed three counts, but in 1994, Swindall reported for a one-year stint in prison.[45]

- **Rep. Donald Lukens (R-Ohio), 1989:** Sentenced to a jail term and fined $500 after a jury convicted him of paying a sixteen-year-old girl $40 to have sex with him. Lukens served only thirty days of a six-month term—but in 1996 was sentenced to *thirty months* in prison for having accepted bribes from a trade school while he served in Congress.[46]

- **Sen. Jesse Helms (R-North Carolina), 1990:** Though this item technically doesn't make the cut under the criteria we set up, it was such a dirty trick we threw it in anyway. The Helms campaign sent out 125,000 postcards, primarily to black North Carolina voters, claiming that they might not be able to vote, and that they would be prosecuted for vote fraud if they tried. Helms's campaign, the North Carolina Republican Party, and four consulting and marketing firms were charged with violations of the Voting Rights Act. The Helms campaign signed an admission of guilt, but Helms and his staff were never prosecuted.[47]

- **Rep. Wes Cooley (R-Oregon), 1996:** Lied about serving in the Korean War, quit Congress under a cloud in 1996, and was later convicted of falsifying VA loan applications and fined $7,000.[48]

- **Rep. Jay C. Kim (R-California), 1997–98:** Admitted accepting more than $250,000 in illegal campaign contributions, including unlawful donations from corporations and a Taiwanese national. Until that time, Kim's case was the largest criminal campaign finance violation ever committed by a member of Congress. Still, without explanation, U.S. District Judge Richard Paez sentenced Kim to only two months of home detention and a year of probation. The sentence enabled Kim to run again, but he lost his next primary.[49]

- **Sen. David Durenberger (R-Minnesota), 1995:** Sentenced to one year of probation for each of five misdemeanors after he pleaded guilty to billing Congress for his overnight stays in a condominium that he owned. (The senator also rang up $1.5 million in legal fees.)[50]

- **Sen. Bob Packwood (R-Oregon), 1995:** Resigned after the Senate Ethics committee unanimously recommended his expulsion for a "pattern of sexual misconduct in at least 17 instances between 1969 and 1990." Packwood spent his first day of civilian life taking calls from book agents and publishers who were interested in the lascivious content of his incriminating diaries.[51]

- **Rep. E. G. "Bud" Shuster (R-Pennsylvania), 2000:** Received a "letter of reproval" citing "serious official misconduct" after admitting to violating the House gift rule (he took his family to Puerto Rico on a lobbyist client's dime), improper use of official resources, and improper campaign work by congressional employees. The unrepentant congressman called the House's action "overkill."[52]

- **Rep. Tom DeLay (R-Texas), 2004:** While, at this writing, the former majority leader may be just the latest ham sandwich indicted by Texas prosecutor Ronnie Earle, DeLay does show up twice on the House's historical disciplinary report. In 2004, in connection with an energy company fundraiser, the Sugarland Republican was admonished for creating "an appearance that donors were being provided special access." He was also admonished in 2004 for promising Rep. Nick Smith (R-Michigan) that he would support Smith's son's run for Congress in return for Smith's yes vote on a Medicare drug benefit bill.[53]

- **Rep. Randall "Duke" Cunningham (R-California), 2005:** In November 2005, the former Navy Top Gun pilot and Vietnam war ace signed a plea agreement stipulating that he "demanded, sought and received at least $2.4 million in illicit payments and benefits," including cash, checks, meals, travel, lodging, furniture, antiques, rugs, yacht club fees, boats, boat repairs, and moving expenses. The staggering total, of course, topped Rep. Kim's record-breaking greed. As this book was going to press, Cunningham had not been sentenced.[54]

Slicing It by the Scandal

The politicians listed to this point were freelance malefactors, with Democrats outnumbering Republicans 29 to 13, a similar ratio to our Political Graveyard analysis. But sometimes corruption happens in bulk. And when it does, Democrats are there. In fact, the Dems have virtually swept the major congressional scandals of the last twenty-five years. While eighteen congressional Democrats were either convicted in court or disciplined by their own chamber, only three Republicans were caught up in multimember scandals—and one of those had his conviction overturned.

House Bank Scandal

In 1990, *Roll Call*'s Tim Burger reported that a General Accounting Office audit had shown that the House Bank had cashed $200,000 in bad checks in a single year, putting the institution at risk for "material losses in the future." By September 1991, a more thorough GAO probe showed that House lawmakers had written more than four thousand bad checks. "Nearly one-third of the House—the stewards of our tax dollars—were all bouncing checks worth more than $1,000, without even having to repay the debt," said a spokeswoman for the Project on Government Oversight. Four members were convicted in the scandal, all Democrats: Reps. Albert Bustamante (Texas), Carl Perkins (Kentucky), Mary Rose Oakar (Ohio), and Walter Fauntroy (District of Columbia).[55]

House Post Office Scandal

Two Democrats fell in this 1991 scandal involving the trading of postage stamps for cash. Rep. Joseph Kolter pleaded guilty to conspiring to defraud taxpayers and was sentenced to six months in prison. Powerful House Ways and Means Chairman Dan Rostenkowski (whom Lloyd Grove, writing in the *Washington Post*, once described as a "gruff-talking, steak-eating, cigar-sucking, martini-chugging unmade king-size bed of a Chicago politician") pleaded guilty to mail fraud in 1996 and was fined and sentenced to seventeen months in jail.[56]

Abscam

Short for "Arab Scam," this 1980 sting operation netted six Democrats and one Republican after they were captured on film accepting cash bribes from FBI agents posing as Arab businessmen. Rep. Michael Myers (D-Pennsylvania), who was expelled from the House and served about twenty months in prison, earned the distinction of being the first member booted from Congress since the Civil War. Other Democrats convicted were Sen. Harrison Williams of New Jersey, and Reps. John Jenrette (South Carolina), Raymond Lederer (Pennsylvania), Frank Thompson (New Jersey), and John M. Murphy (New York). Rep. Richard Kelly, the Republican, later had his conviction overturned. A grand jury named Rep. John Murtha (D-Pennsylvania) an unindicted coconspirator in the case, but the House ethics committee eventually cleared him. Murtha, a formerly hawkish former Marine, emerged in 2005 as a Democratic hero for speaking out against the war in Iraq.[57]

Keating Five

Four Democrats and one Republican were disciplined by the Senate in the late 1980s scandal involving S&L kingpin Charles Keating and his failed Lincoln Savings and Loan. Keating made it perfectly clear what he wanted in exchange for the $1.4 million he'd given to Sens. Alan Cranston (D-California), Don Riegle (D-Michigan), Dennis DeConcini (D-Arizona), John Glenn (D-Ohio), and John McCain (R-Arizona): "One question . . . had to do with whether my financial support in any way influenced several political figures to take up my cause," Keating said. "I want to say in the most forceful way I can: I certainly hope so."[58]

Koreagate

Tongsun Park came to the attention of the FBI in 1977 when the agency became aware of the Asian businessman's peculiar habit: disbursing envelopes stuffed with as much as $20,000 cash to congressmen as part of a lobbying campaign financed by South Korean intelligence agencies. Though "Koreagate" involved the alleged bribery of more than one hundred members of Congress, only one, Democratic Representative Richard T. Hanna of California, was convicted.[59]

House Page Scandal

Involving one Republican and one Democrat, this scandal demonstrated the tolerance of Democratic voters for corruption. In 1983, in the process of an internal drug probe, a House ethics committee learned that Reps. Dan Crane (R-Illinois) and Gerry Studds (D-Massachusetts) had both engaged in sexual relationships with congressional pages, both seventeen-year-old minors. Crane, a married father of six, was remorseful over his 1980 affair with a female page. Still, he lost his reelection bid in 1984. Studds, who was outted as gay by the episode, was unrepentant about his fling with a teenage boy, and Democratic voters continued to reelect him until he retired in 1996.[60]

In August 2005, constitutional scholar Alan Baker told *The Federal Observer,* "Congressional corruption has no party, no ideology and no gender. It's bipartisan and soaked in history and tradition."[61] Not according to our tally. In case you weren't keeping score, the final count of corrupt and/or criminal members of Congress over the past thirty years was 46 Democrats to 15 Republicans, a ratio of 3 to 1. Put another way, there were about three times as many Democratic crooks as Republican ones.

Not all corrupt Democrats serve in Congress, of course. Some were elected governors of their states. But in that department, unscrupulous Democrats just barely edge out their Republican brethren: combined with clever Googling, a search of the Political Graveyard and Lexis-Nexis reveals six GOP governors who have resigned, been convicted, pleaded guilty, were censured, or were removed from office since 1975. The total for Democrats is seven—with a bonus governor, Don Siegelman of Alabama, under indictment at this writing. (Going back to 1900, the total is Dems 14, GOP 12.)

The constellation of corruption shines locally as well: one slippery Dem was elected mayor of the most powerful city in the world.

"I'm Marion Barry, Mayor of Washington"

"Bitch set me up," Washington, D.C., Mayor Marion Barry famously said when federal agents caught him in the Vista International Hotel smoking crack—and insisting on sex—with a former girlfriend. "I shouldn't have come up here," the married mayor exclaimed. "[Expletive] bitch."[62]

It was January 18, 1990. Marion Barry and his acolytes painted the arrest as a racist, politically motivated plot against a popular black leader. He was popular, yes, having risen to power as a champion of the poor, albeit in association with such criminals as H. Rap Brown, a 1960s radical whose murder conviction a judge upheld in May 2004. But in his own eyes, Marion Barry was larger than life. He whisked about the city in limousines flanked by a security detail larger than the president's. And when talking up the ladies (even those he'd already met), he enjoyed introducing himself using his full, formal title. "Hello," he would say, "I'm Marion Barry, Mayor of Washington."

Despite his outsized self-image, or perhaps because of it, Barry wafted scandal in his wake the way a hooker wafts cheap perfume:

- In 1981, he faced allegations that he had used cocaine or was present when others used it during a Christmas party at a downtown bar.

- In 1984, amid a grand jury investigation, Barry admitted visiting the home of Karen Johnson, thirty-two, for more than a year. Johnson was cited for contempt of court for refusing to testify before the grand jury on alleged cocaine use by Barry, and was later convicted of cocaine distribution.

- In 1987, federal agents uncovered financial records suggesting that friends of Barry had paid Johnson for her silence. Johnson told investigators the figure: $25,000. That same year, model Grace Shell confirmed that Barry had made unwelcome advances toward her, including a visit to her Capitol Hill apartment. "The man never got what he wanted, and I know what he wanted," she said.[63] Also in 1987, Barry met a woman named Bettye Smith in the Bahamas, but told the press the relationship was not romantic.

- In December 1988, two police detectives investigating drug use allegations against Barry associate Charles Lewis at a Ramada Inn left the hotel after learning Barry was in the room. Four months later, Lewis was arrested and convicted of cocaine possession and distribution. While in custody, he told police he smoked crack with Mayor Barry in a hotel room in December 1988.

As allegations continued rolling in, Barry protested that federal authorities were conspiring with the press to "get me out of office." The final shoe fell on January 18, 1990, at the Vista International Hotel, when FBI officers busted Barry. A jury found Barry guilty of one count of cocaine possession and deadlocked on twelve other charges, including a perjury count that alleged Barry had tried to obstruct justice when he allegedly lied to a grand jury investigating reports of drug use by a former D.C. employee.

Barry appealed to Judge Thomas Penfield Jackson for leniency, saying his crimes were "out of character for me," but the judge wasn't buying. Declaring that the mayor had shown "persistence, until the moment of his sentencing, in a formal attitude of denial," Jackson sentenced Barry to six months in prison.[64]

But for Barry, jail time proved only a minor setback, and Democratic voters proved their low standards. In 1994, two years after he got out of jail, Barry ran again for mayor—and won.[65]

Are such scandals merely isolated incidents? Or do they underscore a Democratic political ethos that winks at crime and scandal until such time as voter amnesia sets in? Democrats answered that question when they tapped Massachusetts's senior senator, Edward "Teddy" Kennedy, to deliver a key speech at the 1988 Democratic National Convention. The DNC dispatched Kennedy nineteen years after police dispatched John Farrar, a scuba diver and captain of the search and rescue division of the volunteer fire department in Edgartown, Massachusetts, to Dike Bridge on Chappaquiddick Island, near Martha's Vineyard.

Why Couldn't Mary Jo Have Been Driving the Car?

It was July 19, 1969. A car had gone over the bridge into Poucha Pond, Farrar was told. At the scene, he donned his gear and plunged into the water. Once under, Farrar saw an Oldsmobile sedan balanced on the brow of its windshield and, he would learn later, facing the opposite direction from what it had been traveling when it sailed off the bridge.

"The car must have been going at a pretty good clip to land almost in the middle of the channel, " he would later say.[66] Farrar thrust his torso through the car's open window. The Olds's roof was below him, the floorboard above. Looking up, Farrar found the body of a young woman, her head cocked back, her face pressed into the footwell. The woman's hands clutched the front edge of the back seat, as though she were straining toward the footwell. Her position showed that she had not been knocked unconscious by the impact of a crash, Farrar later testified. The woman "was holding herself in a position such as she could avail herself of the last remaining air in the car."[67]

As soon as Farrar grabbed the woman's leg, he realized she was dead. Her flesh was stone-like from rigor mortis. "Instead of life-saving, I was evidence-gathering," he said. "Because I was the only person who would be able to observe this situation, it behooved me to think about what I saw underwater to be able to report it."[68]

Sen. Ted Kennedy, however, was not as conscientious about reporting the whereabouts of Mary Jo Kopechne, twenty-eight.

The story of Mary Jo's death has been told before, but never so well as by Leo Damore, whose 1988 book, *Senatorial Privilege: The Chappaquiddick Cover-Up*, at last pulled back the veil from Kennedy's gutless and self-serving criminal negligence and the cover-up that has enabled him to cling to power for more than four decades. In 1969, Damore covered the Chappaquiddick incident for *The Cape Cod News*. Later, as an author, he arranged for access to files on Chappaquiddick that had long been locked away in a district attorney's vault. Investigators of the accident, several of whom deeply regretted letting the Kennedy family glamour blind them to Ted Kennedy's guilt, allowed Damore access to their personal notes on the incident. Finally, and most devastatingly, Kennedy's cousin, Joe Gargan, a trusted family insider, decided he had protected Ted Kennedy long enough.

Gargan was there that night after the accident and, in interviews for *Senatorial Privilege,* told Damore exactly what he saw.[69]

Sen. Ted Kennedy had been driving the doomed Oldsmobile, license number L78 207, having left a sailing regatta victory party at the Lawrence Cottage on Chappaquiddick, attended by six married men and six single women. For such an intimate party, it was awfully well-stocked with booze: investigators later learned that Kennedy's chauffeur had purchased three half gallons of vodka, four fifths of scotch, two bottles of rum, and two cases of beer for the guests. Three witnesses later confirmed that Kennedy had been drinking all day. [70]

Even today, no one knows exactly what time the senator left the party with Mary Jo. He didn't say goodbye to anyone and neither did she, and she left her purse behind. But in the early morning of July 19, Deputy Sheriff Christopher "Huck" Look spotted an Oldsmobile, with a man and woman inside, pull off the pavement onto a private dirt road near the Dike Bridge. Look later said he thought the driver spotted him, because the car first parked, then took off in a cloud of dust.[71]

Look caught a glimpse of the license plate: it began with an L7 and had a 7 at the end.

Investigators determined that at twenty-five miles per hour, it would have taken one minute and forty-five seconds from the time Look spotted the Olds for Kennedy to drive the length of Dike Road before launching off into Poucha Pond. Based on Look's testimony, the accident would have occurred around 12:45 a.m. But no one except Kennedy, his attorney, and another lawyer friend knew about the accident until more than nine hours later.

First, Kennedy slogged out of the pond and trudged back to the cottage. He returned to the bridge forty-five minutes later, with Joseph Gargan, his cousin and lawyer, and Paul Markham, a lawyer and former U.S. attorney. The two lawyers immediately stripped naked and dove into the water.[72]

"All I was interested in was saving the girl . . . ," Gargan later told Damore. "I felt there was only one thing to do and that was get into that car as quickly as possible. Because if we didn't, there was just no chance in the world of saving Mary Jo."[73]

The water was swift and, operating in the dark, they had to feel their way around the car. The current kept sweeping them away from the Oldsmobile, but they battled their way back, struggling to pry open the doors. Again and again, Gargan and Markham surfaced for bites of air. During this time, Gargan remembers seeing Kennedy lying on his back on the Dike bridge, knees drawn up, rocking back and forth, moaning, "Oh my God. What am I going to do? What am I going to do?"[74]

What he did was ask the other men to drive him back to the cottage to establish a story. Why couldn't Mary Jo have been driving the car? he suggested aloud, after Gargan and Markham, exhausted and nearly drowned, pulled themselves ashore. Why couldn't she have let him off and driven to the ferry herself and made a wrong turn? Kennedy suggested that when he was back on the mainland, Gargan could "discover" the accident and report to police that Mary Jo had been alone in the car. Gargan refused. [75]

Between 7 and 8 a.m. on July 19, a high school science teacher and teenager fishing off the bridge noticed the glint of metal reflecting off a dark shape in the water. They headed for the nearest cottage, where a summer renter telephoned police. John Farrar, the rescue diver who examined the Chappaquiddick accident scene, was convinced that Mary Jo Kopechne had not only survived the crash, but had also lived for some time by breathing a pocket of trapped air. Farrar did not believe that she had drowned, but instead had died by asphyxiation as the oxygen in the air she was breathing was used up and replaced with carbon dioxide: "She was alive, easily an hour."[76]

Farrar repeatedly made similar pronouncements, until the press began to paint him as obsessed with the accident and "anti-Kennedy." But during a later grand jury hearing, Dr. Werner Spitz, deputy chief medical examiner for the State of Maryland, confirmed Farrar's opinion. "It is apparent to me from the record that she lived for a certain time underwater. . . . So she breathed, that girl. She *breathed!* She wasn't dead instantaneously."[76]

Farrar said that Mary Jo Kopechne could have been saved had Kennedy immediately reported the accident. A diagram of his findings underwater, Inquest Exhibit #14, showed that Mary Jo died straining toward an air pocket trapped inside the car. The final water level barely filled the entire floorboard space, and ultimately stopped its rise just inches past Mary Jo's nose and mouth. Kennedy would later claim he didn't report the accident until more than nine hours later because he had been "in a state of shock." This though he plotted story versions, made at least seventeen damage-control phone calls, and dispatched Gargan to sanitize the party cottage.[77]

Prosecuting attorneys discussed charging Kennedy with manslaughter, and the district attorney in the case later told Damore he believed a grand jury would have indicted Kennedy on exactly that charge—if the D.A. had given them the case. Meanwhile, the press and public were barred from the inquest. After the inquest documents were made public, many people believed what Gargan already knew: that Kennedy had not told the truth about the accident. In the end, a powerful senator from a powerful family was allowed to plead guilty to the misdemeanor of leaving the scene of an accident. He received no judicial punishment. On July 25, 1969, Kennedy made an anguished confession to a national television audience (one Gargan later said was "made up, all of it"), asking the people of Massachusetts to "think this through with me," about whether his role in Mary Jo Kopechne's death should prompt him to resign from the Senate.[78]

The answer, it turned out, was no. The people of Massachusetts resoundingly reelected Ted Kennedy, and continued to do so, paving his way to address a national television audience from the 1988 Democratic National Convention. In that speech, it became clear that Democrats are confident that voter amnesia inoculates their party from scandal—even leaving a girl to suffocate. Kennedy attacked the Republican presidential candidate, vice president George H. W. Bush, attempting to tie him to every questionable action of the Reagan administration. He hammered off a list of issues, punctuating each one with an indignant rally cry: "Where was George?!"

The Iran-Contra scandal?

"Where was George?!"

The national deficit?

"Where was George?!"

DNC strategists clearly hoped to raise questions in voters' minds about what Bush knew and when he knew it. But no one at DNC headquarters seemed to grasp the irony of having "Chappaquiddick Ted," who himself went missing that dark morning in a fit of criminal negligence, bellowing, "Where was George?!"

But Republicans did. Within two days, they printed up T-shirts bearing the answer to the senator's question: DRY, SOBER, AND HOME WITH HIS WIFE.[79]

ROOTS OF THE ROT

THE DEMOCRATIC PARTY'S
CRIMINAL LEGACY

"[T]he old slave-owner and slave driver, the saloon-keeper, the ballot-box-stuffer, the Ku Klux Klan, the criminal class of the great cities, the men who cannot read and write, commonly, and as a rule, by the natural law of their being, find their congenial place in the Democratic Party."

—SEN. GEORGE F. HOAR (R-MAINE), 1889[1]

WHEN HE RAN FOR PRESIDENT IN 1960, JOHN F. KENNEDY was very popular among Chicago Democrats, including a fellow named Edward Myles. There was, however, a problem: like many other Chicagoans who voted for Kennedy, Ed Myles was dead.[2]

The 1960 presidential election was one of the closest in U.S. history, with Kennedy winning by a popular-vote margin of a bare 9,000 votes out of 68 million ballots cast. In the Electoral College, Kennedy ended up with 303 votes to Nixon's 219. But if Illinois (27 electoral votes) and Texas (24 electoral votes) went for Nixon, the result would be a Republican victory—Nixon with 270 electoral votes and Kennedy with 252.[3]

While plenty of scandalous tales about Kennedy's tragically short-lived presidency have since become public, reporters have tended to fixate on and fantasize about the trivial and the salacious—was there some connection between JFK's acquaintance with Marilyn Monroe and his 1963 assassination? Usually brushed aside is a more important and substantial question: Was Kennedy's election legitimate?

But elephants never forget, and bitter memories of the 1960 election were a major reason Republicans had little sympathy for Democrats who in 2000 and 2004 howled with rage over claims of GOP election mischief in Florida and Ohio. On talk radio and Internet chat boards, Republicans scoffed at accusations from Democrats. Confusing ballots in Palm Beach County? Long lines outside polling places in Cleveland? What was that, Republicans demanded to know, compared to the clear criminality of Chicago Democrats in 1960?[4] Like so much else in the mythical history of the Democratic Party, the vaunted legend of Kennedy's "Camelot" era conceals a sordid tale of crime and corruption.

There is no doubt that Democrats in Chicago (Mayor Richard Daley was Kennedy's national campaign manager) engaged in vote fraud in 1960. As Earl Mazo of the *New York Herald-Tribune* and historian Stephen Hess later wrote: "The Daley organization's all-out effort—employing every time-proven big-city trick, from voting tombstones and floaters to spoiling Republican ballots and tallying the 'votes' of those who had once lived on streets evacuated for [the construction of] superhighways—was a marked success." A major motivation for this "all-out effort" in Chicago, Mazo explained, was Daley's desperation to defeat a Republican district attorney "whose aggressiveness in local law enforcement gravely threatened the Democratic machine's survival."[5]

The key to stealing an election is knowing how many votes you need. On Election Night 1960, the Daley machine held back Chicago's results until Republican-leaning areas in the city's suburbs and in downstate Illinois had reported their totals. This tactic caused a temporary panic among Kennedy's staff, when television returns showed Nixon leading in Illinois. "I damn near collapsed," remembered Sargent Shriver, Illinois campaign manager for his brother-in-law, John Kennedy. "I was devastated. I thought that the fact that I had lost my state, Illinois, would mean that Kennedy would lose the presidency."[6] But then Daley's Chicago came through with enough votes to give Illinois to Kennedy by a margin of 8,858 votes out of 4.7 million votes cast in the state.

The Democrats' "chicanery," as Mazo called it, was widespread in Chicago:

- In Ward 5, Precinct 22, one voter put six paper ballots into the ballot box.[7]

- In Ward 4, Precinct 77, the Democratic precinct captain voted twice.[8]

- In Ward 4, Precinct 31, a man who had died, and his son who had moved away, both voted.[9]

- In Ward 27, Precinct 27, there were 397 votes—but only 376 voters.[10]

- In Ward 4, Precinct 6, a man calling himself Estes Hemphill showed up to vote, but was not listed among the precinct's registered voters. The man said that he had recently "moved from 4140 South Berkeley to 104 East 41st Place" and was allowed to vote. After the election, an investigation showed that no such person lived at 4140 South Berkeley, and 104 East 41st Place was a nonexistent address.[11]

The vote rigging was blatant enough to convince the *Chicago Tribune* that "the election of November 8 was characterized by such gross and palpable fraud as to justify the conclusion that [Nixon] was deprived of victory."[12] An article about the Chicago vote in *Look* magazine carried the emphatic headline: "How to Steal an Election."[13] Forty years later, Earl Mazo had no doubts: "There's no question in my mind that it was stolen," he told the *Washington Post*. "It was stolen like mad."[14]

More than 650 Chicago election officials were charged as part of a special prosecutor's investigation, but the judge appointed to the case,

Thomas Kluczynski, was a Daley loyalist who consistently ruled in favor of the defense, and the charges were dropped. Eventually, three poll workers from the 28th precinct were the only Chicago officials to serve jail time for their part in the stolen election.[15]

Democratic vote fraud was a national phenomenon in 1960. "Illinois was not the only scene of 'irregularities' in the Kennedy-Nixon fight," columnist Christopher Matthews admitted forty years later. "There were close tallies and serious questions about the counts in Arkansas, Missouri, New Mexico and Texas, home to Kennedy running mate Lyndon Johnson."[16] Texas was a story of its own. "Organization Democrats were in command of every gear in the Lone Star State's election machinery, from precinct tally clerk to state Board of Canvassers," Mazo observed. "The state board, which ran the whole election operation in Texas and was also court of last resort on vote tallies, was made up of three party stalwarts, two of whom happened to be managers of the Democratic campaign in Texas." Mazo asserted there were "thousands" of fraudulent results like that one in Angelina County, where in one precinct 86 people voted, but the reported vote was 148 for Kennedy, 24 for Nixon. Meanwhile, in Fannin County, where there were fewer than 5,000 registered voters, more than 6,000 votes were cast.[17] By such methods, the Kennedy-Johnson ticket won Texas by 46,000 votes out of the 2.3 million cast in the state—less than 2 percent of the total, in the home state of the Democratic vice-presidential candidate.

But the 1960 vote-count was by no means a Democratic original. Mayor Richard Daley's operation in Chicago resembled in some ways Boss Tweed's Tammany Hall machine in New York in the 1800s when, as Tammany operative George Plunkitt said, a politician could "become a millionaire through honest graft."[18] While the Democratic Party's monopoly control of politics in New York and Chicago made men rich in those cities, many others grew wealthy from "honest graft" in the "Solid South," where one-party rule made the scandal-ridden Democrats virtually bulletproof. Huey Long in Louisiana, Lyndon Johnson in Texas,

Eugene Talmadge in Georgia—these were just a few of the beneficiaries of the unshakeable partisan loyalty of Dixie's "yellow dog Democrats."

It was on such a troubled foundation—patronage-peddling urban machines in the North and white segregationists in the "Solid South"—that the modern Democratic Party was built.

Tammany and Treason

Amid the confusing political swirl surrounding the origins of the Democratic Party, Aaron Burr played a pivotal role. A Princeton graduate and grandson of the famous New England clergyman Jonathan Edwards, Burr put aside his law studies to join the patriot army when the Revolutionary War broke out in 1775. He served with distinction, briefly served on General Washington's staff, and rose to the rank of lieutenant colonel. In 1779, Burr fell seriously ill, left the army, and went back to studying law. He became a popular and successful lawyer in New York, won election to the state assembly in 1784, was appointed the state's attorney general in 1789, and the next year was elected U.S. senator, defeating Phillip Schuyler—Alexander Hamilton's father-in-law.[19]

Hamilton and Burr had both been officers in the Revolution, and both had been young attorneys in New York after the war. If they were rivals before the 1790 election, they were enemies afterward, and in the Senate, Burr naturally aligned himself with Jefferson against Hamilton (though Jefferson would later say he never really trusted Burr). Jefferson's Virginia and Burr's New York were then the most populous and powerful states in the Union, so the alliance the two men formed in 1792 had the potential not only to checkmate Hamilton and the Federalists, but to dominate the federal government. This alliance was to become the Democratic Party.[20]

But the Federalists were still a mighty force, and in 1796, they dealt a defeat to the newborn Democrats. John Adams was elected president, and under the original provision of the Constitution, the vice-presidency went to the second-place candidate, Jefferson. Burr was defeated for reelection to the Senate that year, but his ambition was undeterred. He returned to New York City and, with the help of a social club called the St. Tammany Society, quickly built a mighty political machine—the legendary Democratic dynamo known to history as Tammany Hall.[21]

Burr got himself elected to the New York legislature in 1797, but accusations of corruption cost him reelection two years later—just in time to make Burr available as a vice presidential candidate in the 1800 election. This was the big showdown Jefferson had been looking for, and Burr played a key role. With the help of his Tammany machine, Burr swung New York to the Republican (Democratic) column, but the strategy nearly backfired. When the Electoral College votes were counted, Jefferson and Burr each had seventy-three votes, which sent the election to the House of Representatives. There, the vote remained deadlocked for six days and thirty-six ballots. Finally, due in large part to Hamilton's influence, the Federalists backed down and the House elected Jefferson, with Burr as vice president. Though he disliked Jefferson, Hamilton truly detested the cunning and ambitious Burr. "His private character is not defended by his most partial friends," Hamilton wrote of Burr in one letter.[22]

Burr's behavior during the deadlocked election resulted in his estrangement from Jefferson. Though he disclaimed any intention of diverting votes from Jefferson, Burr refused to promise that he would not accept the presidency if the House elected him—even as Burr's supporters in the House refused to switch their votes to Jefferson. Isolated in Washington and with little influence in the Jefferson administration, Burr's remorseless ambition went spinning in new directions. In 1804, while still vice president, he ran for governor of New York and was defeated largely due to the opposition of Hamilton, who denounced Burr as a "dangerous man." At some point during the campaign, Hamilton said something so insulting about his rival that Burr felt justified in challenging Hamilton to a duel. When the pair faced off famously in New Jersey on July 11, 1804, Burr shot Hamilton, fatally wounding him. Having shot dead the nation's first secretary of the Treasury, the vice president became a fugitive from justice, fleeing murder indictments in both New York and New Jersey to serve out his term in Washington. During his remaining months as vice president, Burr presided over the impeachment of a federal judge, Samuel Chase, provoking one journalist to remark, "It was the practice in Courts of Justice to arraign the *murderer* before the *Judge*, but now we behold the *Judge* before the *murderer*."[23]

Even as he finished out his vice-presidential term, however, Burr was plotting the scheme that would permanently stain his name with infamy. Exactly what he planned to do has been a subject of dispute for nearly two centuries, but it is certain that Burr organized a private military expedition to make a conquest in the West. He may have been planning to invade Mexico—illegal enough, since to do so would be a violation of the federal Neutrality Act. More likely, he aimed to capture New Orleans in the newly purchased Louisiana Territory and, with the assistance of disgruntled frontiersmen, to establish a separate western republic, perhaps encompassing the entire Mississippi and Ohio river valleys, with himself as president.[24]

As farfetched as such a plan might sound, Burr was not the first to contemplate it. America's western frontier had been the scene of schemes and scams for decades, when the land across the Appalachians was claimed by the fading empires of France and Spain. Before Jefferson bought Louisiana from the French in 1803, and while Spain still claimed Florida, these thinly populated frontiers had fired the imagination of many adventurers. During Washington's presidency, the French diplomat Edmund Genet had intrigued with Revolutionary War hero George Rogers Clark to conquer New Orleans, then held by the Spanish. A few years later, Tennessee Sen. William Blount was caught conspiring with the British to oust Spain from both New Orleans and Florida. So it was a familiar story in August 1804 when Burr approached the British envoy in Washington and suggested his own plot.[25]

"I have just received an offer from Mr. Burr the actual vice president of the United States," diplomat Anthony Merry wrote in a letter to the

British foreign office, "to assist His Majesty's Government in any manner in which they may think fit to employ him, particularly in endeavoring to effect a separation of the Western part of the United States from that which lies between the Atlantic and the mountains, in its whole extent."[26]

This was treason, plain and simple, and what Burr wanted most from the British was money. When this was not forthcoming, Burr then sought to get money from Spain, only to be rebuffed again. While he lined up his relatives and friends to support this conspiracy and pursued foreign money and military assistance, Burr also formed a pact with the U.S. Army commander in the New Orleans district, General James Wilkinson, who was secretly on Spain's payroll. Burr and Wilkinson devised a secret code, and eventually Burr found financial support from an expatriate Irish nobleman, Harman Blennerhassett.[27]

Heir to Castle Conway in Ireland's County Kerry, Blennerhassett had fled to America after his advocacy of Irish independence antagonized the British. Blennerhassett brought with him a beautiful young wife, who was also his niece, and the incestuous couple had set themselves up in fine style in a mansion on an island in the upper Ohio River. The exiled Irishman agreed to back the cunning Burr, and the autumn of 1806 found Burr's crew building flatboats on Blennerhassett Island. The plan was for this makeshift flotilla, bearing firearms and other supplies along with several hundred men, to journey down the Ohio to the Mississippi, along the way rendezvousing with Burr, who would be bringing more men from Tennessee and Kentucky. Once this force was united . . . well, what Burr planned next has never been fully explained.[28]

In Natchitoches, Louisiana, General Wilkinson received a coded letter from Burr, alerting him that the time had come to launch their prearranged plot. Even decoded, the exact plan is not clear. A naval officer who was in on the plot was "going to Jamaica to arrange with the admiral there and will meet us at Mississippi," Burr wrote. Burr would bring a force of five hundred to one thousand men down the river and join forces with Wilkinson at Natchez, Mississippi, in early December. Once united, they would decide whether to capture or bypass the territorial capital at Baton Rouge. And then? The coded letter didn't say, but Wilkinson did not intend to find out. Instead, the general sent a message to President Jefferson, warning of the danger posed by Burr's conspiracy—but not telling the president of his own role in the scheme.[29]

Soon the scheme unraveled, but not before involving men who were, or would become, among the most famous in American history. Among the first to raise the alarm about Burr's plot was the Tennessee militia commander, General Andrew Jackson. When a federal prosecutor tried to indict Burr in Kentucky, the accused appeared before the grand jury with his defense attorney, a young fellow named Henry Clay, who served later as a Democratic congressman. And when Burr was finally brought to trial in Richmond, Virginia, the presiding judge was Supreme Court Justice John Marshall. Fortunately for Burr, Marshall—who was Jefferson's cousin—was a Federalist, and a man of high principle. Marshall insisted on a very narrow definition of treason. Burr was acquitted, but he was ruined just the same.[30]

Patronage, War, Slavery, and Graft

During the thirty years after Burr went west to plot his treason, a profound change swept across the American political landscape. For one thing, the Federalist Party faded from the scene. Jefferson saw to that by inaugurating what was to become known as the spoils system, ousting Federalist officials and appointing his own party's favorites in their place. Describing the results of Jefferson's first term, biographer Willard Sterne Randall writes: "He evicted eighteen of thirty federal judges; thirteen of twenty-one United States attorneys, eighteen of twenty U.S. marshals. He purged Hamilton's old power base at the Treasury, sacking fifteen of sixteen revenue supervisors, including all but one collector of customs in ports from Maine to Georgia." Jefferson's purge, which was replicated in the governments of those states where the Democratic-Republicans also won victories, had the effect of stripping the Federalists of both political power and social prestige. Jefferson was "banishing from power many of the oldest and best-established families in America," writes Randall, who calculates that among the ousted Federalists, 27 percent had been officers in the Revolutionary War.[31]

Jefferson and his immediate successors as president, James Madison and James Monroe, each served two four-year terms, thus establishing twenty-four consecutive years of one-party control of the White House, the so-called Virginia Dynasty. During that era, Democratic congressmen Henry Clay and John C. Calhoun emerged as leaders of the West and South. The "War Hawks," as the Clay-Calhoun faction was known, demanded war with England, claiming the issue was the British navy's kidnapping of American merchant seamen. But there were other, less noble reasons. In the Great Lakes region, the British had stirred up the local Indian tribes, who menaced the fast-growing American settlements in the old Northwest Territory. And to the south, England's Spanish ally still controlled Florida, a haven for hostile Indians and runaway slaves. The hawks expected to end these problems with a war that they declared would be a fairly simple affair.[32]

The hawks pushed a war declaration through Congress, and Madison signed it—thus beginning one of the worst managed military crusades in American history. The New England states mostly boycotted the war, refusing to send their state militias, and eventually gathering at Hartford, Connecticut, to contemplate the possibility of seceding from the Union rather than support "Mr. Madison's war." The Democrats hadn't prepared sufficiently for war, and the United States had an army of only seven thousand men. The British captured Detroit, and the War Hawks' plans for invading Canada were bungled. In the spring of 1813, the Americans captured and burned Toronto, but the continued efforts to conquer Canada had the result of weakening the defenses at home, and in August 1814, the British captured Washington, D.C., burning both the White House and the Capitol in reprisal for American depredations in Canada.

There were disasters and triumphs and finally a peace treaty was negotiated, but news didn't reach America in time to prevent Jackson from
inflicting a whipping on the British at New Orleans, two weeks after the
treaty was signed.[33]

Prosperity followed peace, but that peace was soon disturbed by a new
quarrel: slavery.[34] The war that New England had opposed made a hero of
the slave-owning Democrat, Jackson, whose 1829 inauguration prompted
one Supreme Court justice to observe: "The reign of 'King Mob' seemed
triumphant."[35] Like Burr before him, Jackson was a dueler—in 1806, an
argument over a horse race in Nashville turned ugly, insults were
exchanged, and soon Jackson and Charles Dickinson faced each other
with pistols at the deadly range of only twenty-four feet. Dickinson fired
first, striking Jackson in the chest, but the bullet missed Old Hickory's
heart, and the general then calmly aimed and shot Dickinson dead.[36]

(At this point, perhaps the loyal Democratic reader is wondering:
"Where is my party? Treason, plots of imperial conquest, murderous
duels, slavery and warmongering— this doesn't remotely resemble the
peace-loving, tolerant party of freedom and equality that I support!" Hang
on, dear Democrat. It only gets worse.)

As the nation drifted toward division and war over slavery, Tammany,
Aaron Burr's old political base in New York City, was under new management. Like many liberal institutions, the Tammany Society started off
nobly enough. Founded in 1786, it was a social and fraternal organization
that adopted as one project a move to improve the image of America's
native population, the Indians. By 1798, though, Tammany's activities
had grown increasingly politicized, and by 1800, as noted before, Burr had
expanded Tammany into a political machine that he pressed into the service of his election. During the early nineteenth century, Tammany locked
arms with the Democratic Party and expanded its control over New York
City politics.

"The records show that Tammany was . . . from the beginning, an evil
force in politics," historian Gustavus Myers observed. By the mid-1850s,

Tammany was ready to elect its first mayor, Fernando Wood, with the support of what can fairly be called a coalition of criminals: "The disreputable classes, believing that his success meant increased prosperity to themselves, energetically supported Wood, and the liquor-dealers formally commended him. In the city at this time were about 10,000 shiftless, unprincipled persons who lived by their wits and the labor of others," Myers wrote. The historian also noted that a part of this "shiftless, unprincipled" constituency concentrated its efforts on "turning primary elections, packing nominating conventions, repeating and breaking up meetings. Most of these were Wood's active allies."[37]

Elected in 1854, Wood initially appeared to be an honest reformer, closing the saloons on Sundays and taking measures to crack down on gambling and prostitution. But within a year, the new mayor revealed himself to be "reckless and unprincipled," and "the blackness of his administration exceeded anything known before." Under Wood's administration, the "saloon power had grown until it controlled the politics of the city," supplying "a crowd of loafers and bruisers" as a political street army, so that the mayor was "backed by the dregs of the city" in his bid for a second term, which he won on an election day "enlivened with assaults, riots and stabbings."[38]

It was during Wood's term as mayor, in 1857, that the famous gang war between the "Dead Rabbits" and the "Bowery Boys" was fought, leaving eight dead and scores injured. Wood angered city residents by putting illiterates, criminals, and foreigners on the police force. Two-thirds of the police he hired were Irish, part of Wood's effort to secure the votes of a rapidly growing minority. "The police being so disorganized, the criminal classes ran the town. . . . [G]amblers, brothel-keepers, immigrant runners and swindlers of every kind bought [votes] and cheated for [Wood's reelection]." Wood quadrupled the city's taxes even as the economy slipped into recession, and millions of dollars of tax money went into the pockets of Wood and his cronies, or else was spent on "charitable" causes intended to buy political loyalty from key constituencies. So shocking was

Wood's corruption that the leaders of Tammany expelled him and chose a Tammany man to oppose him. Wood responded by forming his own organization, Mozart Hall, and getting himself elected mayor again.[39]

With Lincoln's election in 1860, Southern states began seceding, and war soon came with the bombardment of Fort Sumter. In a strategy that would be emulated by future Democrats, Tammany Hall managed to be both for the war and against it. Tammany and Wood's Mozart Hall issued stirring patriotic proclamations in support of the war, and Tammany raised a regiment of volunteers. But the "real sentiments" of New York Democrats "were to the contrary," Myers noted. On the anti-war side, Mayor Wood gave a speech calling for New York City to secede from the Union and establish itself as a neutral port, and both he and his former Tammany allies "did their best to paralyze the energies of Lincoln's administration." Wood mended fences with Tammany and got himself elected to Congress in 1862, the same year that Democrat Horatio Seymour was elected governor of New York with the strong backing of Tammany.[40]

Seymour, in true Democratic fashion, proclaimed himself strongly in favor of maintaining the Union, but criticized Lincoln's prosecution of the war—particularly the Emancipation Proclamation and a law enacted to draft soldiers into the Union army. Democrats and their allies in the press encouraged resistance to the draft, suggesting to their immigrant supporters that Lincoln's policies amounted to forcing them to die for blacks who were taking away their jobs. As the *New York Herald* put it: "The Irish and German immigrants, to say nothing of native laborers of the white race, must feel enraptured at the prospect of hordes of darkeys overrunning the Northern States and working for half wages, and thus ousting them from employment." The result of such agitation was nothing less than the deadliest race riot in American history.[41]

In July 1863, less than two weeks after the Battle of Gettysburg, New York City posted the first list of names of men chosen for the draft. The draft list was based on the voting rolls, and the city's Democrats had illegally naturalized thousands of Irish and other immigrants as part of their political operations. The list of draftees was thus heavy with Irish names, enraging the immigrants. A mob of fifty thousand destroyed the draft offices and, yelling "to hell with the draft and the war," went hunting for black men. Dozens of blacks were lynched, stores looted, and buildings burned—including the Colored Orphan Asylum. The rampage continued for four days, and it was only with the help of thirteen Union army regiments (including troops who had rushed straight from the Gettysburg battlefield) that order was restored. The exact number killed in the riot has never been established. Some have estimated the death toll as high as one thousand, though Democrats claimed this was a Republican smear, and that there was "no evidence that any more than 74 possible victims of the violence . . . died anywhere but in the columns of partisan newspapers."[42]

Despite the efforts of Democrats like Wood and Seymour, the Confederacy was defeated. War was followed by Reconstruction in the South, and several years of booming prosperity in the North. In New York City, Tammany reached its zenith (or nadir) during the postwar era, under the leadership of Democratic state Sen. William Marcy Tweed. Controlling patronage jobs in the city, Tweed and his colleagues siphoned off an estimated $30 million in graft before being exposed with the aid of state Democratic Party chairman Samuel J. Tilden. But though Tweed was arrested and died in prison, Tammany remained a powerful and corrupt force for the next eighty years.[43]

This era produced important political consequences. White Southerners, embittered by the war and Reconstruction, would remain loyal to the Democratic Party, giving rise to the "Solid South." They would be joined by most of the immigrant ethnic minorities—especially the Irish, but also later the Italians, Jews, Poles, and Serbs. In 1876, in what would become known as "the corrupt bargain," Republican leaders secured the presidential election of Rutherford B. Hayes in return for agreeing to withdraw federal troops from the South. Black voters, who had supported the GOP during Reconstruction, were soon at the mercy of Democrat-led state legislatures and denied the right to vote across the South. This political alignment would remain in place into the 1960s.

This combination of corrupt big-city machines and the "Solid South" was an unsavory alliance that drew the attention of Republican Sen. George F. Hoar as early as 1889. The Republicans had had their own share of scandals in the administration of President Ulysses F. Grant. But, as Hoar saw it, this had not really damaged the party, because the Republican Party "stands for something. It is on the growing side of the great political issues of the time. It has positive policies, not merely negative policies."

More than that, Hoar said, despite the wrongdoing of Republican officials, the party itself was composed of decent, respectable people: "The men who do the work of piety and charity in our churches; the men who administer our school systems; the men who own and till their own farms; the men who perform skilled labor in the shops; the soldiers, the men who went to war and stayed all through; the men who paid the debt and kept the currency sound, and saved the nation's honor; the men who saved the country in war and have made it worth living in peace, commonly, and as a rule, by the natural law of their being, find their place in the Republican party."

Then, turning his attention to the Democrats, Hoar observed: "The Democratic party is made up, in substance, of the great bulk of the old owners of slave-labor and slave plantations, and of their children; of that portion of the population of our great cities and towns that were brought up where there were no free schools; of the keepers of liquor-saloons and those under their influence and control. Its strength is greatest where free elections are unknown and where the great historic frauds on the ballot have been committed in the past."[44]

Hoar was a vigorous advocate of trade protectionism and other doctrines that would be rejected by modern Republicans (among other things, he advocated the "extirpation of Mormonism"). And he was a New Englander writing at a time when memories of the Civil War were fresh, when Republicans regularly "waved the bloody shirt" and condemned

Democrats as the party of "Rum, Romanism and Rebellion."[45] But Hoar had identified key characteristics of the Democratic Party: its alliance with criminals, its calculated appeal to the poorly educated and immoral, and its reliance on vote fraud and crooked districts to win elections.

4

THE GANG'S ALL HERE

DEMOCRATS AND THE MOB

*"My father is no different than any powerful man,
any man with power, like a president or senator."*

—MICHAEL CORLEONE[1]

THE 1932 DEMOCRATIC NATIONAL CONVENTION WAS DEADLOCKED. For three ballots in Chicago, the contest for the presidential nomination wavered between two New Yorkers, former Gov. Al Smith—the party's presidential candidate in 1928—and incumbent Gov. Franklin D. Roosevelt. That was when the Roosevelt forces sought the assistance of an unofficial delegation to the convention. These delegates weren't exactly idealistic reformers. Their names included Frank Costello, Lucky Luciano, and Meyer Lansky.

As Luciano recalled years later in his authorized biography, the New York mob arrived in Chicago the week of the convention and stayed in plush suites at the Drake Hotel. Their hosts were local mobsters, who had taken over the city's organized crime operations after Al Capone was sent to federal prison in May 1932. One of the Chicago hosts was Joe Accardo, suspected of being one of the masterminds of the notorious 1929 St. Valentine's Day Massacre that wiped out Bugs Moran's gang. Accardo was known as "Joe Batters" because of his propensity for delivering deadly beatings with a baseball bat. Bootleggers, heroin smugglers, pimps, gamblers, racketeers, and cold-blooded killers—the gangsters who gathered in Chicago were among the most brutal and vicious criminals in America. And FDR needed their help.[2]

By the time of the 1932 convention, Luciano could brag that he and Costello controlled Tammany Hall, and it was no idle boast. Tammany and the mob had been intertwined for decades. In 1903, when two rival New York gangs, the Five Points Gang and the Eastman Gang, got into a bloody turf battle that left three men dead, Tammany leader "Big Tom" Foley intervened to broker peace. A Tammany judge released gang leader Monk Eastman without any charges, perhaps because Eastman regularly provided muscle for the Democrats' brutal electioneering campaigns. One of the Five Pointers who got away was Johnny Torrio, who would later serve as mentor to a young hoodlum named Alphonse Capone.[3]

"Big Tim" Sullivan, a Lower East Side saloon-keeper and Democratic state senator, was the de facto boss of New York City in the first decade of the twentieth century. Sullivan, who controlled New York's police on behalf of pimps and gamblers, was legendary in his ability to deliver votes for Democrats. In the 1892 election, Tammany put young Sullivan in charge of the Lower East Side; the vote in Big Tim's precinct was 395 for Democrat Grover Cleveland to 4 for Republican Benjamin Harrison. Sullivan was outraged: "Harrison got one more vote than I expected, but I'll find that feller." When Sullivan died in 1913—demented from advanced syphilis and disgraced by scandal—his funeral was attended by 75,000 mourners, including sixteen congressmen and four U.S. senators.[4]

Arnold Rothstein, most famous as the gambling kingpin who fixed the 1919 World Series in the "Black Sox" scandal, was a Sullivan protégé who for many years acted as the mob's go-between with Tammany leaders. The arrival of Prohibition in 1919 was a boon for Rothstein, who organized what biographer David Pietrusza called "the biggest liquor-smuggling ring in the history of the world." Rothstein bankrolled and protected such bootleggers as Jack "Legs" Diamond, Dutch Schultz, Bugsy Siegel, Carlos

Gambino, and Albert Anastasia, men who would become among the most infamous gangsters in history. Lanksy and Luciano were the chief operators of Rothstein's ring, and as the booze and jazz poured out of New York speakeasies during the Roaring Twenties, the elegantly-dressed Rothstein was a famous figure on Broadway, his name linked in gossip columns to Ziegfeld showgirls. Rothstein, who more or less invented the "floating" crap game that moved from location to location to avoid police harassment, was the inspiration for the character of Nathan Detroit in *Guys and Dolls*.[5]

By September 1928, Rothstein was well on his way to setting up a lucrative heroin-smuggling operation when he lost $300,000 in a three-day card game with some out-of-town high rollers. He suspected he'd been cheated and refused to pay up. Less than two months later, he was shot dead. The man suspected of killing Rothstein, George "The Hump" MacManus, had been the host of the rigged card game. Rothstein's death cleared the way for Lansky, Luciano, and Frank Costello to emerge as masters of New York's underworld, with Costello taking the lead role as the mob's ambassador to Tammany Hall.[6]

So it was that, at the 1932 Democratic convention, FDR needed Costello's help. This was ironic enough. Roosevelt was a reformer who loathed Tammany Hall, and as governor of New York had waged war against the city's gangsters and politicians, including Mayor Jimmy Walker, whom he would eventually drive from office. FDR had appointed a judge, Samuel Seabury, to head an investigation into the city's corruption, and Seabury was making things uncomfortable for the New York mob. The mobsters went to Chicago for the convention, ready to make a deal, with Tammany delegates as their bargaining chip. When the first three rounds of balloting failed to yield a nominee—Tammany was holding out for Al Smith—Roosevelt's advisers were forced to approach Frank Costello.[7]

"We waited until the very last second," Lucky Luciano recalled years later, "and we had Roosevelt and Smith guys comin' out our ears. They all knew we controlled most of the city's delegates. . . . When Frank got the word that Roosevelt would live up to his promise to kill the Seabury investigation. . . . It was in the bag for him." As Luciano put it: "I wouldn't say we elected Roosevelt, but we gave him a pretty good push." But Al Smith was not fooled. When Costello informed him of the deal with Roosevelt, the former governor warned his mob pal, "Frank, Roosevelt'll break his word to you. This is the biggest mistake you ever made in your entire life by trusting him. He'll kill you."[8]

Smith was at least half-right right. During his remaining months as New York's governor, Roosevelt continued to push the Seabury probe, but it focused mainly on corrupt city judges and other officials. The gangsters lost some of their protection, but they managed to buy more. In 1943, a wiretap on Costello's phone captured his conversation with Thomas Aurelio, who had just won the Democratic Party nomination to New York's state supreme court:

> **Costello:** "Congratulations. It went over perfect. When I tell you something is in the bag, you can rest assured."
> **Aurelio:** "It was perfect. It was fine."
> **Costello:** "Well, we have to get together and have dinner some night real soon."
> **Aurelio:** "That would be fine. But right now, I want to assure you of my loyalty for all you have done. It is unwavering."[9]

In 1951, a Senate investigation of organized crime concluded that Costello was "strong in the councils of the Democratic Party of New York County."[10] Through its Tammany Hall connections, the mob remained a force in New York politics into the 1960s. But the long trail of corruption, beginning with Aaron Burr's use of Tammany Hall in the 1800 election, runs all the way through the history of the Democratic Party and connects the party's three most famous twentieth-century presidents—Roosevelt, Truman, and Kennedy—directly to some of America's most notorious gangsters.

The Kingfish and the Pendergast Man

While mobsters were running New York and picking presidents, the state of Louisiana was under the thrall of one of the most vicious demagogues in American history, Huey Long. A brilliant lawyer, Long was elected governor as a Democrat in 1928 after making a heart-breaking appeal to Louisiana's poor: "Where are the schools that you have waited for your children to have that have never come? Where are the roads and highways that you spent your money to build, that are no nearer now than ever before? Where are the institutions to care for the sick and disabled?" Long was as good as his word, instituting new corporate taxes to pay for roads, schools, bridges, and hospitals. But Long was also power-mad and used his popularity to elect a legislature that voted vast powers to the governor. Every policeman in the state reported to Long, and he controlled practically every government job in Louisiana, including tax collectors and schoolteachers. Newspaper editors who criticized him were beaten, kidnapped, or imprisoned, and he was guarded by a machine gun-wielding security detail.[11]

Elected to the Senate, Long soon gathered a national following and began attacking President Roosevelt, whom he had supported in 1932. Long's charge was that the New Deal was insufficiently radical. Instead, he promoted his own "Share the Wealth" program, which included the following proposals:

- Fortunes would be limited to $5 million.

- No one's income could be greater than $1.8 million a year or less than $2,000.

- Children would receive a free education from kindergarten through college.

- Every family would be entitled to a $6,000 homestead grant and a radio, an automobile, and a washing machine.[12]

To promote his left-wing agenda, Long sought support from anti-Semitic demagogues such as Father Charles Coughlin and Gerald L. K. Smith, as well as from the segregationist Democratic governor of Georgia, Eugene Talmadge. With the slogan "Every Man a King," Long's ideas were widely appealing to poor people in the midst of the Great Depression, especially those too ignorant of economics to ask whether the government could get enough money to pay for such a scheme. Such was the threat of this rival brand of class warfare that FDR's team commissioned a secret poll to determine how popular Long was. The result shocked them: Long had the support of some four million voters. That wasn't enough to challenge Roosevelt for the 1936 presidential nomination, but if Long were to run on a third-party ticket, his votes would be enough to prevent Roosevelt's reelection. That possibility was averted when Long was assassinated in September 1935, by a young doctor disgruntled because his father-in-law, a Louisiana judge, had been gerrymandered out of a job by Long.[13]

While Long's newfangled demagoguery held Louisiana under its grip, Missouri was suffering from a more traditional Democratic disorder—domination by the corrupt machine in Kansas City. The machine was founded by James Pendergast, an alderman who owned saloons and gambling dens. As early as 1902, more than two-thirds of the Kansas City police force was under his control, and he brought his younger brother, Tom, into the operation. One of the tricks of Tom Pendergast's Democratic Party operation was to keep lists of vacant lots. On Election Day, the Democrats would gather up "prostitutes, thieves . . . anybody we could get on the voting registration books," then transport them to the polling places. The lawlessness and corruption of the city prompted a federal judge to declare: "Kansas City is a seething cauldron of crime, licensed and protected."[14] As one historian put it, Pendergast "controlled not just the political machine that bore his family name but the local Mafia as well."[15] A gangster named Johnny Lazia ran the Kansas City mob until he was charged with tax evasion and threatened to "blow the lid" on the city's corruption. He was gunned down at his home.[16]

Lazia was killed in 1934, the same year that a Pendergast-backed judge was elected Missouri's U.S. senator. His election was due to a campaign of terror by the Kansas City gang that left four men dead, with vote fraud on a massive scale. The new senator's name was Harry Truman, and though his biographers say that Truman was never personally corrupt, his loyalty to the Pendergast machine was complete. Years later, when Tom Pendergast was sent to prison for income-tax evasion, Truman said: "He was my friend when I needed him, and I will be his." When, in 1944, Truman was tapped to become FDR's vice president, the choice outraged many Democrats, who derisively referred to the selection as the "Second Missouri Compromise." Interior Secretary Harold Ickes called Truman's selection evidence of "the seeming dominant position that corrupt city bosses now have in the Democratic national organization," while Eleanor Roosevelt remarked icily: "It looks to me as though the bosses had functioned pretty smoothly."[17]

The story of how Truman became vice president, over the objection of so many Democrats, takes us back to the streets of New York. During the brutal labor struggles in the city's garment industry, both the unions and the owners used hired muscle—guys like Monk Eastman, "Little Augie" Orgren, Lucky Luciano, and Legs Diamond all did their share of strong arming. Most brutal of all was Louis "Lepke" Buchalter, who led a gang of vicious killers that became known as "Murder Incorporated." After eliminating Orgen, Buchalter took over his rival's operation, providing security for unions that included the Amalagamated Clothing Workers of America (ACWA). At least two murders of which Buchalter was suspected—those of factory owner Guido Fererri and trucker Joe Rosen—were allegedly ordered by the ACWA boss. Buchalter was sent to the electric chair in 1944, refusing a deal that would have spared his life if he had "named names." Before his execution, Buchalter said ominously: "If I would talk a lot of big people would get hurt. When I say big, I mean big. The names would surprise you."[18]

In FDR's White House, few names were bigger than that of Sidney Hillman, head of the ACWA and founder of the Congress of Industrial

Organizations (CIO). Hillman was named to key positions as labor advisor to the National Recovery Administration and later the Wartime Production Board. Hillman's connection with Buchalter led many to speculate that Hillman was one of the "big people" whom Buchalter might have implicated had he decided to talk to investigators. Yet when Democratic National Committee chairman Robert Hannegan suggested Truman as FDR's running mate in 1944, Roosevelt told Hannegan, "Clear it with Sidney"—the labor boss's approval was all that was needed.[19]

A year before Truman was picked as FDR's vice president, a train crew in a Chicago railyard saw a strange sight: a drunk with a bottle of whiskey in one hand and a pistol in the other was standing on the tracks. As they watched, the man raised the pistol to his head and blew his brains out. So died Frank Nitti, chief lieutenant to Al Capone. One day before his suicide, Nitti and seven others had been indicted on federal conspiracy and extortion charges, accused of plotting to take over a key movie-industry union. Nitti had masterminded the scheme, and when it went sour, his criminal cohorts gave him the bad news: he had to take the rap or . . . well, this *was* Chicago. Nitti had just gotten out of prison and didn't plan on going back, and so he ended his life on the tracks.[20] He might not have pulled the trigger had he known that his colleagues would spend only three years behind bars, thanks to their friends in the Truman administration.

In the hotly contested 1946 congressional elections, Chicago reporter Jim Doherty began hearing curious talk on the streets: Republicans in the Italian-American community were being pressured to vote Democrat. "The word is out, we all got to go Democratic this time," one source told him. One of Doherty's editors heard an even more explicit explanation: "We have got the word. We have to go Democratic this time so four guys can get out on parole." And that fall, Doherty later testified, "Those Italian Republican leaders delivered ten thousand or fifteen thousand votes to the Democratic organization."[21]

Meanwhile, in Dallas, Texas, a lawyer named Maury Hughes found he had a generous new client—a trucking company owner from Chicago, seeking his services on behalf of federal inmate Paul Ricca, one of Frank Nitti's coconspirators. In addition to being a lawyer, Hughes was a prominent Democrat and a childhood friend of Tom Clark, Harry Truman's attorney general. Soon, other lawyers were added to the legal team: Paul Dillon, lawyer for the Pendergast machine in Kansas City, and A. Bradley Eben, whose mother worked in the White House as an assistant secretary to Truman. By August 1947, Ricca and his associates walked out of the federal pen at Leavenworth as free men. When a congressional committee tried to investigate the parole scandal, Attorney General Clark was uncooperative, and Truman issued an executive order to prevent the committee from obtaining key documents in the case. According to Sam Giancana's brother Chuck, the Mob went all out to reelect Truman in 1948, saying, "We own him. We own the White House." And in the hotly contested election, with the Democrats split three ways, the famous "Dewey Beats Truman" headline might have been true, had it not been for the help of the Democrat's gangster friends: "Boy, does Truman owe Chicago," Giancana said. "Thirty thousand votes . . . that's all he won by. Jesus, we had to beg, borrow, and steal to swing the son of a bitch. . . . No way the man doesn't know who got him elected."[22]

Sixteen years later, an FBI wiretap caught a Chicago gang boss explaining how they arranged the paroles for Capone's former underlings: "The trick was to get to Tom Clark"—but the attorney general was worried about negative publicity if the notorious mobsters were turned loose. As the FBI listened, the gangster explained how the deal was finally made with Clark: "If he had the thick skin to do it, he'd get the next appointment to the Supreme Court." And in October 1949, Truman did just that, appointing Tom Clark to a seat on the nation's highest court.[23]

Sweet Home, Chicago

In Chicago, Sam "Mooney" Giancana's syndicate went all out to elect Richard Daley as mayor in 1955. The *Chicago Tribune* warned that

Daley's election would mean that "the political and social mores of the badlands are going . . . to have a powerful influence" at city hall.[24] But the Outfit controlled the city's First Ward, where it delivered an overwhelming 13,275-to-1,961 margin that helped Daley win, and Daley repaid the favor. The head of the Chicago civil service commission was replaced with a man who had been head of a mob-controlled union. The First Ward alderman intervened with the new mayor to ensure that Daley chose the mob's handpicked man to head the ward's police precinct. Throughout his twenty years as mayor, Daley demonstrated a decidedly laissez-faire policy toward the operations of the Chicago syndicate.[25]

The Chicago mob had other powerful friends. During Prohibition, one of the most successful bootleggers was not a mobster but a Harvard-educated Boston banker, who was well-known to some of his occasional customers such as Costello, Lansky, and Luciano. His specialty was smuggling in Canadian whiskey. In 1926, Canadian investigators were attempting to discover if American bootleggers were cheating the Canadian government out of excise taxes. One of the firms they investigated was the Hiram Walker distillery, which had increased production at its facility in Canada by 400 percent to meet the increased demand brought on by Prohibition. Joseph Kennedy's name appeared over and over in the Hiram Walker books, along with the names of Al Capone and other gangsters. Since Capone controlled bootleg traffic from Canada across Lake Michigan, it is almost certain that Kennedy would have had to do business with Capone in order to smuggle his Canadian whiskey purchases into the United States.[26]

Corroboration of the Capone-Kennedy connection is mostly anecdotal, but Joe Kennedy's later ties to organized crime are indisputable, because the gangsters knew the man they were dealing with. In the Roaring Twenties, Kennedy was just another young businessman smuggling whiskey, but by 1960, he was a former ambassador and influential Democrat, angling to get his son, Sen. John F. Kennedy, elected to the White House.

Nearly three decades had passed since Joe Kennedy's whiskey-running days, and he no longer had any direct mob ties in Chicago. So he enlisted the help of go-betweens—including John's buddy Frank Sinatra, who knew Giancana through the mob's Las Vegas operations—to contact Mooney Giancana. With further aid from a Chicago judge, Kennedy set up a face-to-face meeting with Giancana in the judge's chambers. The exact terms of their agreement are unknown, but afterward, Giancana sought approval from "the boys"—his associates Arcado, Paul Ricca, and Murray "Curley" Humphreys. Arcado and Ricca voted in favor of the deal, but not Humphreys, who considered Kennedy "untrustworthy." Humphreys recalled that his buddy Luciano had been double-crossed by FDR, and Humphreys' wife, Jeanne, wrote in her journal that her husband had other reasons to distrust Kennedy, dating back to Prohibition: "Something to do with a booze delivery that Joe had stolen. [Humphreys] said Joe Kennedy could not be trusted as far as he, Murray, could throw a piano."[27]

Humphreys was right. The Chicago gangsters worked with the Daley machine to help JFK carry Illinois in 1960, but just weeks after the election, word leaked out that the president-elect's younger brother, Bobby, was being considered for the post of attorney general. The Kennedy family's maverick, Bobby, had made a name for himself as chief counsel for the McClellan Committee, a Senate investigation of ties between labor unions and organized crime. Once he took office as attorney general, Bobby Kennedy quadrupled the size of the Justice Department's organized crime division and cracked down hard—especially on the mob in Chicago, to the chagrin of Giancana. Some conspiracy-minded writers have suggested that Giancana or other mobsters played a role in John F. Kennedy's 1963 assassination, but journalist Gus Russo—whose 2001 book *The Outfit* exhaustively chronicled the relationship between the Chicago mob and the Kennedy family—discounts such theories. Russo notes that Humphreys told his wife: "We're not connected with it, but they got the wrong one"—a wish that Bobby Kennedy would have been killed instead. That sentiment was echoed by another mobster, caught on an FBI wiretap telling an associate: "They killed the good one. They should have killed the other little guy."[28]

Since the days of FDR, Truman, and JFK, Democrats have cleaned up their ties with the mob: they now call it "support for organized labor."

THE UNION LABEL

LABOR UNIONS' DEATH-GRIP
ON THE DEMOCRATS

"The Democratic Party is a wholly owned subsidiary of Big Labor."
—LINDA CHAVEZ[1]

THE CROWD HUSHED AS A MAN WEARING A BLACK HOOD made his way to the witness table near the front of the historic, paneled hearing room where Congress once deliberated the fate of President Richard M. Nixon. The man took his seat at the table, shielded from the gallery of spectators by a three-sided cardboard partition. Only members of the House Crime Subcommittee could see him.[2]

Committee chairman Bill McCollum, a Florida Republican, gaveled the room to order.[3] "There will be no photographs permitted of this witness," he said. Then McCollum told the man he could remove his hood: "Mr. Fino, you're now in the clear."[4]

Ron Fino was—and may still be—a man with a Mafia contract on his head. He grew up the son and nephew of "made" Mafioso killers in Buffalo, New York. As a boy, he used to visit his father, Joe Fino, and his Uncle Nick in Attica state prison. Upon graduating from high school in 1964, he joined Laborer's International Union of North America (LIUNA), and from 1974 to 1989, served as business manager of LIUNA

Local 210 in Buffalo. For eight of those years, he was a national union official—and also an informant for the FBI.[5]

Disgusted by the mob's theft of workers' union dues, and disillusioned by the union's acquiescence, Fino detailed for U.S. Justice Department officials the extent of Mafia control over LIUNA: that, for example, mobsters had for years systematically pillaged LIUNA's federally funded training programs; that they had drained more than $50 million from union pension trusts; that the mob had corrupted an FBI employee in Cleveland; that Arthur E. Coia, the union's No. 2 man in New England and father of future LIUNA president Arthur A. Coia, answered to both Mafia don Raymond Patriarca (whose union philosophy, caught on tape, was "Hit them, break their legs to get things your way") and to the Genovese crime family in New York. And much, much more.[6]

Fino met with FBI agents more than four thousand times delivering unprecedented detail on the staggering scope of the Mafia's union chokehold. But in 1989, a Mafia soldier named Danny Domino sent word to Fino via a relative: the mob knows "you've been cooperating with the Justice Department, and been doing it for years. There's a contract on you. Danny says get out of town fast."[7]

Fino did, living on the run for seven years, sometimes hiding out on military bases, seeing his family perhaps once a year.[8] Finally, on July 24, 1996, he risked his life to appear before the House Crime Subcommittee to tell Congress what he knew.

And for that Democrats openly mocked him.

"Is that bulletproof?" Rep. Melvin Watt asked about the partition that shielded Fino from view. "I just want to know if I'm in danger if somebody opens fire."

The gallery chortled.

"Mr. Fino," said Rep. Charles Schumer, now a senator on that chamber's Judiciary Committee, "do you believe space aliens are linked to the mob?"

How is it that Schumer, of New York, a state terrorized for decades by the "Five Families" of La Cosa Nostra, would question the sanity and truthfulness of Fino, the son and confidant of powerful Mafiosos, a man intimate with organized labor's criminal underbelly, a man who had tried to do the right thing and received for his pains a price on his own head?

In a word: money.

"Fino's testimony struck at the heart of an illicit alliance in which a Mafia-dominated union provided multimillion-dollar campaign contributions and Justice Department racket-busters were shackled," wrote Eugene H. Methvin in the *Weekly Standard* in August 1998.[9]

Methvin, who served from 1983 to 1986 on the President's Commission on Organized Crime, and directed its investigation into labor-management racketeering, revealed that the House subcommittee investigating LIUNA in 1996 had received confidential information that federal prosecutors had been thwarted in their plan to take over and clean up the union. But subcommittee Democrats, including Schumer, blocked subpoenas that would have forced testimony from insiders who might have uncovered the fix.[10]

Many suspected the fix came from Bill and Hillary Clinton, whose cozy relationship with LIUNA's mob-linked Arthur A. Coia was key in triggering the McCollum hearings. (More on that in Chapter Eleven.) Schumer, meanwhile, soon received his reward. Less than a year after the LIUNA hearings, he announced he would run for the Senate in 1998. The Laborers PAC kicked in $10,000, the maximum campaign contribution allowed by federal law.[11] In all, unions poured $227,428 into his campaign. In his 2004 campaign, Big Labor continued to back Schumer, by then the senior senator from New York, contributing $178,750 through union PACs—that we know of.[12] Of the more than $27 million he raised, he did not disclose the origin of more than $3.5 million, or 13 percent of funds received.[13] That's more than six times the amount of funds of "undisclosed" origin received by the average member of Congress in the 2002 election cycle, according to the Center for Responsive Politics.

Now one of the Senate's most influential Democrats, Charles

Schumer serves on the powerful Senate Judiciary Committee, where—as evidenced in judicial confirmation hearings of John Roberts in 2005 and Samuel Alito in 2006—he measures candidates for the federal bench based not on their ability to fairly interpret the Constitution, but on their personal philosophies relative to a leftist agenda that matches that of Big Labor blow by blow.

In their seminal 2004 book *Betrayal,* Linda Chavez and Daniel Gray chronicle Big Labor's cannibalizing effect on the national economy and its death grip on Democrats at all levels of government. The authors boldly call the Democratic Party a "wholly owned subsidiary" of organized labor. [14]

It will not shock any American drawing breath that Democrats and unions toe the same ideological line (big government, higher taxes, affirmative action, a living wage, gay rights, considering Barbra Streisand a savvy political analyst), or that organized labor annually pumps millions of dollars into Democratic politics. But the results of a 1996 Federal Election Commission (FEC) investigation floored a lot of people: unions aren't just *in league* with the Democrats, or philosophically simpatico, but in *control* of the party, with *veto power* over the plans, projects, and needs of the Democratic National Committee (DNC) and its state affiliates. According to an internal DNC document from the 1996 campaign, "When the DNC and its National partners including . . . the AFL-CIO and the NEA agree on the contents of a plan, each national partner will give their funding commitment to the state." Before any DNC or state party plans could be implemented, however, they had to be "submitted with a signature page" showing the "formal sign off" of the AFL-CIO.

"This integration of the NEA into the Democratic Party goes a long way toward explaining how a monopoly that today leaves nearly two-thirds of African-American and Hispanic fourth-graders illiterate has insulated itself against political accountability," wrote *Wall Street Journal* chief editorialist William McGurn.[15]

The DNC and the AFL-CIO sued to keep the FEC from releasing

this information to the public. But the union watchdog group Landmark Legal Foundation snapped up the report before a judge could act. [16] As Chavez and Gray put it: "Obviously, Democrats don't want the details of their unholy alliance with Big Labor known to the American people, but union leaders also need to cover up their infiltration of the Democratic Party. Labor bosses continue to speak in terms of fighting for the rights of working men and women. . . . Thus they obscure the fact that they have essentially abandoned the interests of those working people in order to enhance their own political power."[17]

In the 2003–2004 election cycle, 225 union PACS contributed $53,728,129 to candidates running for federal office. Of that, $46,420,851—or 86 percent—went to Democrats.[18] An analysis of the top all-time donors is even more revealing: Of the top ten donors between 1989 and 2004, eight are labor unions. Among the top twenty, fourteen are unions. Among the top ten donors, unions contributed a combined total of $198,952,722—95 percent to Democrats. From that mountain of cash, Republican candidates received only $10.5 million.[19]

That's only the hard money. According to some estimates, unions spend as much as $800 million dollars *a year* on politics,[20] a combination of cash and in-kind contributions, including advertising; "volunteers" released from their regular jobs to work on behalf of political campaigns; and armies of paid political operatives. For example, the National Education Association—the nation's most politically powerful union—employs 1,800 full-time political operatives, who are paid out of the forced dues collected from teachers.

So what? you may be asking. Can't labor organizations support any candidates they wish? Sure. The problem is that, in many cases, labor unions are shot through with crime, corruption, and violence, with some still controlled by various incarnations of the mob.

Imagine the headlines were it the case that *over the past seventeen years* the top donors to the Republican Party turned out to be Enron, WorldComm, Tyco, and other corporations caught up in the pension and stock manipulation scandals of the early 2000s. Imagine the uproar were it revealed that those companies had veto power over GOP plans and policies. Yet that is precisely the case with the Democratic Party. Consider the crime and corruption in the first ten months of 2005 alone among eight of the top ten donors to Democratic federal candidates, as tracked by National Legal and Policy Center's *Union Corruption Update.*[21]

American Federation of State, County & Municipal Employee Unions (AFSCME)

- March 9: A federal grand jury indicted former AFSCME Local 2719 treasurer Deborah Dewitt on charges of mail fraud and embezzlement. Dewitt, sixty-two, a resident of Verona, Pennsylvania, and a former Pittsburgh city employee, allegedly wrote union reimbursement checks of an unspecified amount to herself during the period of April 1999 to April 2001. Her M.O. was to receive checks from the union, report a larger amount to the bank for cashing, and pocket the difference. In one case, Dewitt received a check from the local for $87.15, but cashed it at the bank for $2,087.15 and kept the change.

- September 7: Elizabeth Fiske, AFSCME ex-bookkeeper and office secretary for Council 38 in Arkansas, indicted in U.S. District Court, Eastern District of Arkansas, on sixty-three counts of embezzling $32,793 in union funds.

- September 20: Gary Gourley, formerly president of AFSCME Local 1522 in Connecticut pleaded guilty to embezzling $63,084 in union funds.

National Education Association (NEA)

- February 17: Michael Koehler, former business manager of Local 965 in Milwaukee, was resentenced for embezzling $135,198 in union funds. In November 2002, Koehler had been sentenced to two years and one month in prison, plus three years supervised release, and ordered to make full restitution. But he failed to provide financial records and make restitution, so a Wisconsin district judge tacked an extra ninety days of community confinement onto the end of his prison sentence.

- September: Wayne Kruse, former president of the Lawrence (Kansas) Education Association, an NEA affiliate, pleaded guilty to one count each of theft and forgery in connection with stealing more than $97,000 from $240,000 in dues payments deducted from union members' paychecks between November 2003 and August 2004. Because Kruse had no prior criminal record, Douglas County District Court Judge Jack Murphy sentenced him to two years probation.

Communication Workers of America (CWA)

- January 13: Former secretary-treasurer James Pearson was sentenced to three years probation after pleading guilty in October 2004 to embezzling $28,686 in union funds.

- September 6: George P. Strollo, former treasurer for Communications Workers of America Local 81495, pleaded guilty in U.S. District Court, Western District of New York, to falsifying union records to conceal thefts.

Service Employees Union International

- March 22: Charles Cart, former Democratic Party boss for Sussex County, pleaded not guilty in federal court on charges of embezzlement and money laundering that bankrupted a New Jersey local. Cart is also charged with creating a bogus consulting position for an associate who collected $84,000 from the union between August 2000 and July 2001 for services he never provided. The associate allegedly kept $7,000 per month while passing $56,000 on to Cart.

Laborers (LIUNA)

- June 21: For years, Laborers Local 91 dictated the terms of hiring at construction sites in Niagara County, New York. Nonunion workers and any contractor foolish enough to hire them faced vandalism, assault, and extortion. In a predawn raid in 2002, federal agents arrested more than a dozen union members. In late spring 2005, two Local 91 "enforcers," Anthony Cerrone and Andrew Shomers, pleaded guilty to racketeering. Salvatore Bertino went down next. The former local vice president, fifty-three, pleaded guilty in June to racketeering conspiracy. At his hearing, Bertino admitted to five incidents in which Local 91 President Mark Congi directed him and others to engage in extortion. Seven other union officials, including Congi, were also indicted.

- September 21: Joseph Calcagno, former business manager/secretary treasurer for Local 1162, was sentenced in U.S. District Court, District of Massachusetts, to two years probation for making false entries in the local's financial records. He also was ordered to make $66,632 in restitution to the union for improper expenses.

Carpenters & Joiners Union

- June 8: Julie Messick, former treasurer for Carpenters Local 2001, was sentenced to one year of probation for embezzling $11,800 in union funds.

Teamsters (International Brotherhood of Teamsters)

- August 19: The City of Chicago created the Hired Truck Program to outsource hauling work to private trucking companies—in the process creating a corrupt system in which city officials accepted bribes to award or extend contracts. Through July 2005, thirty-two former city workers and trucking officials were charged in an FBI investigation that ran for about two years. In August, the Justice Department indicted Anthony Affetto, sixty-six, of Chicago, and

Robert Mangiamele, sixty-two, of Mount Prospect, Illinois, charging that they had paid bribes to Donald Tomczak, the city's ex-first deputy water commissioner. Tomczak admitted to taking bribes and shaking down campaign contributions from trucking firms for a total of nearly $400,000.

Tomczak is a Democrat.

That hit parade is only a partial listing of the crime and corruption infesting just the top eight union donors to Democratic politics—and only for 2005. (Remember, there are four more unions among the Top 20 all-time donors.) A complete accounting of crime and corruption would have taken up two chapters in this book.

The Democratic Party claims to represent the interests of "working families." Yet the party accepts millions in campaign contributions each year from unions, some of which have officials who routinely steal from working families, embezzling from the pension and training funds those families entrust to their care. Why?

And why do Democrats, who claim to be on the side of teachers, take millions of dollars each year in influence money, skimmed directly from the paychecks of rank-and-file teachers, then lobby each year for the federal government to spend more money on education, claiming teachers don't get paid enough? For that matter, why does the party, which claims to be fighting for schoolchildren, submit itself to the control of unions whose bosses steal taxpayer money and, like Gwendolyn Hemphill, use it to shower themselves—and their political beneficiaries—with expensive perks and gifts?

On August 31, 2005, a federal jury convicted James Odell Baxter II, fifty-one, and Gwendolyn Hemphill, sixty-four, of twenty-three counts of conspiracy, mail and wire fraud, embezzlement, false statements, money laundering, and other charges in connection with their roles in looting the Washington Teachers Association (WTU) treasury of nearly $5 million between 1995 and 2002. Baxter is formerly the WTU treasurer. Hemphill is the former assistant to disgraced WTU President Barbara Bullock, who had already pleaded guilty to mail fraud and conspiracy. By the time of Hemphill's conviction, Bullock was already enjoying her nine-year stay at a federal penitentiary.[22]

The trio, it seemed, had taken to using the WTU treasury as their personal bank account. Baxter used union credit cards to make at least $537,000 in personal purchases and wrote union checks to himself, including some designated as "pension payments."[23] Hemphill used a signature stamp to convert union checks into cash and misspent at least $492,000 collected from rank-and-file teachers.[24] On one occasion, the three crooks stole $720,000 from teachers by directing its district Washington, D.C., in writing, to withhold an extra $144 in dues per teacher during one pay period in June 2002.[25]

In December 2002, the FBI found out what happened to a big hunk of the money. Investigators searched the homes of Baxter, Bullock, and Hemphill, unearthing the urbanites' equivalent of Aladdin's treasure cave. The Bureau affidavit listing the loot was two single-spaced, margin-to-margin pages long and included: a 288-piece set of Tiffany silverware; a full-length mink coat, a black cashmere cape with fox trim, and a three-piece mink scarf set; handbags from Fendi, Gucci, Dolce & Gabbana, Ferragamo, Bally, Louis Vuitton, and Chanel; caches of Herend luxury porcelain, William Yeoward glassware, and a Baccarat crystal vase with spiral steps up the side; jewelry from Neiman-Marcus, a ring and silver watch from Tiffany, and strands of baroque pearls in white and gray; stacks of framed art and sculptures from fine artists and high-end galleries; ladies' clothing from Versace, Chanel, St. John, and Myong Lim.[26]

Oh, and a double-barrel shotgun.

Bullock, meanwhile, spread the wealth: in 2000, she used a WTU American Express card to donate $9,000 to the Democratic National Committee and $2,000 to Hillary Clinton.[27]

But that wasn't the only place the scandal intersected with the

Democrats. Prior to the revelation that she was likely a thief, Hemphill had been known in D.C. as a Democratic Party insider, a "savvy hostess, dishing out barbecued ribs and political gossip . . . ," wrote the *Washington Post's* Craig Timberg after the scandal broke. "She was the kind of woman who, decade after decade, seemed at the right place at the right time as mayors came and went . . ." By 2002, she had ensconced herself as Democratic Mayor Anthony A. Williams's campaign manager and executive director of the city's Democratic Party.[28]

While drawing a full-time union salary, she worked virtually full time to reelect Williams. Hemphill later admitted she used a WTU credit card to pay for such things as $1,200 worth of T-shirts given to delegates to the 2000 Democratic National Convention and a $20,000 party for a top mayoral aide featuring a band, an open bar, and . . . barbecued ribs.[29] Again, all money stolen from taxpayers and classroom teachers.

Meanwhile, Bullock and Hemphill—both full-time union staffers— threw their weight around in the mayor's office. According to a former official at the D.C. Office of Boards and Commissions, Hemphill routinely submitted names of people she wanted appointed to government boards.[30] And under Williams, the WTU negotiated a contract raising salaries of its members by 20 percent over three years. (A concession, perhaps, for the fact that union leaders were robbing members blind.) The mayor's senior aides also helped Bullock and Hemphill secure for teachers free or discounted legal services, a perk that cost D.C. taxpayers about $1 million a year.[31] In addition, the women exercised enormous influence over hiring and firing decisions in city jobs. For example, mayoral aide Mark A. Jones said Williams told him to hire Hemphill's husband as director of the D.C. Office of the Public Advocate.[32]

As Chavez and Gray put it, the alliance between organized labor and the Democratic Party is a "corrupt bargain."[33] Regardless of the political views of their memberships, unions funnel money to Democrats. Democrats then work to pass laws and policies that align with the union agenda—an agenda that results in a more lenient criminal justice system, substandard schools, and bigger government, all of which require more money from taxpayers who funded the whole mess in the first place. The relationship between Democrats and organized labor cannot be compared to corporate financing of Republican campaigns—first, because business contributions are voluntary, while most union contributions are compulsory (if not stolen outright, as in the case of Barbara Bullock); and second, because corporations spread their donations more evenly between the national parties compared with unions, which buy Democrats in bulk.

In some cases, Democrats and unions buy each other. In 2001, U.S. Attorney Mary Jo White indicted Teamsters President Ron Carey on charges of lying, both to federal investigators and a grand jury, in connection with an elaborate campaign-finance swindle that implicated the Teamsters, other unions, the future head of the DNC, and, as seems par, at least one person named Harold Ickes.[34]

The indictment was a long time coming—and, it turned out, full of holes—revolving as it did around the 1996 election for Teamsters president. That race pitted the incumbent Carey against Jimmy Hoffa, the son of James R. Hoffa, the mob-controlled Teamsters boss who disappeared from the parking lot of the Machus Red Fox restaurant near Detroit right around the time he was to meet "Tony Jack" Giacalone and "Tony Pro" Provenzano, a pair of Jersey Mafiosos.[35] (Go figure.)

Teamsters' ties to such wise guys are legendary. By the time Carey was elected to his first term as Teamsters president in 1991, the union was already under the control of a federal Independent Review Board (IRB), the result of racketeering charges brought against the union by a tough U.S. attorney named Rudy Giuliani.[36] Carey, a registered Republican at the time, ran on the promise of kicking the mobsters out of the union. But once in office, he switched parties, bringing the Teamsters back into the Democratic fold just in time for the 1992 elections.[37]

Prior to the Democratic National Convention in New York that summer, Carey hooked up with Harold Ickes Jr., Bill Clinton's New York campaign chairman. Ickes was an accomplished labor lawyer, having accomplished much on behalf of unions charged with crimes, particularly racketeering. The firm's client roster included a number of mob-infested unions, a fact that would delay for a year Ickes' appointment as Bill Clinton's White House chief of staff. [38] But the Carey-Ickes meeting was a match made in heaven. Once he secured his White House job, Ickes wrote Bill Clinton a memo detailing the importance of the Teamsters—and likely their cash and political foot soldiers—to the administration. Ickes urged the new president to get acquainted with Carey on a personal basis.[39] From 1992 to 1996, the Teamsters delivered millions in campaign contributions to the Clintons and the DNC.[40] Then, facing a tough reelection race against Hoffa and a campaign finance dilemma of his own, Carey, through intermediaries, called his marker due.[41]

To battle corruption and restore democracy to the Teamsters, the federal government had provided for the election of union officers by secret ballot, with the entire election overseen by a federally appointed officer.[42] Meanwhile, Teamsters rules forbade the use of General Treasury funds to promote any particular candidate for union office. But Carey had a problem: his campaign manager, Jere Nash, had conducted polling that showed Carey's lead over Hoffa narrowing. So Nash commissioned Martin Davis of The November Group, a political consulting firm in D.C., to create a direct-mail campaign to drum up support for the incumbent. The price tag: $700,000.[43]

That's a lot of cash. Coincidentally, the Teamsters general fund was full of cash. But how to get at it? In September 1996, Davis, working with Nash and a Massachusetts telemarketer named Michael Ansara, came up with a plan: they would induce wealthy donors to contribute money to the Carey campaign so that the candidate could pay his direct-mail bill. In return, the Teamsters would contribute from their general fund a multiplied amount to the wealthy donors' pet causes. Davis, Nash, and Ansara consulted the union's Government Affairs director William Hamilton Jr. He agreed to dip into the Teamster's treasury as long as the contributions could withstand later scrutiny.[44]

In October 1996, the collaborators tested the plan with a very rich fellow named Charles Blitz, who wanted to financially bless two liberal causes, Citizen Action and Project Vote. On October 24, Ron Carey authorized Hamilton to donate $475,000 to Citizen Action's Campaign for a Responsible Congress, a group that during that election cycle would mount a $7 million get-out-the-vote drive on behalf of Democratic candidates.[45] Carey also authorized a $175,000 to Project Vote, a liberal outreach to senior citizens and minority voters.

For his part, Blitz raised approximately $185,000 in checks and donated them to the hilariously named Teamsters for a Corruption-Free Union (TCFU), the committee Carey had created to receive contributions from non-Teamsters. Upon learning that Carey had approved the donations to the Citizen Action and Project vote, Ansara released the checks payable to the TCFU to the Carey campaign's New York City attorneys, who used them to pay part of The November Group's bill for the pro-Carey direct mailing campaign.[46]

And around it went. Carey approved similar money-swapping schemes with the National Council of Senior Citizens (an AFL-CIO front group), the AFL itself, the Service Employees International Union, and the Association of Federal, State, County & Municipal Employees. In all, he spent at least $885,000 in member dues to ensure his own reelection.

November Group consultant Martin Davis later confessed to federally appointed Teamsters election monitor Ken Conboy that he thought a similar scheme might work with the Democratic National Committee. Prior to Carey's reelection campaign, the Teamsters had already intended to make contributions to the national Party and its affiliates during the 1996 federal campaign.[47] Davis's plan was to up the ante: the Teamsters, in exchange for contributions to the Carey campaign from wealthy donors identified by the DNC, would use dues money from the union's general fund to donate even more to the party than they'd originally planned to.[48]

In the spring and summer of 1996, Davis approached the DNC and Clinton-Gore '96 Reelection Committee officials, including a man named Terry McAuliffe, with the idea. Would the DNC, Davis wanted to know, raise $100,000 for the Carey campaign in exchange for bigger donations from the Teamsters?[49] According to Conboy's later report, either the Clinton-Gore '96 Reelection Committee or the DNC told Davis that summer that they'd found a willing donor, a Filipino woman from California.[50,51] Unfortunately, the woman turned out to be ineligible under the Teamsters election rules and . . . well, the feds were watching. Davis continued to urge McAuliffe and other DNC players to identify someone eligible to donate. He also asked Hamilton, via Nash, to postpone donating to the DNC until the party came up with someone who could fork over cash to the Carey campaign. That request was memorialized by a note, written by hand on an August 10, 1996, memorandum. The memo was from the DNC's Richard Sullivan, asking the Teamsters to hold up their end of the bargain and hand over contributions totaling approximately $1 million. Davis forwarded the memo to Hamilton after jotting a note on it: "I'll let you know when they [the DNC] have fulfilled their commitments."[52]

The DNC never succeeded in locating an eligible donor to the Carey campaign. But Conboy, the election supervisor, concluded that "despite the fact that no funds were raised for the Carey campaign through the DNC swap scheme, it is clear that the individuals who participated in the scheme violated the Election Rules." Nash and Davis pleaded guilty to the fundraising scheme.[53]

Carey beat Jimmy Hoffa by a slim margin to retain the union presidency. But on July 16, 1997, Carey appeared before a grand jury to answer questions about the campaign finance scam. Part of the conversation went like this:

> **Grand Jury:** At any point in time in 1996 were you told either by someone in the Teamsters organization or at the Carey campaign, were

you ever told that there was any link between contributions that the [Teamsters were] making to any organization, whether it was a political action committee, Citizen Action, or other unions, and help that your campaign, that the Carey campaign, was receiving in its fundraising efforts?

Carey: No. And if I had, I would have got to the bottom of that and heads would have rolled.

Grand Jury: You would have stopped it in its tracks?

Carey: Absolutely.[54]

Conboy apparently didn't believe Carey, because he invalidated the election and expelled him from the union.[55] The evidence against him, which included affidavits and eyewitness testimony, also earned him seven counts of lying to investigators in U.S. Attorney Mary Jo White's 2001 indictment. Still, a trial jury acquitted Carey after he told them he knew nothing of the campaign-finance quid pro quo.[56]

Ms. White's indictment, meanwhile, was remarkably void of any mention of the Democratic National Committee. It is worth noting that she began working on the case four years earlier, under the supervision of Clinton Attorney General Janet Reno, but did not indict Carey until four days after George W. Bush became president—a full twenty-two months after Teamsters Governmental Affairs director William Hamilton was convicted on multiple felony counts in connection with the scheme.[57] For her part, Reno refused to appoint a special prosecutor to investigate allegations that Harold Ickes had lied to a Senate committee investigating the Teamsters scandal, drawing fire from House Republicans.

"Ickes told Congress the Clinton administration did nothing to help the Teamsters," said Pete Hoekstra of Michigan, who chaired the House panel that held hearings on the scandal. "But internal Clinton administration documents . . . show a different story."[58]

Terry McCauliffe went on to head the DNC. There, he, along with

Ickes, would later be implicated in a scheme to sell seats on taxpayer-financed foreign trade missions in exchange for campaign contributions—in keeping with Democrats' long history of illegal meddling in foreign affairs.

6

INTERNATIONAL CRIMINALS

THE PARTY OF TREASON AND SUBVERSION

"Congressmen who willfully take actions during wartime that damage morale
and undermine the military are saboteurs who should be arrested,
exiled or hanged."

—ABRAHAM LINCOLN

NOT CONTENT WITH STARVING, TORTURING, AND MURDERING their own people, Communist governments in the Soviet Union and Cuba in the late 1970s launched an outreach program. The objects of their benevolence: the Caribbean and Central America.

In El Salvador, the Farabundo Marti National Liberation Front (FMLN), a Marxist guerilla army, had stepped up attacks on the nation's noncommunist national government. In Nicaragua, the Sandinista Liberation Front had seized power from the corrupt dictator Anastasio Samoza. And on the tiny Caribbean island of Grenada, Marxist Maurice Bishop and the New Jewel Movement had staged a coup in 1979, transforming the nutmeg capital of the world into a totalitarian Communist outpost. Fidel Castro and the Kremlin provided military aid to their revolutionary brothers in all three countries. A senior Soviet general was on hand when Bishop signed military agreements with Cuba, North Korea, and the USSR.[1]

To the deeply anticommunist Ronald Reagan, Grenada was of particular concern. Though only 133 miles square, the island's Caribbean location would make it, with Cuba, the second Communist state within attack range of the American mainland. Bishop had begun constructing an airport, ostensibly to receive tourists, but with a runway of military length—10,000 feet—perfect for Soviet aircraft. Meanwhile, Cuban and Soviet military instructors had quickly built the island's People's Revolution Army into the largest fighting force in the region.[2]

Unfortunately for Bishop, Communists tend to eat their own. In 1983, his erstwhile friend and deputy prime minister, Bernard Coard, overthrew Bishop in a coup and, as is the custom among old Communist friends, had him executed. Grenada plunged into chaos, and six Caribbean nations, fearing the new regime, urgently petitioned the Reagan administration to intervene, though according to the prime ministers of Barbados and Jamaica this formal appeal was privately "requested" by the United States.[3]

In addition to strategic factors, the presence in Grenada of about a thousand Americans, most of them medical students, cemented the president's decision. In October 1983, he ordered Operation Urgent Fury, an efficient U.S. military invasion that within a few weeks wrested control of the island from its captors, and restored free elections and noncommunist rule.[4] The Stalinist Coard was sentenced to death and tossed into prison, where he remains today, appealing violations of his constitutional rights.[5]

In 2004, Coard was nearly freed, though, when Grenada High Court Judge Kenneth Benjamin overturned his life sentence.[6] Benjamin's decision was reversed, but the fleeting possibility of Coard's freedom likely set Democrats' hearts aflutter. Though the American forces that freed Grenada were greeted by citizens as liberators, and U.S. citizens kissed the ground upon returning to their own country, Democrats were apoplectic that Reagan had acted in defense of liberty.[7]

"There is no legitimate reason for the United States to seek to overthrow other governments we don't like," said Michigan Sen. Carl Levin.[8]

"This is Wednesday, and we must be in Grenada or Nicaragua or Lebanon or God knows where tomorrow," fumed then Representative (now Senator) Barbara Boxer of California, ratcheting up the rhetoric. "If we follow the reasoning put forth by many of my colleagues on the [Republican] side of the aisle, we may well be cheering on American forces in dozens of countries all over the world."[9] Meanwhile, U.S. journalists mocked the Reagan administration's claim that Coard's cooperation with the USSR and Cuba threatened U.S. national security. "The dreaded 'Soviet menace' advances . . . ," wrote *Washington Post* columnist Richard Cohen.[10]

That the Soviet-trained PRA greeted the American landing force with Soviet-made 12.7 mm guns tended to argue against Cohen's snarky quotation marks. So did thirty thousand pages of documents recovered from the Bishop regime. The contents of the papers "incriminated many prominent Americans," wrote leading British investigative journalist Chapman Pincher in *Traitors: The Anatomy of Treason*.[11] Among them: Barbara Lee. The Berkeley leftist, formerly a confidential aide to Black Panther "Minister of Defense" Huey Newton, was elected to Congress in 1998. But in 1983, she still served as an aide to then Congressman Ron Dellums.[12]

Dellums, also a Berkeley radical and Democrat, had not abandoned the Communist struggle, but like other moles and sympathizers on the U.S. payroll, continued to prosecute it by other means. Among the papers Bishop and his officers left behind were the minutes of a politburo meeting that included the following notation: "Barbara Lee is here presently and has brought with her a report on the international airport done by Ron Dellums. They have requested that we look at the document and suggest any changes we deem necessary. They will be willing to make the changes."[13, 14]

According to U.S. intelligence, Bishop's airport had been designed to host Soviet warplanes. The Reagan administration suspected that it would ultimately become the first Soviet base in the Western

Hemisphere. Dellums, who opposed that view—and any potential U.S. military action it might trigger—made a "fact-finding" trip to Grenada and issued an airport report of his own.[15] He concluded that the facility being built was "for the purpose of economic development and is not for military use." His report also slammed the administration's Soviet suspicions as "absurd, patronizing, and totally unwarranted."[16]

Dellums neglected to mention, however, that he was a patron of Maurice Bishop's, a fact that became clear when U.S. liberators also brought home letters to Bishop from his lover, Ron Dellums's aide Carlottia Scott. "Ron has become truly committed to Grenada," Scott wrote, " . . . he's really hooked on you and Grenada and doesn't want anything to happen to building the Revo[lution] and making it strong. . . . The only other person that I know of that he expresses such admiration for is Fidel."[17]

So it was that a U.S. congressman and two aides apparently conspired with a Marxist dictator to conceal Soviet strategy and subvert American national security efforts during the Cold War. Dellums was never disciplined for his acts—but he did announce in October 2005 to a pack of cheering liberals that he is planning to run for mayor in Oakland in 2006.[18]

Barbara Lee, whom the politburo minutes showed willing to make enemy-authored changes to a U.S. government report, succeeded Dellums in the House and is now in her fourth term. Frighteningly, in 2005, she was among a group of women nominated for a Nobel Peace Prize. "It's an honor to be included with all of these women who have done so much to promote peace on our planet," Lee said, reportedly with a straight face.[19]

Carlottia Scott went on to become the political director of the Democratic National Committee in 1999. That the DNC would make such an appointment, that Democrats would also endorse Lee's later appointment to the House International Relations Committee, and that the party took no action against Dellums, points up three critical—and related—problems. First, Democrats tolerate apparent treason. Second, despite its spectacular failure across the globe, leftist Democrats are still clinging to the Marxist dream. Finally, because of that dream, Democrats also tend to nurture subversion. Today, subversive Democrats even have an official club: the Congressional Progressive Caucus.

The Progressive Caucus was founded in 1992 by Reps. Bernie Sanders of Vermont (an avowed socialist who has the good sense to advertise himself as an independent), Peter DeFazio of Oregon, Lane Evans of Illinois, Maxine Waters of California, and the arguably treasonous Ron Dellums.[20] When he helped launch the caucus, Dellums was an official with the Democratic Socialists of America (DSA) and, during his three decades in the House, worked closely with the committed Marxists and Soviet KGB agents at the Institute for Policy Studies, a sort of boot camp for American communists. The DSA is "the largest socialist organization in the United States and the principal U.S. affiliate of the Socialist International."[21]

Until 1999, the DSA hosted the Progressive Caucus Web site, and the caucus's Web site linked back to the DSA.[22] Today, the ties are less visible, but can be found in dual memberships. For example, New York Congressman Major Owens is a member of both the DSA and the Progressive Caucus. With such close ties, it is instructive to learn what the DSA believes. Here's the group in its own words:[23]

- "We are socialists because we reject an international economic order sustained by private profit."

- "The current assault on the welfare state led by corporate and conservative elites is also an attack on political democracy."

- "A democratic commitment to a vibrant pluralist life assumes the need for a . . . representative government to regulate the market. . . . In the 21st century this will increasingly occur through international, multilateral action."

- "Free markets or private charity cannot provide adequate public goods and services."

- "No country, even a superpower like the United States, can guarantee peace and stability, never mind justice. Only a multinational armed force can intervene in conflicts to enforce generally accepted standards of human rights and democratic practices."

- The DSA supports a "massive redistribution of income from corporations and the wealthy to wage earners and the poor and the public sector to provide the main source of new funds for social programs, income maintenance, and infrastructure rehabilitation."

- The DSA supports a "massive shift of public resources from the military . . . to civilian uses."

To put it plainly: the DSA is working full time to eradicate the American system of free enterprise, individual rights, and limited government that has enabled citizens—and refugees—to enjoy the greatest personal liberty and highest overall standard of living the world has ever known.

Of course, the DSA knew there would be uncooperative cranks like us. That's why the collective urges its members to cloak its agenda in more palatable political garb. In one document, the DSA urges its "youth section" to "stress our Democratic Party strategy and electoral work. . . . The Democratic Party is something the public understands, and association with it takes the edge off. Stressing our Democratic Party work will establish some distance from the radical subculture and help integrate you to the milieu of the young liberals."[24]

But deep in a document called "Where We Stand: The Political Perspective of the Democratic Socialists of America," the group states its goals more baldly: "Many socialists have seen the Democratic Party, since at least the New Deal, as the key political arena in which to consolidate this coalition, because the Democratic Party held the allegiance of our natural allies. Through control of the government by the Democratic

Party coalition, led by anti-corporate forces, a progressive program regulating the corporations, redistributing income . . . and expanding social programs could be realized."[25] Progressive Caucus cofounder Bernie Sanders may in 2006 attempt to export this plan to Congress's upper chamber, when he runs for the U.S. Senate. He will be in good company there, as Sens. John Kerry, Tom Harkin, and others also dabble in subversion.

In the spring of 1985, on the eve of a major Senate vote on aid to Contra forces battling Nicaraguan President Daniel Ortega's Sandinista regime, Kerry and Harkin flew down to visit with the Communist leader, a Soviet ally. Ortega's brutal regime had harassed and tortured labor leaders, issued death threats to Jews, murdered religious leaders (one Protestant missionary had his throat slit and his ears cut off, but lived), and attacked native Indian tribes, forcing them from their land and packing them off to concentration camps. "The revolution can tolerate no exceptions," said security chief and interior minister Tomas Borge. [26]

Though they hail from the party of tolerance, Kerry and Harkin, while in Managua, held a press conference to announce a study that listed dozens of lies the administration had reportedly told Congress about the Sandinistas, as well as fifteen allegations of illegal acts. The study, it turned out, was authored by the people at Ron Dellums's old hangout, the Institute for Policy Studies. Kerry and Harkin then jetted back to the States carrying a three-page "peace proposal" given to them by Ortega. Secretary of State George Schultz was outraged. "It's presumably not lawful for citizens to appoint themselves as negotiators for the United States," he declared.[27]

Meanwhile, House Democrats had done their part to subvert the administration policies in Nicaragua. Ten members, including Rep. Matthew McHugh of New York and Jim Wright of Texas, in 1984 signed the infamous "Dear Commandante" letter, which they then sent to Ortega. In essence, the letter advised Ortega to dial back his overt Marxist behavior long enough for Democrats to see to it that Reagan's Contra aid proposal failed in Congress. Rep. David Bonior was even more helpful. With great access to media, he stumped for the Sandenistas. While not perfect, he said, "if we measure the errors of Nicaragua, if we lay them side by side with what might be called the errors of our own administration, which seem greater to me . . . who would we conclude poses the greatest threat to the stability of the region, Nicaragua or the present administration?"[28] Reagan lost the vote, and Ortega promptly embarrassed his congressional shills by hopping a plane to Moscow to firm up ties with the Soviets.

Bonior would later join the Congressional Progressive Caucus, where he remains today. In preparation for his 2006 Senate bid, Bernie Sanders has relinquished the caucus chair to the patriot Barbara Lee, who will colead with Lynn Woolsey of California. At this writing, sixty-one House Democrats belong to the group. That means that nearly one in three Democrats in the U.S. House of Representatives supports, on some level, transforming the nation from a free republic into a socialist utopia. [29]

Let's return, for a moment, to the DSA's assertion that "since at least the New deal," the Democratic Party held the allegiance of socialists' natural allies. Who were these natural allies? Not women, since few at the time were involved in partisan politics. Not organized labor, since labor at the time was mostly white, mostly male, and very anti-immigrant. (The largest union, the AFL-CIO, was also staunchly anticommunist, though the opposite is true under current President John Sweeney, a DSA leading light and a major Democratic contributor.)

The truth is, socialists' most powerful "natural allies" at the time of the New Deal were the communist spies and American traitors that infested the Roosevelt and Truman administrations.

In *Treason: Liberal Treachery from the Cold War to the War on Terrorism*, Ann Coulter details the depth to which Soviet spies had penetrated the Roosevelt and Truman administrations—and the extent to which Democrats ignored and defended the spies when they weren't promoting them to higher office.[30]

The 1920s and '30s in this country saw the fomenting of a quiet rebellion. Inspired by the Marxist-Leninist illusion of a society without property, without class, in which each worker contributed to the collective good, the American bourgeoisie organized in the cities. Tiny klatches of working-class intellectuals met in Communist cell groups, soaking in the revolutionary warmth of the socialist *idea*, safely sequestered from the grim realities of famine and mass murder unfolding across the Soviet countryside.[31]

In 1938, the year before the Communist Party USA reached its official American heyday with an enrollment of 66,000,[32] a man named Whittaker Chambers broke with the Communist Party, "reversing the faith of an adult lifetime, held implacably to the point of criminality."[33]

Chambers had worked in Washington as a Communist organizer, carrying stolen documents between New York and Washington. The documents were eventually delivered to Boris "Sasha" Bykov, head of an underground cell group that included Chambers and a man named Alger Hiss.[34] But Joseph Stalin's Great Purge, in which millions of peasants, intelligentsia, kulaks, and professionals were executed, imprisoned, tortured, or starved, convinced Chambers to leave the party. In a plea that lasted well into the night, he tried to convince Hiss to leave too, but Hiss said that he could not because of his loyalty to his friends.[35]

Later, Alger Hiss would claim he never knew a man named Whittaker Chambers. By then, Hiss, a Harvard man, had risen to become an assistant to the secretary of state under Democratic President Franklin D. Roosevelt. He was also one among two dozen Soviet spies whose names Chambers divulged to Roosevelt's assistant secretary of state, Adolf Berle, in a private meeting. Berle immediately warned the president, who laughed and suggested that Berle perform upon himself an anatomically impossible act. Then Roosevelt promoted Hiss, making him a trusted advisor.[36]

Berle also told Roosevelt's undersecretary of the Treasury, Dean Acheson, that Chambers had said that both Alger Hiss and his brother, Donald, were Soviet agents. Acheson, apparently a more careful man than Roosevelt, swiftly launched an investigation of Janet Reno proportions: he asked Donald Hiss if he was a Communist. Hiss said no. Case closed.[37]

It was not until 1948, nearly a full decade later, that anyone important took notice of what Whittaker Chambers had to say. By then, Chambers was a senior editor at *Time* magazine, and the House Un-American Activities Committee (HUAC) called him to testify. Again, Chambers named Alger Hiss as a Soviet spy and testified that he had known him in the Communist underground. Hiss, a dashing intellectual popular in Capitol social circles, appeared before the committee and blithely denied ever knowing Chambers. And the notion that he was a Soviet agent? Come now.[38]

Coulter writes what happened next: "Springing naturally to their traitorous positions, the adversary press vilified HUAC for persecuting the charming State Department official. Hiss's performance was universally acclaimed as a smashing success. Chambers was portrayed as a 'vulgar impostor' who had snowed the 'gullible' committee. He was a rumpled journalist at *Time* magazine, without social pedigree. . . . There were titters about a 'Red Scare' sweeping Congress."[39]

If anything was red and scary, it was the scab of treachery that Chambers peeled back to reveal a Democratic administration teeming with a Communist infection, and despite repeated warnings, doing nothing. One member of the HUAC, a Republican congressman from California named Richard Nixon, believed Chambers. His dogged pursuit of the truth ultimately revealed the extent to which Joseph Stalin was pulling Roosevelt's strings like those of a hapless puppet. Among the Soviet operatives influencing American policy:[40]

- Harry Dexter White, assistant secretary of the Treasury, who installed at least eleven other Soviet agents on the Treasury Department payroll. Though the FBI repeatedly warned that White was a Soviet spy, Harry Truman later appointed him the top U.S. official at the International Monetary Fund.

- Lauchlin Currie, administrative assistant to Roosevelt and deputy administrator of the Board of Economic Welfare.

- Laurence Duggan, head of the Latin American Desk at the State Department.

- Frank Coe, U.S. representative on the International Monetary Fund.

- Solomon Adler, senior Treasury official.

- Klaus Fuchs, atomic scientist.

- Duncan Lee, chief of staff to the head of the Office of Strategic Services, an intelligence agency that was the precursor to the CIA.

- Harry Hopkins, special advisor to President Roosevelt, described by former KGB agent Oleg Gordievsky as a Soviet agent "of major significance."

And where would we be without blood ties to the Clinton administration? Harold Ickes, secretary of the interior under Roosevelt—and father of little Harold Ickes, Bill Clinton's future chief of staff—was a member of the Stalinist front group League for Peace and Democracy.

Then, of course, there was Alger Hiss, who would, during the ten years after Roosevelt first ignored Chambers's warning, rise to become assistant to the secretary of state. It was Hiss who whispered advice in Roosevelt's ear at Yalta, the conference at which the American president ceded control of much of Eastern Europe to Joseph Stalin, dooming millions to poverty, political persecution, and death.[41]

Throughout Chambers's ordeal, Democrats decried the outing of Soviet agents as a "witch hunt." Even after Alger Hiss's guilt was established beyond doubt, the party embraced him, and he spun out his days on the cocktail party and lecture circuit. And even after the Venona Project in 1995[42] declassified Cold War–era Soviet cables, confirming the guilt of the men listed above, Democrats continued to revile as "McCarthyism" the fight to expose them. This though Sen. Joseph McCarthy's later hearings on Communists in federal government had nothing to do with Whittaker Chambers.

In retrospect, it defies the imagination that for ten years, the Hiss boys and their highly placed network of Soviet agents spread like Ebola through a Democratic administration, not only escaping even the most cursory investigation, but rising in influence and authority. To what end? To turn the Republic into a socialist state.

To what end now does the Congressional Progressive Caucus work? To turn the Republic into a socialist state.

The sixty-one members of the Caucus would probably state the goal in terms that make better sound bites: social justice . . . equality . . . environmental responsibility . . . and certainly no purges. But if the history of applied Marxism has taught us anything, it is that human beings, in our fallen condition, cannot create a society in which an all-benevolent nanny-state distributes evenly the resources and materials necessary for living. Greed interrupts. Power beckons. Vice pervades. World history has shown us the human toll of societies that embrace the Marxist illusion:[43]

The Soviet Union: 20 million dead
China: 65 million dead
Cambodia: 2 million dead
North Korea: 2 million dead
Afghanistan: 1.5 million dead
Eastern Europe: 1 million dead

These people died after torture or imprisonment, were executed singly, or murdered en masse. The figures above do not include people who died in planned wars or famines related to the Communist struggle. Still, nearly one in three Democrats in the U.S. House uses his or her tax-funded salary to subvert the American system of national sovereignty and individual rights in favor of a nightmare.

What would that look like? Perhaps like Barbara Lee collaborating with a Marxist dictator. Or like Progressive Caucus member Rep. Sam Farr of California, who in June 2003 explained why he flies the United Nations flag outside his Capitol Hill office, instead of his hometown banner like most of his colleagues: "If the UN didn't exist, we'd be inventing it right now . . . [as] the only way to build up the infrastructure around the globe for the human rights, labor, and environmental conditions that are fair and equitable," he said.[44] Compare Farr's statement with one from the DSA: "Democratic socialists area dedicated to building truly international social movements—of unionists, environmentalists, feminists, and people of color—that can together elevate global justice over global competition."[45]

Or perhaps the caucus's mission of subversion would look like Reps. David Bonior and Jim McDermott (both CPC members), and Mike Thompson (not a CPC member), who in September 2002, at the height of tensions between Baghdad and Washington over Iraq's development of weapons of mass destruction, traveled to enemy territory to kiss the ring of Saddam.

For more than a decade, the Iraqi thug had thumbed his nose at international weapons inspectors, shifting and hiding the materials, facilities, and personnel involved in his country's WMD program. McDermott, Bonior, and Thompson knew this. Only two months before their subversion junket, Khidir Hamza, Saddam's former chief nuclear weapons engineer, had testified before Congress:

Saddam's government kept a tight lid on its science and engineering military teams at the same time it allowed UNSCOM and the IAEA to demolish most of its weapons production sites. That these science and engineering teams were capable was made manifestly clear in the aftermath of the Gulf war. Within less than a year these teams rebuilt successfully most of Iraq's services infrastructure. These included rebuilding the destroyed control rooms of the power stations, the major telephone exchanges and oil refineries. Elated by their success Saddam kept these teams as contracting entities to the government for the civilian sector with a much reduced load and assigned them the rebuilding of the needed facilities for the WMD program. This provided them with a cover of civilian contractors with actual work to prove it but at the same time their WMD work continued unhindered. Thus the computer we used for the nuclear weapon design is now located in a hospital in Saddam city at the outskirts of Baghdad. If an inspector should arrive at the site he or she will be shown contracts for the civilian sector.[46]

Still, McDermott, Bonior, and Thompson pranced around Baghdad, taking in the sights, posing for pictures, chatting up Iraqi officials. Speaking publicly, Bonior counseled "neutrality" on how weapons inspections in Iraq should proceed: "We've got to move forward in a way that's fair and impartial. That means not having the United States or the Iraqis dictate the rules to these inspections."[47] The United Nations had already dictated the rules, though, as columnist George Will noted at the time: "The only permissible inspections would be those permitted by the 1998 agreement Saddam reached with his servant [U.N. General Secretary Kofi] Annan . . . [in which] various inspections are forbidden, such as any at eight presidential sites—about 12 square miles of facilities with thousands of buildings."[48] But McDermott, with Jesse Jackson–like diplomacy, said he had it from reliable sources (Saddam's henchmen) that weapons inspectors would be "allowed to look anywhere." Speaking to Iraqi officials, the congressman said that he believed that President Bush "would mislead the American people," but that we should "take the Iraqis on their value—at their face value."[49] McDermott and his colleagues exhibited all the earmarks of the "blame America first" syndrome in which enlightened progressives lionize non-Western, non-Christian cultures, and not only demonize America, but *blame* the United States for every ill that befalls a less prosperous nation. In that respect, Bonior did not disappoint. He used his visit to Iraq to rail against the "horrendous, barbaric, horrific" number of cases of childhood leukemia and lymphomas he claimed were caused by U.S. weapons dropped in Iraq during the Gulf War.[50]

Speaking of the Bush administration, McDermott also said, "I believe that sometimes they give out misinformation. . . . It would not surprise me if they came up with some information that is not provable, and they've shifted. First they said it was Al Qaeda, then they said it was weapons of mass destruction."[51] Democrats, Baathists, and members of the Screen Actors Guild now reading this book are likely sputtering: "McDermott was right! We didn't find any WMD in Iraq!"

That's true if you don't count the fact that two Iraqi scientists, newly freed by American forces, in April 2003 went on the Arab news channel Al-Jazeera and said they had watched vandals loot a Tawitha nuclear facility of 200 barrels of milled uranium oxide, or "yellow cake." Or the dozen or so sarin and mustard rounds, 7-pound block of cyanide salt, vial of live botulinum, and 1.77 metric tons of low-enriched uranium recovered by coalition forces.[52] Meanwhile, in 2005 and 2006 (heading into the first general election since the Democrats got spanked in 2004) it made tasty propaganda for the party to denounce President Bush's reading of intelligence on Iraq as the cowboy ravings of a Texas jingo justifying his own mad gallop toward war. Even had Democrats been telling the truth, Bush didn't ride alone:

- **Sen. Robert Byrd (D-Virginia), October 3, 2002:** "The last UN weapons inspectors left Iraq in October of 1998. We are confident that Saddam Hussein retains some stockpiles of chemical and biological weapons and that he has since embarked on a crash course to build up his chemical and biological warfare capabilities. Intelligence reports indicate that he is seeking nuclear weapons."[53]

- **Ted Kennedy (D-Chappaquiddick), September 27, 2002:** "We have known for many years that Saddam Hussein is seeking and developing weapons of mass destruction."[54]

- **Al Gore, September 23, 2002:** "We know that he has stored secret supplies of biological and chemical weapons throughout his country."[55]

- **And the noted patriot Sen. John Kerry (D-Massachusetts), in 2002:** "I will be voting to give the President of the United States the authority to use force—if necessary—to disarm Saddam Hussein because I believe that a deadly arsenal of weapons of mass destruction in his hands is a real and grave threat to our security."[56]

Kerry, for once, was being consistent. He was among several signers—including Sens. Dodd, Kerrey, Feinstein, Inouye, Levin, Lieberman, Daschle, Mikulski, Breaux, Johnson, Landrieu, and Lautenberg—of a letter urging the President after "consulting with Congress and consistent with the U.S Constitution and laws, to take necessary actions, including, if appropriate, air and missile strikes on suspect Iraqi sites to respond effectively to the threat posed by Iraq's refusal to end its weapons of mass destruction programs."[57]

Wait: the Democratic senators wrote *that* letter to Bill Clinton in 1998.[58] Apparently it would have been lawful and constitutional for a *Democrat* to bomb Saddam—pantywaist air strikes and crashing helicopters in deserts being favorite Democratic methods of punishing rascally Islamo-fascists who kidnap and murder Americans. But it was *illegal*, many Democrats said in 2005, for George W. Bush to prosecute a ground war based on the very same threat.

Under a *Republican* president, when their country was engaged in a war approved by 296-133 votes in the House and 77-23 in the Senate, Democrats began . . . what shall we call it? . . . *lying*.

Almost exactly a year after he said, "We have known for many years that Saddam Hussein is seeking and developing weapons of mass destruction," Sen. Kennedy told reporters that the Iraq war was a "fraud made up in Texas."[59]

On Veteran's Day 2005, Sen. Kerry said, "This administration misled a nation into war by cherry-picking intelligence and stretching the truth beyond recognition."[60]

But a 2004 bipartisan investigation of prewar intelligence analysis laid that blame for faulty intelligence at the CIA's doorstep, not at the White

House. The Senate Report on the U.S. Intelligence Community's Pre-War Intelligence Assessments on Iraq 2004 found "no evidence" that the intelligence community's "mischaracterization or exaggeration of the intelligence on Iraq's weapons of mass destruction capabilities was the result of political pressure."[61] Even *The Nation*, the progressive national magazine of record, discussed the Senate's bipartisan findings under the following headline: "Senate Report Whacks CIA, not Bush." (Still, writer David Corn was so disappointed with the Senate's findings that he strained to find ways to blame the President: "Bush and his lot overstated the overstatements of the intelligence community," Corn wrote.)[62]

And what of Khidir Hamza? In his July 2002 congressional testimony, the former Iraqi nuclear weapons chief said that "with the more than 10 tons of uranium and more than one ton of slightly enriched uranium in its possession, Iraq has enough to generate the needed bomb grade uranium for three nuclear weapons by 2005."[63]

Is Hamza an overstated overstatement of a fraud made up in Texas?

Where, one wonders, are the principled Democrats? They must be out there: intellectually honest party members who will stand up and admit that President Bush could not have gone to war without informed Democratic support. Instead there is only silent assent to the party's weird, dissociative story that Democrats *sincerely believed* the intelligence on Iraq—most of which was collected during the Clinton administration—but Bush, in a diabolical, warmongering plot, somehow *knew* the intelligence was faulty. This though Intelligence Committee Democrats had, as former vice-presidential candidate and Sears Catalog underwear model John Edwards told reporters, "day after day, week after week" [64]*for years* seen such intelligence and concluded that Iraq was a nuclear, chemical, and biological threat—while Bush was still the governor of Texas.

Democrats want to have it both ways: they want to whine that they were gullible dupes apparently incapable of their own competent intelligence analysis *and* they want to be put in charge of the country and the national defense. For the basest of reasons—to win majority power in

2006—congressional Democrats at this writing are misleading the American people, lying to them in time of war, sowing doubt among American forces, twisting daggers in the hearts of parents who have lost children, and shilling for the enemy. Constitutionally, that may not be treason. But it appears perilously close.

7

AIDING AND ABETTING

DEMOCRATS' PRO-CRIMINAL POLICIES

"Those who rob Peter to pay Paul can always count on Paul's support."
—LOWELL PONTE[1]

THE VIDEO SHOCKED AMERICA. IN FEBRUARY 2004, GRAINY footage from a security camera at a Florida car wash showed the image of eleven-year-old Carlie Brucia being approached and led away by a man with tattoos on his forearms. It was the last time anyone, except her killer, saw the Sarasota sixth-grader alive.[2]

Carlie had spent Saturday night, January 31, at a friend's house and about 6:15 p.m. Sunday left to walk to her home, about a mile away on McIntosh Lane. Around the same time, a surveillance camera caught the image of a cream-colored Buick station wagon turning around on the car wash lot. A couple of minutes later on the video, a man in a mechanic's uniform approaches the girl and grabs her by her wrist. At five feet tall and 120 pounds, Carlie was big for her age. But the tattooed man was much bigger. The car wash video showed him speaking to her for two or three seconds, then leading her away, out of camera range.

The car wash stands next to an ice-cream parlor and mini-golf course where Carlie liked to hang out with friends. Separated from McIntosh

109

Lane by a small patch of grass, the car wash parking lot was a shortcut home that Carlie knew well. That's why, when she failed to return home, her parents began searching for her within minutes. When they couldn't find her, they called police. Officers soon hit the streets with search teams and police dogs. The next day, owners of the car wash turned over a surveillance video to police, providing them with clear-cut evidence confirming their worst fears: Carlie had been abducted. Florida officials issued an "Amber Alert," and television news programs broadcast the car wash video repeatedly, and showed school photos of Carlie, a smiling, chubby-cheeked girl with long blonde hair.

Parents across the country reacted with horror at the footage, which showcased the apparent ease with which a criminal could snatch a child off the street, just a few hundred yards from the safety of her home. The abduction video horrified Ed Dinyes, too, but for a different reason.

Dinyes recognized the man shown grabbing Carlie's arm as his friend and coworker, Joseph P. Smith, thirty-seven.

"Just by his gait, I could tell it was him," said Dinyes, Smith's best friend. A year earlier, the two men had become partners in an auto-repair business. While Smith battled a drug habit, Dinyes tried to help him get on the right track. Another friend had tried to help, too, by loaning Smith a car: a cream-colored Buick station wagon. Dinyes would later tell reporters that until he saw the car wash video, "I never would have thought (Smith) was capable" of such a crime.

But he had no doubt that the tattooed man on the video was his friend and quickly called police, who soon arrested Smith. Police also impounded the Buick, which investigators were "certain . . . was used in the abduction," according to Sarasota County Sheriff Bill Balkwill.[3]

Smith was arrested on a Tuesday—February 3, 2004—but refused to tell police anything about what happened to the girl. Authorities and citizens combed the landscape around Carlie's neighborhood for three more days until, on Friday, her body was found in the woods behind a church, three miles from the car wash. Carlie's sixth-grade classmates remembered her as outgoing and friendly. Officials later said her killer had first raped her, then strangled her. Ed Dinyes said believing Joe Smith could do such a thing was a "big pill to swallow," until he later learned about Smith's extensive criminal history.

By the time police found Carlie's body, lots of other people who had been shocked by the girl's abduction were shocked even more to learn that someone with Smith's record hadn't been put behind bars long before. "He shouldn't have been out on the street," said Carlie's father, Joe Brucia. Ed Dinyes shared his sentiment: "Hell, I'm one of his best friends and I even called his parole officer trying to get his probation [revoked]."[4]

Indeed, if Smith had received the maximum sentence for each of his arrests in the eleven years before Carlie was murdered, he would have spent forty-six years in prison. Barely three months before he kidnapped the Sarasota girl, Smith tested positive for cocaine while on probation for an earlier crime. But state Judge Harry Rapkin didn't see the need for any action. And when Smith fell behind on court-ordered restitution payments, Judge Rapkin again refused to revoke his probation, despite Smith's record as a career criminal.[5]

Judge Rapkin is a Democrat.

Criminal Leniency

In Florida, state judges are elected and officially nonpartisan. But in reality, judges often purposely retire midterm, giving the governor an opportunity to appoint a politically *simpatico* jurist.

Joe Smith would ultimately become the beneficiary of a long line of Democratic appointees to the Florida bench. A native of New York, he was twenty-six when he moved to the Sunshine State in early 1993, and immediately began compiling a criminal record. Before the state charged him with kidnapping, raping, and murdering Carlie Brucia, Smith's record featured thirteen criminal charges (not counting probation violations), including four separate incidents involving violence against women. A month after he arrived in Florida, Smith slammed a motorcycle helmet into a twenty-one-year-old woman's face.

This unprovoked attack on a stranger—the woman was walking home from a nightclub after midnight—could have landed Smith fifteen years in prison. Instead, prosecutors offered him a plea deal. Sarasota Circuit Judge Lee Haworth sentenced Smith to sixty days in jail and two years' probation. Haworth later modified the sentence so that Smith could serve his time on weekends.

Over the next few months, Smith was charged in separate incidents of driving on a suspended license, contempt of court, and fleeing to elude police. In November 1994, Smith was arrested on domestic violence charges, but no prosecution resulted and no probation violation notice was filed. Two years later, Smith was accused of stealing tools from a construction site, but no charges were filed.[6]

In 1997, Smith's behavior careened out of control, and he was arrested in two separate assaults on women. In the first incident, M. H. Syin, a newspaper copyeditor, told police Smith approached her in a supermarket parking lot at 1:30 a.m. and tried to lure her to a remote corner of the lot. After a 911 call, police arrived and confronted Smith, discovering a steak knife with a five-inch blade hidden in his shorts. He pleaded guilty to a misdemeanor weapons charge and was sentenced to a year's probation.

Less than four months later, however, police arrested Smith again. A twenty-year-old woman told investigators she was walking down the street when Smith grabbed her and tried to drag her into some nearby bushes, threatening her: "If you don't quit screaming, I'll cut you." She managed to escape and was rescued by a passing motorist. Smith went to trial, where a jury acquitted him after he swore that he had only been trying to save the woman from being hit by a passing car.[7]

Never law-abiding for long, Smith was again arrested in March 1999, May 2000, and September 2001, each time on charges ranging from heroin possession to passing forged prescriptions. In the 1999 incident, Smith had enough drugs in his possession to lead officers to suspect him of dealing. But the state attorney's office under Democratic Attorney General Bob Butterworth charged him with drug possession, a lesser crime, and Circuit Judge Nancy Donnellan, an elected judge whose party affiliation is unknown, placed him on probation.

The 2001 arrest—for passing a forged prescription and also violating probation—could have landed Smith in jail for ten years. But Judge Haworth, who had sentenced Smith to sixty days in jail for attacking a woman, this time sentenced the career criminal to seventeen months. Smith served thirteen months, the longest prison term of his extensive criminal career prior to his arrest for kidnapping Carlie Brucia.[8]

Serving more than a year in prison seems to have done nothing to discourage Joe Smith's life of crime. He was released from prison on January 1, 2003. Eight days later, police found a hypodermic needle and two packets of cocaine in Smith's car, and an officer noticed fresh injection marks on his arms. Facing as much as five years in prison, Smith instead got three years' probation in a plea deal approved by Democratic appointee Judge Robert Bennett. But in October 2003, Smith tested positive for cocaine and his case came before Judge Rapkin.[9]

Harry Rapkin is a New Jersey native who came to Florida to attend the University of Miami. He returned to New Jersey to attend law school at Seton Hall, but the beautiful Sunshine State climate brought him back to practice law in Venice, Florida. As much as he loved the sunshine, he loved lawyering, later explaining that he got "a good feeling out of helping good people at a bad time in their life." He wanted to become a judge, he said, because "I thought I could help people."[10] Among the people he helped was Democratic Sen. Bob Graham, with a $500 donation in 1991. The next year, Democratic Gov. Lawton Chiles appointed Rapkin to a circuit court bench, the same year he appointed Judge Bennett, who after Carlie Brucia's murder would defend Rapkin as "one of the toughest sentencing judges we have."[11]

When Smith failed his October 2003 drug test while on probation, officials noted that Smith was recently hospitalized at a drug treatment center after an attempted suicide. Judge Rapkin called for no additional action. On December 30, 2003—exactly thirty-three days before Carlie Brucia's disappearance—Smith's case again came before Judge Rapkin. This time, probation officials reported that Smith was $170 behind on restitution payments. But Judge Rapkin refused to take action, instead asking the probation department to prove that Smith had the means to pay and writing a note on the file: "I need evidence that this is willful!"[12]

Willful or not, Joe Smith's failure to meet the terms of his probation could have sent him back to prison. Instead, he remained free, and Carlie Brucia died. "The system failed Joe, and it failed that little girl," said Ed Dinyes, who had tried to get his friend's probation revoked.[13] But in this case, "the system"—in the person of Judge Harry Rapkin—refused to take responsibility for turning loose a killer. After local and national news media (led by Bill O'Reilly of Fox News) reported on Smith's extensive criminal record and Rapkin's role in the case, the judge called a press conference. "Why are you all looking for someone to blame?" Rapkin asked. "All I did was follow the law. It's my job."[14]

Incredibly, it was not the first time Rapkin's mishandling of a probation case had been blamed for a young girl's death. That 1994 case involved a convicted sex offender who had violated probation. Prosecutors wanted Richard Lee Walker sentenced to fifteen years in prison, but Rapkin gave him only four weekends in jail. Weeks later, Kristy Degg, the fourteen-year-old daughter of Walker's girlfriend, disappeared. Kristy's body was found in a shallow grave and, though the case remains unsolved, Walker was the prime suspect in the girl's death. But Sandra Degg has no doubt who killed her daughter—and she blamed Rapkin for failing to lock up Walker. "We have two dead girls now," she said after Carlie Brucia's death.[15]

Other area residents shared that sentiment. One man took his anger to the courthouse, protesting with a sign that declared: "Judge Rapkin, Carlie's blood is on your hands. Resign now." The protester told a reporter: "I'm just tired of judges letting criminals loose on the streets."[16] Despite such criticism over his role in freeing Carlie's killer, the judge insisted that he was in fact tough on crime. "They call me, 'Hang 'Em High Harry,'" Rapkin told reporters, blaming the public for failing "to understand what rationally happened."[17]

One comment by the Democratic judge showed clearly that he was the one who lacked rational understanding: "Bad people, I send to prison. Drug addicts, I try to rehabilitate." In other words, even after he turned loose a violent dopehead who had kidnapped, raped, and murdered an eleven-year-old girl, Rapkin still believed that "bad people" and "drug addicts" were mutually exclusive categories.[18]

Liberal Theory, Criminal Reality

In Harry Rapkin's defense, when he freed Joe Smith, the judge was not aware that this criminal was going to kidnap, rape, and murder a sixth-grader. Judge Rapkin, who retired rather than face reelection in 2004, clearly felt he was treated unfairly by the media. He called Bill O'Reilly "scum."[19] Even Fox News fans might admit that O'Reilly is sometimes sensationalistic, with a habit of lecturing and interrupting guests he disagrees with, and slamming anyone who refuses an invitation into his "No-Spin Zone." Rather than scapegoating Judge Rapkin, being "fair and balanced" would require mentioning a point made by the Florida journalists who investigated Joe Smith's many encounters with Florida's criminal justice establishment: "[N]early everyone in the legal system who came in contact with Smith gave him the benefit of the doubt at least once."[20]

In one sense, Judge Rapkin was a victim of the law of large numbers. Any judge who handles a lot of cases involving petty criminals and drug offenders might eventually be caught with the hot potato, becoming the judge of record for the final release of a small-time crook whose next crime is a major felony. And the fact that Carlie Brucia's abduction was caught on videotape gave her murder the kind of arresting visual "hook" that TV news can't resist. Of all the cops, probation officers, and judges who dealt with Joe Smith's case during his ten-year criminal career in

Florida, Judge Rapkin just happened to be the last guy to deal with the monster who committed this nationally televised crime.

So much for fairness—now for the balance. Even if Harry Rapkin was just the unlucky loser in a game of judicial roulette, his handling of the Smith case exemplifies some of the basic failings of the liberal approach to criminal justice that has long caused critics to accuse Democrats of being "soft on crime":

An emphasis on the rights of criminals—One of the distinguishing traits of liberalism is a focus on certain constitutional rights, such as the Fifth Amendment's protection against self-incrimination, or the Fourteenth Amendment's guarantee of "due process." While liberals have shown contempt for Second Amendment gun ownership rights and the protection of private property against government's power of "eminent domain," liberal lawyers and judges over the years have pushed to enlarge the rights of criminal defendants. As a result, a single procedural slip-up is now enough to overturn a conviction. In the case of Joe Smith, this may explain why Judge Rapkin never saw his full criminal record. "Criminal history information is not routinely included with probation violation reports," the *Sarasota Herald-Tribune* reported.[21] To include that information might be prejudicial to the defendant. Even if such background information were included in a probationer's case file, of course, it would likely include only a record of convictions, not arrests. Joe Smith had been charged with four violent attacks on women, but in one of those cases, he plea-bargained down to a simple weapons charge and in another, he went to trial and was acquitted. So even if Harry Rapkin had received a complete case file on Joe Smith, it probably would have left out the arrest reports that might have tipped the judge to the fact that this probationer—who on paper looked to be a more or less decent working-class guy with a drug problem—in fact showed a clear tendency toward violent attacks on women.

Failure to recognize patterns of criminal behavior—The American system of justice prevents juries from considering a defendant's prior criminal record as evidence of guilt. Each defendant is innocent until proven guilty, and the fact that an accused car thief has the proverbial "record as long as your arm" can't be introduced by prosecutors. This is a sound principle of justice, so long as it is limited to the courtroom question of whether the suspect is guilty of the crime of which he is accused. But liberals wish to expand this idea beyond the courtroom, so that neither the cop on the beat nor the judge in his chambers can be allowed to consider the fact that criminal behavior tends to follow patterns. There is such a thing as suspicious behavior, but police can get in trouble if they act on a hunch (who's that shady-looking stranger hanging out on the corner?) without "probable cause." The 9/11 terror attacks were committed by nineteen young Arab males, but airport security has to search Irish grandmothers or risk accusations of unconstitutional "racial profiling."[22] Now consider the case of Joe Smith. Even had Judge Rapkin been aware of his entire criminal record—including every arrest, every dropped charge, every acquittal—the liberal approach to criminal procedure may have prevented him from drawing a common-sense conclusion: "Chronic dopehead, history of violence against women, suicidal depression, wanton disregard for the law—this guy is desperate and maybe dangerous. Let's lock him up for a few months, just in case."

The criminal as victim—Harry Rapkin wanted to be a judge so he could "help people," and the people he tried to help specifically included dopeheads like Joe Smith: "Drug addicts I try to rehabilitate." Many people might suggest that locking Smith up for thirty days would have at least kept him away from drugs for a while and given the addict time to reflect on his problem. But jail time apparently doesn't qualify as a method of rehabilitation. Beyond that, in explaining why he didn't lock up Smith after he fell $170 behind on his court payments, Judge Rapkin protested that Florida doesn't have "debtor's prisons."[23] Translation: Smith is poor, therefore it is unjust to expect him to pay the fines and fees required under the terms of his probation. Never mind that Smith might be able to pay if he wasn't spending his money on more dope, or that he might not be so poor if his dope habit didn't make it hard for him to keep a steady job.

In his widely praised analysis of modern liberalism, *The Vision of the Anointed,* economist Thomas Sowell has noted the tendency of liberals to classify some people as "mascots" deserving of extra sympathy and protection.[24] Poor people, racial minorities, mental patients, homosexuals, and drug addicts are just a few of the categories of mascots whom liberals proudly defend against what they perceive as oppression and injustice. As a poor drug addict, Joe Smith was a double mascot and thus, in the liberal perspective, doubly deserving of lenient treatment. If he'd also been, say, a gay Latino schizophrenic, Smith might have qualified for a "genius grant" from the liberal McArthur Foundation.

The vanishing victim—In recent years, advocates for the victims of crime have sought to balance our criminal justice system, to correct what they see as a tendency to ignore the fact that innocent victims have rights, too.[25] This gives the suffering crime victims an important visibility in the justice system, correcting a problem that psychiatrist Dr. Willard Gaylin has noticed in regard to murder: "[T]he dead person ceases to be a part of everyday reality, ceases to exist. We inevitably turn away from the past, toward the ongoing reality. And the ongoing reality is the criminal; trapped, anxious, now helpless, isolated. He usurps the compassion that is justly his victim's due. He will steal his victim's moral constituency along with her life."[26]

Along with stealing Carlie's life, Joe Smith smashed apart a family. "I lost the love of my life," Carlie's mother, Susan Schorpen, told the jury from the witness stand, taking deep breaths to keep from breaking into sobs. "I cry for her at all hours of the day. I cry for her at night. I'm broken. I will never heal." The jury convicted Smith in December 2005 and recommended that he be sentenced to death for what he did to Carlie Brucia.[27]

Judge Harry Rapkin says he is "totally heartbroken" over Carlie Brucia's death.[28] She is one victim who probably will never vanish from his conscience. But victims vanish all the time in the minds of other Democrats.

A "Promising" Young Rapist

On December 2, 2003, Rep. Lynn Woolsey wrote a letter to a judge on behalf of one of her constituents: "Stewart Pearson is a young man from a supportive family. I believe he has a promising life ahead of him, and urge you to consider these factors when deciding upon a suitable sentence."[29]

Stewart Pearson is a rapist. In July 2003, seventeen-year-old Tina Phan was sleeping on a sofa in her family's Terra Linda, California, home when Pearson struck, using a chemical-soaked rag over her mouth and nose in an effort to knock her unconscious. Phan struggled, but Pearson, who also had a knife, overpowered her and raped her. She testified that he told her "he had done the same thing before, and that he intended to do the same thing again."[30]

With the testimony of Phan—who had known Pearson for years—and overwhelming physical evidence against him, Pearson pleaded guilty to rape two months after committing the crime and was assigned a January 2004 sentencing date. It was while he was awaiting sentencing that Woolsey, on her official congressional letterhead, wrote to the judge on behalf of the rapist, possibly because the rapist's mother worked in the Democrat's district office in Marin County.

"I have known Stewart and his family for almost six years," Woolsey wrote to the judge, seeking leniency for the "promising" convicted rapist. When the Democrat's advocacy on behalf of this criminal became public, prosecutors and victim advocates were stunned.

"It is hard to imagine that after someone has committed a brutal crime like that [Woolsey's office] would want to write a letter. . . . People should be better informed before they write letters to the court," said Marin County Deputy District Attorney Alan Charmatz, the lead prosecutor on the case, who called Pearson's crime "as bad as it gets."[31]

"My question is, why is Lynn Woolsey advocating for this rapist?" asked Gloria Young, director of a local rape crisis center. Confronted by reporters, Woolsey, a liberal feminist, seemed surprised that her actions were controversial. "Obviously, in my eyes he is not a criminal," Woolsey told the *Marin Independent Journal.* She followed that up with the incredible claim: "I knew nothing about the incidents. I had no idea what the courts had found out."[32]

Syndicated columnist Michelle Malkin pointed out the irony:

Woolsey has continually raked in campaign cash based on her reputation as a tireless champion for women's and children's rights. . . . She aggressively pushed for the Violence Against Women Act, the Domestic Violence and Sexual Assault Victims' Housing Act, the Stalking Prevention and Victim Protection Act, the Date-Rape Prevention Drug Act, the Protection of Women in Prison Act, and the Battered Immigrant Women Protection Act. Woolsey has promoted women's rights in Afghanistan; called for stronger prosecution of rapists in East Timor; performed in the "Vagina Monologues" to show her solidarity with victims of rape, domestic abuse and genital mutilation; and crusaded for the "United Nations Convention to Eliminate Discrimination Against Women" to show how much she cares for the oppressed women of the rest of the world.[33]

Yet when given the opportunity to intervene on behalf of a rape victim in her own district, Woolsey took the side of the rapist. In response to media attention, Woolsey apologized "for making a horrible situation worse,"[34] but that was not enough for Tina Phan.

"I don't accept her apology," the rape victim said. "She represents the rapist who took advantage, the people that vote for her are saying the same thing and supporting the rapist. . . . [S]he is basically saying he should be let off the hook."[35]

And, of course, Marin County Democrats let Woolsey off the hook, reelecting her with 72 percent of the vote in November 2004.[36]

The Cop-Killer, a Democratic Hero

Shortly before 4 a.m. on December 9, 1981, a Philadelphia police officer observed a Volkswagen Beetle with its lights off driving the wrong way on a one-way street. When the officer attempted to arrest the driver of the Beetle, William Cook, an altercation ensued. At that point, the VW driver's brother appeared on the scene. Wesley Cook, a cab driver, had been parked in his taxi nearby and apparently witnessed the struggle between his brother, William, and Officer Daniel Faulkner. Wesley Cook carried a .38-caliber revolver in a shoulder holster. He pulled out his pistol and shot Officer Faulkner in the back. The officer managed to return fire before collapsing. When other police units arrived on the scene, the twenty-six-year-old policeman was dead—with a .38 slug in his brain—and Wesley Cook had been wounded with a .44-caliber bullet from the policeman's revolver.[37]

You have probably never heard of Wesley Cook before, but there are many people across America and around the world who idolize him. Some years before he killed Officer Faulkner, Wesley Cook had changed his name to Mumia Abu-Jamal.[38]

The "Free Mumia" campaign—based upon the claim that Cook aka Abu-Jamal was the victim of a racist frame job—became the radical cause celebre of the 1990s, as rock bands and movie stars joined the effort to spare Abu-Jamal the death penalty. A former radio reporter who had once been "Minister of Information" for the Philadelphia chapter of the Black Panther Party, Abu-Jamal began sending out tape-recorded commentaries that were aired on National Public Radio and were eventually turned into a best-selling book, *Live from Death Row*. Emblazoned on posters, shirts, and bumper stickers, "Free Mumia" became a popular slogan among campus left-wingers, spotted frequently on protest signs at antiglobalization rallies in the late 1990s and early twenty-first century.[39]

Foremost among those who proclaim Abu-Jamal's innocence are congressional Democrats like Rep. John Conyers of Michigan, Rep. Chaka Fattah of Pennsylvania, Rep. Cynthia McKinney of Georgia, and Rep. Barbara Lee of California.

"The struggle to free Mumia is part of the struggle to free all of us," said Ramsey Clark, a Democrat who served as attorney general in Lyndon Johnson's administration.[40] (Clark, dangling from the far-left fringe, also defended the Palestinian Liberation Organization [PLO] when the group was sued by survivors of wheelchair-bound Leon Klinghoffer, sixty-nine, whom PLO terrorists pushed over the side of the cruise ship *Achille Lauro* into the Mediterranean during a 1985 high-seas hijacking. At this writing, Clark is passionately defending the mass-murdering despot Saddam Hussein.)[41]

In an August 2000 rally for Abu-Jamal outside the Democratic National Convention, two-time Democratic presidential candidate Jesse Jackson ascended the stage and led the crowd chanting, "Free Mumia." At a rally three months earlier, former New York Mayor David Dinkins declared: "I join with you in saying Mumia deserves a new trial, an unbiased judge and a competent lawyer. We go the extra mile to say that not only Mumia, but everyone who's been denied justice, deserves these things."[42]

That Jamal was "denied justice" is rather a strange claim, given the facts of the case. The ballistics evidence alone—Officer Faulkner was killed by bullets from the .38 owned by Abu-Jamal, who was in turn wounded by the policeman's gun—would be enough to make for an open-and-shut case. No fewer than five witnesses told police on the scene that they had seen Abu-Jamal shoot the policeman: "One even stated that Jamal took the time to bend down and fire the final shot into the wounded officer's face from less than a foot away and that the officer's 'whole body jerked' when the shot hit his face."[43]

Abu-Jamal's defenders claim he was the victim of a right-wing racist conspiracy, a bit far-fetched since the district attorney responsible for his prosecution was Ed Rendell, a Democrat who has since served two terms as mayor of Philadelphia, been chairman of the Democratic National Committee, and been elected governor of Pennsylvania. The trial prosecutor was Rendell's assistant, Joseph McGill, who has handled over one hundred homicide cases and calls the case against Abu-Jamal "the strongest I ever had."[44]

If anyone should be interested in exonerating Abu-Jamal, it would be his brother, William Cook, who was on the scene and saw everything that happened. But to this date, Cook's only statement about the murder of Daniel Faulkner is the one he gave cops when they showed up immediately afterward: "I ain't got nothing to do with this." Abu-Jamal, who acted as his own attorney during his trial, did not even call his own brother to testify in his defense. Stuart Taylor Jr., writing in *American Lawyer* magazine in 1995, argued on legal and constitutional grounds that Abu-Jamal should get a new trial, but admitted that there was "evidence that tips me toward finding Jamal guilty beyond a reasonable doubt. . . . That evidence is the 14-year-long silence of both Jamal and his brother, William Cook, about what happened. Neither of them has ever said how Faulkner was killed, or even denied explicitly that Jamal killed him. Not on the day of the murder. Not at Jamal's trial. And not during the 14 years since."[45]

Despite the overwhelming evidence of Abu-Jamal's guilt, his supporters continued to proclaim his innocence. After the *Village Voice* ran an article in 1999 distorting the record of the case, the left-wing weekly received a letter from a woman in Los Angeles, who noted that "after reviewing the actual facts . . . for more than three years, the nine-member Supreme Court of Pennsylvania unanimously agreed that there was no credible evidence or testimony pointing to Abu-Jamal's innocence." The letter was signed by Maureen Faulkner, who was twenty-four when her husband, Officer Daniel Faulkner, was murdered by Abu-Jamal.[46]

In 1999, after the state supreme court had refused to block Abu-Jamal's execution, Conyers, McKinney, and Lee were among those who signed a letter appealing for Gov. Tom Ridge to spare Abu-Jamal's life: "We earnestly plead with you for clemency," the letter said, invoking "the highest cherished virtues of which humanity is capable—compassion and mercy." Compassion and mercy were not exactly what Abu-Jamal showed on that night in 1981 when he shot Officer Faulkner in the head at point-blank range.[47]

Eventually, however, the cop-killer's Democratic supporters were victorious. In December 2001, a week before Christmas and a little more than twenty years after Officer Faulkner was gunned down on Locust Street, a federal judge overturned Abu-Jamal's death sentence. This did not satisfy his supporters, one of whom called the ruling a "political maneuver to diffuse international pressures," while another said, "Unless the judge called for the release of Mumia, then he hasn't done anything fair."[48] The "Free Mumia" crowd continues to call for a new trial, hoping to put back on the streets of Philadelphia the man who, according to two witnesses, said after shooting Officer Faulkner: "I shot the motherf—r, and I hope the motherf—r dies."[49]

Pro-Gangster Democrats

Perhaps inspired by their success in sparing Mumia Abu-Jamal from death, pro-crime Democrats soon found another celebrity killer to support: Stanley "Tookie" Williams, who was convicted of murdering four people in cold blood. Williams faced the death penalty in California in December 2005 because of a pair of robberies that netted less than $300 total. But Democrats as far away as Iowa, Massachusetts, and New York praised the murderer as "a powerful voice for peace."[50]

In the early-morning hours of February 28, 1979, Williams and three accomplices robbed a 7-Eleven convenience store on Whittier Boulevard in Los Angeles. Williams wielded a sawed-off 12-gauge pump shotgun. (The High Standard brand shotgun, serial number 3194397, had been purchased five years earlier by Williams, and was Exhibit 8 at the killer's subsequent trial.) Alone in the store was clerk Albert Owens, an Army veteran and divorced father of two who had recently moved back to

California to fight for custody of his daughters. Williams jammed his shotgun into Owens' back.

"Shut up and keep walking," he told Owens, who was forced into the store's stockroom at gunpoint. "Lay down, motherf—r," said Williams. The clerk complied. Williams then fired two shots into Owens' back at point-blank range.

This action—murdering an innocent and helpless man who offered no resistance—mystified even William's fellow robbers. Tony Sims told police: "I asked Tookie, I said, 'What you do?' He say, 'I killed him,' like that. And I say, 'Why you kill him?' He say, uh, 'So it wouldn't be no evidence.'" To another accomplice, Williams laughed as he bragged about the gurgling noise that Owens made while dying: "You should have heard the way he sounded when I shot him."[51]

Williams and his three buddies got only $120—$30 each—from the 7-Eleven robbery. Less than two weeks later, at a South L.A. motel owned by his family, Robert Yang was asleep with his wife when he heard a loud banging. It was the sound of Tookie Williams breaking down the door of the motel office. Once inside, Williams shotgunned to death three people and emptied the cash register before leaving. Robert Yang had heard the gunshots and heard the victims' screams. When he reached the motel office he found three members of his family—his sixty-three-year-old mother, Tsai-Shai Yang; his seventy-six-year-old father, Yen-I Yang; and his forty-three-year-old sister, Yee-Chen Lin—all dying from shotgun wounds. Williams shot Yang's father twice, Yang's mother once in the face, and Yang's sister twice.

All the shots were fired at point-blank range. Williams told friends about this crime in some detail, referring to his victims as "Buddhaheads" and saying that the next time he committed a robbery, he would "blow them away just like I blew them Buddhaheads away." This brutal crime netted Williams about $100, but since he'd acted alone, at least he didn't have to split it with any buddies.[52]

These were the crimes for which Tookie Williams was convicted and sentenced to death. But he was more than just a robber and killer. He was also the cofounder, in 1971, of the Crips gang, which still terrorizes the mean streets of South Los Angeles. In 1971, gang violence was still confined to local, but not often deadly, neighborhood turf battles. But Williams and the Crips patented new methods of brutal, bloody violence, including assault, rape, murder, and the now popular drive-by shooting.

Strangely enough, his role as gang leader was cited as a reason to spare him the death penalty by Democrats like California Assemblyman Mark Leno, who wrote a column for the *San Francisco Chronicle* in which he praised Williams for his "redemptive efforts to steer kids away from violence."[53]

Leno had plenty of company. By December 2005, when all his appeals were exhausted—even the ultraliberal 9th Circuit Court of Appeals (known widely in California as the 9th Circus Court) could find no grounds for overturning Williams's death sentence—Tookie was being praised by Democrats across the country. This was due in no small part to the efforts of Barbara Becnel, who used her position as executive director of a taxpayer-supported community agency to turn Williams into a celebrity, coauthoring a biography of the murderer that became a cable TV movie with Jamie Foxx portraying Williams. Becnel spent a dozen years promoting Williams's image as an advocate of peace after the San Quentin inmate appeared in a 1993 video to endorse a truce between L.A. street gangs. She also helped publicized at least nine children's books Williams says he penned in an effort to steer children away from violence.[54]

In that effort, Williams's failure hit close to home. His son, Tookie Jr., was convicted for murder in the 1994 retaliation slaying of a twenty-year-old woman. Meanwhile, between 1979, the Crips' inaugural year, and 2003, at least 9,747 gang-related homicides occurred in Los Angeles County alone. Between 1979 and 1994, about one in four of these killings was a drive-by shooting, a murder technique introduced and perfected by the Crips.[55]

Williams's Democratic apologists in 2005 claimed he had repudiated all that. Williams himself claims to have begun developing "a conscience gradually, through educating himself," this after "falling in love with words" when a chaplain gave him a dictionary in 1985. But in 1989, Tookie still ruled at least twenty fellow Crips who had joined him on Death Row, and ordered twenty-three-year-old Tiequon Cox to stab another condemned Crip whom Williams's suspected of being an informant. Cox refused the order and instead slashed Williams with a four-inch "shank." Though the wound to his neck could have been fatal, Williams refused to identify his attacker, telling authorities: "I don't know what happened. I don't remember."[56]

Just four years later, he convinced Becnel he was a changed man. Changed? Perhaps, but still unrepentant. In 2003, Williams told *New York Times* reporter Kimberly Sevcik that he was innocent of the four murders of which he'd been convicted. Williams, in fact, never took responsibility for his own crimes, instead condemning "a white-dominated society" he claimed "brainwashed" black people into becoming criminals.[57]

Most of all, Williams insisted on maintaining the gangster code of total non-cooperation with law enforcement. Becnel praised him in 1993 "because he has taken his years in prison like a man, not snitching on or complaining to anyone."[58] Except, of course, about the racist conspiracy that put him behind bars to begin with.

This, then, was the bloodthirsty killer who was the subject of a 2005 petition asking Gov. Arnold Schwarzenegger for clemency. "The execution of Stanley Williams will silence a powerful voice for peace," the petition declared. Echoing Williams's own self-serving rationalizations, the petitions claimed that there were "disturbing signs of racial bias" in Williams's trial, and cast blame on the "jailhouse snitch" who had revealed Tookie's plot for escaping and assassinating a witness.[59] (The petition failed to mention that testimony by the "snitch" was corroborated by Williams's own handwritten notes about this plan.)[60]

Despite every evidence that Williams had never renounced his gangster creed, the petitioners credited Tookie with promoting "a message of redemption, peace and hope," and urged Gov. Schwarzenegger to commute the killer's death sentence "to affirm the human capacity for personal transformation and reinforce the meaning of hope for young people everywhere."

The petition for clemency was signed by a Who's Who of left-wingers, including Gloria Steinem and such Hollywood luminaries as Ed Asner, Richard Dreyfuss, Danny Glover, Tim Robbins, and Susan Sarandon. But more tellingly, *every single politician who signed this dishonest petition was a Democrat*: California state Sen. Gilbert Cedillo, Los Angeles; former New York Gov. Mario Cuomo; state assemblyman Mervin M. Dymally, Los Angeles; U.S. Sen. Tom Harkin, Iowa; former presidential candidate Jesse Jackson; U.S. Rep. Jim McDermott, Washington state; U.S. Rep. Jim McGovern, Massachusetts; and U.S. Rep. George Miller, California.[61]

The Criminal Constituency

Democrats who vouch for the "promising" character of a rapist, who seek "compassion and mercy" for a cop-killer, and who portray a murderous gangbanger as a messenger of "redemption, peace and hope" might protest that they are only interested in defending the rights of such criminals. And there is certainly one right that Democrats want to make sure convicted felons are never denied: the right to vote.

Of course, criminals have no right to vote. The Constitution reserves to the states the power to determine the "times, places and manners of holding elections," and the Fourteenth Amendment specifically recognizes that states may prohibit convicted criminals from voting. As a result, states vary widely in permitting convicted felons to vote. In a handful of states, felons may be barred for life from voting, although these states all have some process for ex-convicts to apply to have their voting rights restored. Other states automatically restore the right to vote after a convict is released from prison, or completes probation or parole. And, believe it or not, convicted felons are actually allowed to vote while in prison in two states: Vermont (that might explain how Democrat Howard Dean got elected governor) and Maine (that might explain how liberal "Republican" senators Olympia Snowe and Susan Collins got elected).[62]

In every state where felons are prohibited or restricted from voting, Democrats have pushed to have those restrictions lifted. Why? Well, here's a hint: these efforts increased remarkably after the 2000 election:

- In Alabama, Democratic state Reps. Yvonne Kennedy and Alvin Holmes and Democratic state Sen. Quinton Ross turned out for a 2004 rally at the state Capitol, seeking restoration of voting rights for many of Alabama's 212,000 "prisoners, ex-felons and parolees."[63]

- In 2005, Iowa's Democratic Gov. Tom Vilsack chose the Fourth of July to sign an executive order that restored voting rights to some fifty thousand ex-convicts—even those who have failed to pay court-ordered restitution to their victims. "This is about the fact that there are individuals who want to be able to be participating members of society and who have made mistakes in their life who have paid for those mistakes," Vilsack told the *Des Moines Register*. This action was seen as boosting the governor's prospects to compete for the 2008 Democratic presidential nomination. "It can do nothing but help Tom Vilsack's national reputation," a Democratic campaign consultant said.[64]

- In Maryland, ex-convicts with one felony conviction were permitted to vote once they had served their time. But that wasn't enough for Democratic Gov. Parris Glendenning and the state's Democrat-dominated legislature, who in 2002 pushed through a law that restored voting rights to ex-cons with two felony convictions. However, there were restrictions: two-time convicts could vote only "if their second or subsequent crime were not violent and if three years [had] elapsed since they completed their sentence." That was too strict for some Democrats, who immediately started organizing ex-convicts to push lawmakers to repeal the three-year waiting period.[65]

- In Virginia, a state where convicted felons are prohibited from voting for life, ex-convicts can petition the governor to restore their voting rights. Democratic Gov. Mark Warner (like Vilsack, a prospective 2008 presidential contender) set new records in granting such applications. In his first three years in office, he restored the voting rights of 2,157 felons, denying only 134 requests. Virginia governors are limited to a single four-year term. Warner's two immediate predecessors, both Republicans, had restored voting rights to only 638 ex-convicts in their combined eight years in office. Not only had Warner given voting rights to more criminals than any previous Virginia governor, he was far and away the national leader as well. "Among governors of the 14 states that deny voting rights to felons, Mr. Warner has restored more voting rights than any other chief executive, according a report from the Sentencing Project," the *Washington Times* reported in April 2005. "[T]here's nobody who is really even close," said Ryan King, research associate for the Sentencing Project, a Washington, D.C., group that advocates for the rights of criminals.[66]

Of course, Democrats' zealous advocacy for the voting rights of convicted thieves, dope dealers, rapists, and murderers is not entirely based in humanitarian concern. It's about votes.

The party has long courted the votes of criminals, going back at least as far as the days when "the dregs of the city" supported Tammany's Fernando Wood in New York. More than one hundred years ago, one Republican noted that "the criminal class of the great cities . . . by the natural law of their being, find their congenial place in the Democratic Party" (see Chapter Three). This has since been conclusively proven by sociologists Christopher Uggen of the University of Minnesota and Jeff Manza of Northwestern University.[67] Research by these two left-wing academics, who support voting rights for felons, revealed several interesting facts:

- Convicted felons would vote for Democrats by an overwhelming 68.9 percent margin.

- "In the 2000 presidential election, more than 4.6 million Americans were barred from voting because of felon disenfranchisement laws."

- "By removing those with Democratic preferences from the pool of eligible voters, felon disenfranchisement has provided a small but clear advantage to Republican candidates in every presidential and senatorial election from 1972 to 2000." For example, at least two U.S. Senate seats won by Republicans in 1978 would have gone to Democrats, if felons had been allowed to vote.

- Had it not been for the disenfranchisement of felons, Democrats would have maintained control of the Senate continuously since 1986.

- Were it not for the fact that Florida prohibits convicted felons from voting, George Bush would never have been president, because the ex-cons would have delivered an extra sixty thousand votes for Al Gore. "If disenfranchised felons in Florida had been permitted to vote, Democrat Gore would certainly have carried the state, and the election. We can thus conclude that the outcome of the 2000 presidential race hinged on the narrower question of ex-felon disenfranchisement rather than the broader question of voting restrictions on felons currently under supervision," Uggen and Manza concluded.[68]

Little surprise, then, that Florida is one of the states where Democrats have been most desperate to overturn the ban on voting by convicted felons. Democratic state Sen. Frederica Wilson tried unsuccessfully to amend the Florida constitution to guarantee voting rights for criminals.

In 2005, a lawsuit seeking to overturn Florida's ban was appealed all the way to the U.S. Supreme Court, which refused to hear the case (as noted, the Fourteenth Amendment specifically allows such prohibitions). That discouraged, but did not dissuade, Florida Democrats like state Sen. Mandy Dawson, who is trying to get a referendum on the ballot to restore voting rights to ex-convicts.[69]

Just because it's illegal doesn't mean some Democrats don't do it, of course. And Democrats haven't waited to change Florida law before soliciting the votes of criminals. With the 2000 presidential election hanging in the balance, it was discovered that "at least 445 felons [had] voted illegally" in Florida. The *Miami Herald* reported: "Nearly 75 percent of the illegal ballots discovered by the *Herald* were cast by registered Democrats. . . . the *Herald* found 62 robbers, 56 drug dealers, 45 killers, 16 rapists and seven kidnappers who cast ballots. At least two who voted are pictured on the state's online registry of sexual offenders." One of the convicted sex offenders who voted in 2000 was Clarence Eden Williams, whose son was surprised when told by the *Herald* that records showed that the seventy-seven-year-old child molester had cast a ballot. "He's got Alzheimer's, and he can't even carry on a conversation anymore," said Clarence Williams III.[70]

Democrats claim that laws against voting by ex-felons "were the product of explicit efforts to disenfranchise black voters after the Civil War."[71] This is not only incredibly insulting to black voters today, it is also false and absurd. Many of these laws pre-date the Civil War; others are (or were) in states like Iowa, with no history of Jim Crow. If such laws in Southern states appear to date to the post-Civil War era, there is a good reason: under Reconstruction, many Southern states adopted new constitutions that, among other things, abolished slavery and enfranchised blacks. Furthermore, an attorney who defended Florida's law noted that about 70 percent of that state's disenfranchised felons are white.[72]

Ironically, the constitutional provision that authorizes states to keep criminals off the voter rolls was intended for the very opposite of the racist reasons claimed by Democrats today. The Fourteenth Amendment refers to "the right to vote at any election," which cannot be "denied . . . or in any way abridged, except for participation in *rebellion*, or other crime" (emphasis added). In addition to recognizing that criminals rightfully could be prohibited from voting, the Radical Republicans of 1868 who forced through the Fourteenth Amendment wanted to enable Reconstruction state governments in the South to disenfranchise *former Confederate leaders* and murderous Klansmen (which, of course, meant disenfranchising Democrats just as do restrictions on felon voting today).[73]

Just as they never let historical facts stand in the way of smearing Republicans as racist, Democrats don't let the Constitution stand in the way of pandering to criminals. In February 2002, Democratic Sen. Harry Reid of Nevada offered an amendment to a voting rights bill that would have prevented states from disenfranchising felons. Such a measure would certainly have been declared unconstitutional by the Supreme Court, but twenty-seven Democratic senators voted in favor of it, including Hillary Clinton, John Kerry, Ted Kennedy, Barbara Boxer, Dick Durbin, and Patrick Leahy. Mrs. Clinton said she supported the amendment because she was opposed to "disenfranchisement of legitimate American voters."[74]

Democrats are not in the least ashamed of their advocacy of voting rights for criminals. In 2002, about one hundred ex-cons showed up at a rally in a Baltimore parking lot to hear Maryland Democrat Secretary of State John Willis explain the importance of voting rights for felons. Baltimore is both a Democratic Party stronghold and a drug-infested swamp that rivals Washington, D.C., in terms of criminal violence. Not surprisingly, people are leaving in droves—the city has lost more than a quarter-million people since 1970. At the Baltimore voting rights rally, Willis explained that the answer to the city's problems is getting more criminals to vote: "We're talking about another 50,000 to 60,000 people in the city that could help hold on to the city's political power."[75]

(This amazingly frank expression of Democratic Party strategy was reported in a newspaper article which noted that most of the ex-cons attending the Baltimore parking lot rally were recovering drug addicts,[76] suggesting a possible bumper-stick slogan: "You don't have to be on drugs to vote for Democrats—but it helps!")

Uggen and Manza, the sociologists who proved that criminal votes could help elect more Democrats, also claim that letting felons vote is popular with Americans. But the real-world evidence is starkly to the contrary. For example, prison inmates had long been allowed to vote in Massachusetts (which probably explains how Ted Kennedy got elected). But in 2000, even voters in that liberal bastion approved by nearly a 2-to-1 margin a state constitutional amendment to end jailhouse voting.[77]

Many Americans are justly horrified at the idea of allowing kidnappers and rapists to vote. Should lawbreakers elect our lawmakers? "Do we want our politicians pandering for the votes of felons? Or making governmental policy designed to win [felons'] votes and serve those constituents?" asks commentator Lowell Ponte. The result of a federal guarantee of voting rights for convicted felons, Ponte says, would be a "felonocracy"—government of the criminals, by the criminals, for the criminals.[78]

No wonder Democrats love the idea.

SCENE OF THE CRIME

CREATING THE URBAN NIGHTMARE

"Modern liberalism was born in the big cities and died there,
a suicide of sorts."

—FRED SIEGEL[1]

IF YOU WANT TO GET KILLED, WASHINGTON, D.C., IS A GREAT spot for it: the homicide rate in the nation's capital is regularly No. 1 in America. The District of Columbia is also the place to be if you're a killer hoping to get away with murder—in 1999, for instance, nearly two-thirds of the city's homicide cases were unsolved. The D.C. police couldn't even find hundreds of their case files, and weren't even able to identify some homicide victims.[2]

So when a twenty-four-year-old Washington intern disappeared in 2001, it was a good bet that D.C. police wouldn't solve the case. Chandra Levy left her apartment April 30, 2001, to go jogging in the city's Rock Creek Park and was never seen alive again. Her disappearance didn't make much news in Washington until it was reported that Levy, from Modesto, California, had been romantically involved with her hometown congressman, Democrat Gary Condit.[3] While police investigators and the media focused on Condit, nobody paid much attention to a man arrested the same week Levy disappeared.

Six days after Chandra went for her last jog, Ingmar Guandique was arrested for attempted burglary after he broke into a woman's apartment near Rock Creek Park. He was booked and released, despite the fact that the El Salvador native was in the United States illegally.[4] A week later, he attacked a thirty-year-old woman jogging through the park. She managed to fight him off. In July, when Guandique attacked a twenty-six-year-old jogger in the wooded park, she screamed, got the attention of a bystander, and forty-five minutes later Guandique was arrested. Convicted and sentenced to ten years in prison, Guandique remains behind bars—for now.[5]

Despite a police search of Rock Creek Park, Chandra Levy's body was not found until more than a year after she went missing, when a man walking his dog discovered her skeletal remains. By then, police had noticed the similarities between Chandra's disappearance and Guandique's two attacks in the park. And the illegal alien's cellmate said Guandique had told him he raped Levy and stabbed her to death. But police bungled a lie-detector test and so it is likely that Chandra Levy's killer will never be brought to justice. Guandique's lawyer denies his client had anything to do with the intern's death, but D.C. police have no other suspects. The only thing the police investigation really accomplished was to destroy the political career of Gary Condit.[6]

Washington's reputation as a haven for criminals might have something to do with its former four-term mayor, Marion Barry, a former civil rights organizer who—in addition to the misdeeds recorded in chapter two—turned the city into his personal fiefdom.

The city once had one of the nation's best police forces, but between 1985 and 1996, murders increased by 169 percent. By the 1990s, the District was spending twice as much on policing as Philadelphia, though its officers couldn't file search warrants (they'd run out of the proper forms) and two-thirds of their patrol cars were out of service in need of repairs.[7]

Washington is in many ways typical of what Democrats have done to urban America. Similar trends afflict nearly every other major city in

America. This decline was not inevitable, nor can it be blamed on racism or Corporate America. A specific set of policies—including a fawning obeisance toward government employee unions and other Democratic Party constituencies—have caused the tragedy of our urban centers. The pattern is tragically consistent: while neighborhoods decay and the poor suffer, big-city Democrats grow rich on graft.

Philadelphia

In the midst of Mayor John Street's 2003 reelection campaign, it was discovered that the FBI had planted bugs in the mayor's office as part of an ongoing corruption probe. Over the next two years, ten people, including the city's former treasurer, were convicted in connection with what became known as the "pay to play" case, in which city contracts were awarded in exchange for bribes. Democratic fund-raiser Ronald White gave more than $10,000 in cash and gifts to treasurer Corey Kemp, who was convicted of twenty-seven counts, including bank fraud, welfare fraud, and tax fraud. White's mistress, Janice Knight, got a series of printing contracts from the city with her lover's help. Two top officials of a Pennsylvania bank were convicted of conspiracy and fraud for, among other things, arranging a sweetheart mortgage deal for Kemp in an effort to obtain city business. Three months after that trial ended, Philadelphia City Councilman Rick Mariano, a Democrat, was indicted on twenty-six corruption-related charges, accused of accepting $30,000 in bribes.[8]

Chicago

Twenty-two people—including eleven city employees—were convicted for their roles in a widespread scandal under Democratic Mayor Richard Daley. The so-called "hired truck" scandal involved shakedowns, kickbacks, and no-bid contracts for trucking companies in a program run by Angelo Torres, an ex-street gang member connected to the city's Hispanic Democratic Organization. Donald Tomczak, the top deputy in the city's water department, pleaded guilty in July 2005 to his part in a scheme that awarded jobs, promotions, and overtime to city workers who campaigned for Democrats in Chicago. Tomczak admitted to leading an "army" of some 250 city workers who went door-to-door to campaign for Democratic candidates and said similar operations were run by other Chicago officials. Tomczak also said he collected more than $400,000 in bribes and political contributions from trucking companies in exchange for city contracts. (The scandal apparently didn't hurt Democrats like Illinois Rep. Rahm Emmanuel, who benefited from the Daley machine's corrupt dealings. Ironically, the only politician voted out of office due to the scandal was a Republican: Donald Tomczak's son, Jeff, who lost his 2004 reelection bid as state's attorney in suburban Will County, after it was revealed the Republican son had gotten $20,000 from his Democratic father's Chicago operation.[9])

Atlanta

Federal investigators uncovered widespread corruption under Democratic Mayor Bill Campbell, who was indicted on multiple charges of bribery, racketeering, and fraud. The mayor was charged with accepting $150,000 in bribes, and his aides were convicted in a series of scandals. In one scheme, the city's chief operations officer accepted tens of thousands of dollars in bribes to steer a computer contract to Vertis McManus, who got a million-dollar contract to sell Atlanta the same software that Oracle had agreed to sell the city for $850,000 less than two months earlier. A special assistant to Mayor Campbell was also convicted in that case. The chairman of Atlanta's civil service board, appointed by the mayor, owned a contracting firm that received at least $950,000 in city contracts. Meanwhile, the former president of a communications firm that won city contracts pleaded guilty to paying bribes to a Democratic commissioner in surrounding Fulton County to get county contracts in 1998 and 1999.[10]

Cleveland

Several officials in the city's water department were charged in a federal investigation of bribery involving city contractors under the administration of Democratic Mayor Michael R. White. One contractor was convicted of overbilling the city by more than $1 million after bribing a department supervisor with a Lincoln Continental, World Series tickets, and $38,000 in cash. In neighboring East Cleveland, Democratic Mayor Emmanuel Onunwor was convicted of accepting nearly $50,000 in bribes. (Onunwor was succeeded as mayor by fellow Democrat Saratha Goggins, who admitted that she stabbed her boyfriend to death in 1982.) The Cleveland investigation led to evidence of related corruption in several other cities, including Houston, where the city's former director of building services, Monique McGilbra, pleaded guilty to conspiracy for steering city business to contractors. McGilbra admitted accepting bribes that included a ski vacation, travel expenses, restaurant meals, tickets to the stage musical version of *The Lion King*, NFL tickets, earrings, gift certificates from Neiman Marcus and Luis Vuitton, and $6,000 in cash. The former chief of staff to Houston's Democratic Mayor Lee Brown also pleaded guilty to bribery charges as part of the federal investigation.[11]

New Orleans

Among the many corrupt Democrat-run cities in America, perhaps none is more corrupt than the Big Easy—"endemic" and "notorious" are among the adjectives used to describe corruption in New Orleans, where votes are bought and sold to elect politicians who shamelessly line their pockets. An investigation of Louisiana's 1996 U.S. Senate race produced evidence that Democrats paid poor New Orleans residents to vote, and that many voted multiple times for Sen. Mary Landrieu. (The Democrat won by fewer than 6,000 votes statewide, thanks to a 100,000-vote margin in New Orleans.) Responding to reports that his campaign operation was handing out $50 checks on Election Day, New Orleans Mayor Marc Morial said, "I call that true red-white-and-blue American politics."[12] Three years after Morial left office, several city officials and contractors faced federal corruption charges. In one case, a thirty-seven-page indictment alleged that Morial cronies skimmed money from an $81 million city contract; an ex-cop was charged with pocketing $800,000; and two city officials were accused of receiving $100,000 each. Meanwhile, Morial's uncle was accused of skimming more than $500,000 from the city transit authority, and Morial's aunt was convicted on federal charges of paying kickbacks to a school official.[13]

When Hurricane Katrina hit New Orleans in September 2005, the consequences of Democratic corruption became national news. For while city officials had been living high on their ill-gotten gains, they had not prepared for massive flooding—though forecasters had long warned of such a disaster in the event of a major hurricane. Morial's successor, Mayor Ray Nagin, failed to evacuate the city, leaving hundreds of transit authority buses flooded and useless. Sen. Landrieu, who owed her office to the New Orleans votes bought by the Morial machine, blamed federal officials for the disaster even as Americans watched in horror while uniformed New Orleans police joined a nationally televised orgy of looting. Hundreds of city police were no-shows during the crisis, and after the storm, officials investigated charges that New Orleans police had, among many other misdeeds, used the emergency as an excuse to steal Cadillacs from a car dealership.[14]

Scores of poor New Orleans residents, trapped for days amid the flood, climbed onto their rooftops and pleaded to be rescued. But one local politician had better plans for the Louisiana National Guard. Five days after Katrina hit, Guard officials said, Democratic Rep. William Jefferson told them he wanted to tour the flooded city. An eight-term congressman, Jefferson was already being investigated by the FBI; Jefferson's brother-in-law, a former state judge, had recently been convicted of mail fraud in a corruption case involving $20,000 in bribes. But when the Guard took the congressman to tour the city, he didn't ask to visit the devastated Ninth Ward. Instead, Jefferson directed the Guardsmen to his own home in an affluent uptown neighborhood, where he retrieved a laptop computer, three packed suitcases, and a large box. When one of the Guard trucks got stuck in the mud, a Coast Guard helicopter sent a rescue diver to

Jefferson's aid. All of this occurred while the Democrat's poor constituents were desperately awaiting rescue efforts, but Jefferson saw nothing wrong with his actions: "This wasn't about me going to my house. It was about me going to my district," he told ABC News.[15]

Of all the scandals that have attached themselves to the Democratic Party, all the bribery, kickbacks, and assorted acts of corruption, the worst crime Democrats committed was their destruction of urban America. In the first half of the twentieth century, America's cities—with their gleaming skyscrapers and bustling economies—were the nation's pride. Public schools in cities like New York, Washington, and Chicago were among the best in the country, and big-city streets were scarcely more dangerous than those in small towns.[16]

In the half-century after World War II, Democratic policies fueled the decline of many cities, but nowhere was that decline so precipitous as in Detroit. Once the greatest manufacturing center in the world, Detroit became "a textbook case of how to kill a city."[17]

"We Burned Detroit Down"

Krikor Messerlian left Armenia in 1920, looking for the American Dream. And where better to find it than in Detroit? The auto industry was booming, paying good wages to young men willing to work hard. Arriving in Detroit at age twenty, Messerlian—known as "George" to coworkers at the Ford plant—soon saved enough money to open his own business, a shoe repair shop in northwest Detroit.[18]

After World War II, northwest Detroit underwent a rapid demographic transition. In 1940, the area around Messerlian's shop was nearly 99 percent white; in 1960, it was 96 percent black. The neighborhood was increasingly plagued by crime, and many businesses left the area. But George and his shoe shop stayed on Linwood Avenue.

In the wee hours of Sunday, July 23, 1967, Detroit police raided a party at an unlicensed after-hours club on Twelfth Street, a few blocks from Messerlian's shop. Finding eighty-two people in the club, police decided to arrest them all. While police waited for paddy wagons to arrive, an angry crowd gathered around the scene. Some in the crowd broke into a nearby clothing store, and soon looting and arson spread across the community. About 2:30 Sunday afternoon, a crowd of looters came down Linwood Avenue and stopped near the dry cleaning shop next door to Messerlian's shop. The owner had asked him to watch the place, and Messerlian came out to defend his neighbor's business, brandishing a twenty-inch-long ceremonial saber. The looters told the little man to get out of their way, but the sixty-seven-year-old Armenian didn't back down. The crowd pushed past him, breaking the windows of the dry-cleaning shop, and Messerlian swung his saber, slashing one of the looters on the shoulder. Suddenly, Messerlian was shoved to the ground, and one of the looters, wielding a broken chair leg like a club, beat the little Armenian unconscious. Messerlian died five days later.

Messerlian was one of forty-three people killed in the 1967 Detroit riot. The riot was so violent that not even the National Guard could restore order, and President Johnson sent in paratroopers from the 82nd Airborne Division. When it was over, more than a thousand people had been injured and more than seven thousand arrested. Entire city blocks were reduced to ashes and smoking rubble. Detroit, once one of the most prosperous cities in America, has never recovered.

What caused the devastation in Detroit? At the time, the riot was seen as part of a pattern—the "long hot summers" of the 1960s, a decade that saw rioting in most of America's largest cities. With few exceptions, the rioters were black, and commentators then and since have tended to blame the violence on such "root causes" as racism, poverty, and police brutality. Most notable was the Kerner Commission, an official federal panel appointed to investigate the riots, which concluded: "White racism is essentially responsible for the explosive mixture that has been accumulating in our cities since the end of World War II." The problem with such explanations, however, is that they don't fit the facts.[19]

Blaming the riots on racism ignores the fact that the rioting occurred in the North, not the South, and intensified after the triumph of the civil rights movement, including the passage of the landmark Civil Rights Act of 1964 and the Voting Rights Act of 1965. "Because the [Kerner] commission took for granted that the riots were the fault of white racism, it would have been awkward to confront the question of why liberal Detroit blew up while Birmingham and other Southern cities—where conditions for blacks were infinitely worse—did not," Harvard professor Stephan Thernstrom has observed. "Likewise, if the problem was white racism, why didn't the riots occur in the 1930s, when prevailing white attitudes were far more barbaric than they were in the 1960s?"[20]

As for poverty explaining the riots, the decade of the 1960s was one of booming prosperity and jobs were plentiful. Economist Thomas Sowell and others have pointed out that African-Americans had been making steady economic gains even before the civil rights movement, and the cities hit hardest by rioting were places where wages for black workers were higher than elsewhere in the country. And if police were guilty of "brutality" in the 1960s, there is no reason to believe cops were more brutal than in previous decades, before urban riots became an annual ritual. Indeed, Supreme Court decisions such as the 1966 Miranda ruling had limited police authority, and leading politicians sought to curb abuses by police.[21]

The idea that oppression and racism caused the riots of the '60s is especially difficult to accept in the case of Detroit. The city's mayor was a crusading liberal Democrat, Jerome "Jerry" Cavanagh. Just thirty-one years old when elected in 1961, Cavanagh moved quickly to fulfill his promises to reform the police, appointing a new chief. Cavanagh began an affirmative action program to hire more blacks in city government and lobbied for federal funds for the city under the "Model Cities" program. When Martin Luther King Jr. came to Detroit in 1963, Mayor Cavanagh marched beside the civil rights leader in a "March for Freedom" down the city's Woodward Avenue. Journalists lauded the liberal mayor, praising Detroit's "power structure," which *Fortune* magazine said had managed "to overcome tenacious prejudice and give the Negro community a role in the consensus probably unparalleled in any major American city."[22]

Blacks were by no means excluded from Detroit's prosperity and progress. As far back as the days when Henry Ford introduced his Model T, the city's auto manufacturers had shown a willingness to hire blacks and other minorities. The same demand for labor that had brought Krikor Messerlian from Armenia to Detroit also lured thousands of African Americans who were glad to leave behind the South's cotton fields and sharecropper shacks to work at factory jobs that paid top wages. By 1967, Detroit boasted the highest rate of black home ownership in the nation and was also home to numerous black entrepreneurs, including former autoworker Berry Gordy, founder of Motown Records, which in the 1960s made Detroit famous as "Hitsville, USA."[23]

If poverty and racism fail to explain the Detroit riot, what does? For all its external appearance of prosperity, Detroit had been steadily losing manufacturing jobs since the end of World War II. Two major contributors were unions and high taxes, which had helped drive jobs out of the city. Unions had generally refrained from striking during the war, but as soon as peace came in 1945, labor bosses launched a devastating series of strikes. Ford and General Motors were among the first targets of the wave of postwar strikes that spread so widely that newspapers referred to the phenomenon as a "workers' revolt." All told, more than 107 million man-days of work were lost due to strikes in 1946, delivering a shuddering blow to a nation attempting to make the transition to the peacetime economy.[24]

The postwar strikes helped fuel a backlash against unions. The first right-to-work laws, which protected the rights of employees who refused to pay union dues, had been passed in Florida and Arkansas in 1944. In 1946, three more states (Nebraska, South Dakota, and Arizona) followed suit, and another six states (Georgia, Iowa, North Carolina, Tennessee, Texas, and Virginia) passed right-to-work statutes in 1947. And the federal Taft-Hartley Act, passed in 1946, included a provision that recognized the legality of such state laws. Right-to-work laws kept unions from gaining the monopoly power they exercised in heavily unionized states like Michigan, where workers could be fired for not paying union dues— and where politicians beholden to Big Labor could be counted on to block any effort to pass right-to-work laws. Over ensuing decades, industry began to shift operations out of the industrial heartland (which by the 1980s would be dubbed the "Rust Belt") to Southern and Western states with right-to-work laws.[25]

Detroit was also losing industrial jobs, residents, and tax revenue to its suburbs. More than 200,000 Detroit residents moved out of the city during the 1950s, but this was not the kind of racially motivated "white flight" that would characterize subsequent decades. Among the new suburbanites of the '50s, "almost none were thinking about race. They were thinking about a tract house, with a plot of crabgrass and lower taxes," as Detroit journalist Jack Lessenberry observed.[26] Seeking cheaper land and proximity to suburban workers, Detroit's automakers began decentralizing production. Between 1946 and 1956, the "Big Three" manufacturers (General Motors, Ford, and Chrysler) spent $6.6 billion on new plants— none of them in Detroit. Twenty-five new plants were opened in Detroit's suburbs, none in the city. Even as the city lost industrial jobs, however, it continued to attract black job-seekers—among them the man who was eventually charged with Krikor Messerlian's murder. The twenty-year-old had moved to Detroit from Alabama only six weeks before the riot.[27]

As in dozens of other big cities, a vicious cycle was taking hold in Detroit. Residents and industrial jobs left, property values stagnated or declined, and the tax base was shrinking. Officials faced a dilemma: cut the city budget or raise taxes. Like Democratic mayors in many other cities, Mayor Cavanagh chose to raise taxes. Inheriting a $28 million deficit in the city budget when he took office in 1962, Cavanagh instituted a city income tax, not only taxing Detroit residents, but also applying taxes to the wages of commuters who lived outside the city. The result—as in other big cities that took the tax-raising approach—was to drive even more jobs and middle-class residents out of Detroit. The residents who remained were more likely to be unemployed, and more in need of city social services, which in turn drove up the cost of government.[28]

But the spark that turned Detroit's troubles into one of the biggest riots in American history was a shift in the leadership and tactics of the civil rights movement. During the 1950s and early '60s, leaders like Martin Luther King had focused their non-violent efforts on ending segregation in the South and had reached out to seek support from whites. That crusade ended victoriously with the passage of landmark legislation in 1964–65. Dr. King quipped that, in signing the Voting Rights Act of 1965, President Johnson had signed the civil rights movement out of existence. Soon thereafter, King and his allies were challenged by young radical leaders, many of whom had taken part in antisegregation protests as members of the Student Nonviolent Coordinating Committee. SNCC leaders like Stokely Carmichael called for "black power," a term whose political meaning was nebulous but which had the intended effect of provoking fear among whites.[29]

In 1966, when five days of looting and arson destroyed much of downtown Cincinnati, one of Carmichael's lieutenants, H. Rap Brown, told reporters that there would be no peace in the city "until the honky cops get out. . . . SNCC has declared war."[30]

Brown brought that war to Detroit in July 1967 when he declared at a rally, "The honky is your enemy," and warned that if city leaders did not meet his demands, "we are going to burn you down." After the riot that left many black neighborhoods in ashes, Brown proudly claimed credit for the violent destruction, telling a Los Angeles crowd in August 1967: "We burned Detroit down and we put America on notice: 'Jack, we built you up and we will tear you down.'"[31]

The Riot Ideology

What happened in Detroit, and in other major cities during the 1960s and afterward, was the development of a pattern that has been called "the riot ideology." This "conventional and deeply corrupting vision" viewed urban violence as a logical response to poverty and racism. Indeed, to many on the Left, rioting was welcomed as a necessary remedy to the deeply entrenched ills of America. "Terrifying as the looting, the shooting, the arson are," declared a 1967 editorial in *The New Republic*, a leading liberal journal, "they could mean a gain for the nation if, as a result, white America were shocked into looking at itself, its cities, its neglect . . . smugness and evasion." Only the passage of liberal legislation and massive taxpayer-funded antipoverty programs, it was argued, could avert massive violence.[32]

While white liberals romanticized rioting (after all, their neighborhoods weren't being looted and burned to the ground), many black leaders learned to capitalize on the tactics and rhetoric of radicals like Carmichael and Rap Brown. In the political kabuki dance of the riot ideology, the role of black leaders was to articulate grievances and issue demands. The role of government officials was to appease the angry resentments of those whom the black leaders—who were usually unelected and often self-appointed—claimed to represent. Failure to meet the demands of black leaders would result in protests, and if protests failed to get the desired result, the threat of riots loomed. Though rioting became less commonplace after the '60s, the danger of such violent outbreaks cast a long shadow over subsequent decades.[33]

By the end of the '60s, the riot ideology had entrenched itself as the urban zeitgeist, producing what writer Tom Wolfe memorialized as "maumauing the flak catchers," or as Siegel calls it, "a racial version of collective bargaining."[34] This process was encouraged and facilitated by the welfare policies of Democrat President Lyndon B. Johnson's so-called "Great Society" program. One of the aims of LBJ's Great Society was to help create institutional structures in poor communities so that the poor could help themselves. This was to be done through Community Action Programs (CAPs), which were "the heart of the Administration's War on Poverty." These programs, one urban planner claimed, would deliver aid in ways that were "bound to operate with more sensitivity to the poor." In addition, the process of administering the programs would presumably provide poor residents "instructive and beneficial" experiences.[35]

Federally funded to the tune of more than $1 billion in their first two years, the CAPs—administered through the Office of Economic Opportunity (OEO)—turned out to be a gravy train for cynical opportunists to advance their own agendas at taxpayer expense. In many cities, mayors appointed the members of the boards that supervised the local programs and, not surprisingly, loaded the boards with their allies and cronies. While the law called for the "maximum feasible representation" of the poor on CAP boards, this proved difficult to achieve. Sergeant Shriver, the Kennedy in-law who ran OEO, testified to Congress that some would-be board members didn't want to be labeled the "poor representative" on the local boards. And joining the CAP board, Shriver said, had other negative consequences: "Frequently . . . as soon as the minority group member is put on the committee, he becomes an 'Uncle Tom.' He was not before he got on. . . . [A]s soon as someone joins the committee they become unqualified thereafter to speak for the people who are not selected."[36]

Unleashing a flood of federal money into the cities, Johnson's "War On Poverty" programs often had bizarre consequences. In LaGrange, Georgia, federal job-training funds were used for a program to teach "cleanliness and work discipline" to black women training to be household maids, employment which paid $4 a day. (The *Washington Post* praised this program at the time as "dignifying the service jobs that are necessary to running a modern home."[37])

Meanwhile, in Oakland, California, it was at the OEO-funded offices of the West Oakland Planning Council in 1966 that convicted felon Huey Newton and his friend Bobby Seale drew up the charter of a "community group" known as the Black Panther Party, which subsequently received community-action grants.[38]

Four decades later, no one doubts that much of the federal money spent to combat poverty was wasted, doing little to improve the lot of the poor. As humorist P. J. O'Rourke has observed, in the first twenty years after LBJ declared his War on Poverty, federal anti-poverty spending amounted to $3.8 trillion—"enough to give every poor person in America $117,000 to start his own war on poverty."[39]

Perhaps the most significant unintended consequence of the War on Poverty was that it turned poverty from a private affliction into a government-run monopoly. Federal policy was to tear down dilapidated older homes to make way for new high-rise public housing projects. This had the unanticipated consequence of shrinking the property tax base because government-owned property is tax-exempt, and the projects quickly became even more dangerous than the privately owned "slums" they had replaced.[40]

By the mid-1990s, cities everywhere were demolishing the high-rise housing projects that once had symbolized the hopes of LBJ's Great Society. Three decades after these towers had been erected as monuments to liberal dreams, even the most passionate advocates for the poor recognized that government housing was a trap, a cemetery where hope died. O'Rourke, who traveled the world as a foreign correspondent for *Rolling Stone* magazine, visited a Newark, New Jersey, housing project in the late 1980s and declared: "I've been in Beirut, where people were living in holes scooped out of rubble. I've been to the Manila city dump, where people were living in holes scooped out of garbage. . . . I've been to rioting Soweto shantytowns and besieged Gaza Strip refugee camps and half-starved contra outposts in the jungles of the Honduras, and I've never been to a place I would less rather live than this housing project in New Jersey."[41]

This crime against the poor was committed in the name of justice and equality, and promoted by left-wing intellectuals who saw burgeoning welfare rolls as a good thing that would enhance the human dignity of the poor and force government to institute revolutionary changes. The welfare explosion of the 1960s was the brainchild of a group of Columbia University professors, including Frances Fox Piven and Richard Cloward, and crusading New York anti-poverty lawyer Edward Sparer. They saw welfare as a means to shatter "patterns of servile conformity" among the poor, transforming them into a force for revolution. They argued that adding millions more to the welfare rolls "would precipitate a profound financial and political crisis," and thus force elected officials to become "lobbyists for change in Washington." To implement this strategy, Sparer sued the city for higher payments to welfare recipients. Sparer also went to court to win decisions that struck down rules that limited welfare eligibility, such as requirements that welfare recipients actively seek work. Such rules, Sparer argued, violated welfare clients' right "to choose one's own standard of morality." This welfare crusade, led by the National Welfare Rights Organization, prompted thousands of working poor people to leave the work force and go on welfare. Like slum clearance, the welfare crusade undermined the fiscal situation of cities, turning taxpayers into tax recipients and requiring city governments to hire more social workers to administer the increasing welfare caseload.[42]

Meanwhile, the cost of government was further increased by public employee unions. The very existence of such unions turns the logic of the labor movement on its head. The purpose of unions is to represent the interests of workers against the interests of the owners of businesses. But government workers are ultimately employees of the taxpayers, so that government worker unions are fundamentally opposed to the public interest—in the words of one New York liberal activist, "not extracting a share of the profits but rather a share of taxes."[43]

This inexorable logic has had a devastating impact on America's cities. Under Democratic Mayor Robert F. Wagner Jr., New York became the first U.S. city to grant collective bargaining rights to city employees. The public employee unions relentlessly negotiated for higher wages, shorter hours, and more benefits, including health insurance that did not require co-payments from the workers (a policy unheard of in the private sector). Contract negotiations were a farce, since unions used membership dues to fund political campaigns to elect pro-union candidates: "During labor

negotiations, the unions would be on both sides of the table."[44] This trans-
lated into forcing governments (which is to say, taxpayers) to pay above-
market labor rates. By 2005, journalist Steve Malanga observed, "Wages
average a hefty 37 percent higher in the public sector, but the differences
in benefits are even more dramatic. Local governments pay 128 percent
more, on average, than private employers to finance workers' health-care
benefits, and 162 percent more on retirement benefits."[45]

Fewer private-sector jobs, more welfare recipients, more public
employees, higher government costs, higher taxes—by the mid-1960s,
Democratic policies had sent the nation's biggest cities into a downward
spiral that could only end in bankruptcy. For Detroit, already devastated
by deadly riots, the worst days were ahead.

Devil's Night

"No American city ever fell as far or as fast as Detroit," Julia Vitullo-
Martin has observed, and the man who presided over Detroit's descent
into depression and decay was a former radical labor activist named
Coleman Young.[46]

As a young man growing up in Detroit, Young became attracted to
Marxist ideology and showed a great skill for getting himself fired from
job after job. When World War II came, Young joined the Army and was
commissioned a lieutenant. Recruited for the famed Tuskegee Airmen, he
washed out during training, a failure for which he blamed the FBI.[47]

After the war, he returned to Detroit and went to work as a UAW
organizer. He later said that he was "full of ideological passion" in those
years, and his passion was pro-Soviet. One fellow labor activist said, "If
Coleman wasn't a Communist, he cheated them out of dues."[48]

A clear indication of Young's leanings came in 1948. He ran for the U.S.
Senate on the left-wing Progressive Party ticket, whose presidential candidate Henry Wallace was the front man for a Moscow-approved effort to
unseat Democrat Harry Truman. That campaign got Young fired from his

union job, and he ended up as executive secretary of the National Negro Labor Council (NNLC), a known Communist front group. He was subpoenaed in 1952 to testify before the House Un-American Activities Committee, where he refused to cooperate and castigated committee members as racists. In 1956, after Soviet leader Nikita Kruschev denounced Stalin's crimes, the Communist Party USA collapsed, as did the NNLC, and Young was a man without a job or a party. He eventually began seeking office as a Democrat, but due to UAW opposition was defeated in three campaigns before finally being elected to the state senate.

Young was elected mayor of Detroit in 1973, narrowly defeating the city's police chief, John Nichols. During his inaugural address, Young sought to address the city's crime problem by declaring: "I issue a formal warning now, to all the pushers, to all rip-off artists, to all muggers. It is time to leave Detroit for Eight Mile Road. . . . Hit the road!" Eight Mile Road was the dividing line between the city and the working-class suburb of Warren. While Young later explained the remark as his way of telling criminals to get out of town, it was widely interpreted at the time as the newly elected black mayor urging Detroit criminals to attack white suburbanites. The mayor's reputation for racial hostility hastened "white flight" from the city. When he took office in 1974, about half of Detroit's population was white; indeed, the support of white liberals was crucial to his election. But the steady exodus of whites from the city became a deluge under Young's mayorality. Between 1970 and 1980, the white population decreased by 418,000, from 56 percent to 36 percent of the population. During the '80s, the trend continued, with Detroit's white population decreasing by another 199,000, down to 22 percent by 1990.[49]

Young never spoke a word of regret about whites leaving Detroit. He actually seemed determined to drive them out, as when he used the city's power of eminent domain to destroy a Polish-American neighborhood, evicting the homeowners and giving the confiscated property to General Motors for expansion of a plant. And when critics accused him of having been co-opted by big business, Young answered: "If I was co-opted, I was certainly willing."[50]

Young demonized white suburbanites, blaming them for all the city's problems. The suburbs were "economically pillaging the city," the mayor declared, "Whites can't stand for black folks to run a damn thing . . . and if we do, they're going to destroy it."[51] He also attacked the city's police department as "predominantly white and racist," saying: "The police are the major threat . . . to the minority community."[52] Young imposed a rigid racial quota system for hiring and promoting police, instituted a residency requirement to justify the firing of scores of white policemen who lived outside the city limits and watered down the entrance exam for trainees. The rookies hired under the mayor's quota system proved less than ideal: several were accused of dealing drugs, and one trainee was suspended after she "accidentally" shot her husband to death with her service revolver.[53]

During his term in the Michigan State Senate, Young's major legislative accomplishment had been passage of a law that required disputes between unions and local governments to be settled by arbitration. As mayor of Detroit, Young came to regret this sop to his old cronies in the labor movement. In effect, the mandatory arbitration law was an incentive for government employee unions to generate an endless list of demands, grievances, and strike threats. Unions had nothing to lose in arbitration, "and always won at least half of what they were asking."[54] Therefore, all union officials had to do was make demands—for higher wages, shorter hours, and more benefits—and arbitrators would force the city to give in. For Detroit in the 1970s, this meant that elected officials had no real control over the city budget; while tax revenues were stagnant or declining, labor costs skyrocketed. Government unions were "undermining democracy," Mayor Young ultimately declared. "Slowly, inexorably, compulsory arbitration destroys sensible fiscal management. Arbitration awards have caused more damage to the public service in Detroit than the strikes they were designed to prevent."[55]

Detroit soon had the highest-paid city employees in the nation, but that was not enough for union bosses, who demanded still more. In 1978, with the city already facing a budget crisis, Detroit's police and firefighters unions sought new concessions from the city. The case was submitted to arbitration, and the unions were awarded salary increases and additional benefits worth $80 million a year. Having already raised taxes, Mayor Young said the city didn't have the money to meet this latest arbitration award. So Detroit laid off more than a quarter of its police officers, reducing the force from 5,400 to 4,000. Crime spiraled out of control—rising 50 percent in a single three-year period—and soon Detroit had the worst crime rate in the country.[56]

Detroit lost jobs and businesses at an incredible rate, as Vitullo-Martin explains: "Between 1972 and 1991, the number of manufacturing, wholesale, and retail establishments declined by over 45 percent." The city's property tax base—reflecting the value of Detroit real estate—"declined by nearly two-thirds, or $3.6 billion, between 1970 and 1990," as Coleman's administration "acquired and tore down whole swaths of Detroit; it issued 41,800 more demolition permits than construction permits."[57]

The sheer destructiveness of Young's policies were explained by one businessman who left Detroit: "Coleman was a racist, and he made it clear that white businesses were unwelcome. . . . We could get robbed, burned out, preyed upon by city inspectors, and Coleman wouldn't do anything. He encouraged attacks on us."[58]

Perhaps inspired by their mayor's policies, Detroit's youth went on their own orgy of destruction, an annual pre-Halloween arson spree known as "Devil's Night." Every October, TV news showed Detroit in flames, as teenagers torched abandoned homes. The phenomenon reached a peak in 1984, when the city experienced 810 fires during a three-day period. Devil's Night even became a tourist attraction of sorts, as suburbanites came into the city to watch the fires. A suburban resident, videotaping a fire in 1988, told a reporter: "Some people like the Fourth of July. I like Devil's Night."[59]

While his city declined, Coleman Young's twenty years in office produced "a mind-numbing series of scandals," including a 1978 investigation which found that four hundred city employees had been illegally collecting welfare payments. Detroit's sordid history of corruption culminated in the 1992 conviction of Young's handpicked police chief, William Hart, on charges of stealing more than $2.3 million dollars from the police department.[60]

"It is no exaggeration to say that Young's legacy includes one of the most corrupt municipal administrations in modern American history," socialist writer Martin McLaughlin observed after Young's death in 1997. But this corruption, he noted, was excused by Young's supporters. "All this rot was covered over by an increasingly strident proclamation of racial politics. Every Young crony who was sent to prison for theft of public funds was declared to be a victim of racism. Every sweetheart deal between the city government and favored contractors was hailed as an affirmation of black economic power."[61]

Amazingly, long after Young was gone, Detroit politicians argued amongst themselves as to which was the true heir to his legacy. In an October 2005 debate between mayoral candidates, Mayor Kwame Kilpatrick—trailing in the polls after his extravagant expenses became a public scandal—invoked "Coleman Young" three times before challenger Freeman Hendrix called him on it: "Mayor Young was a fighter for the little people in this city. Mayor Young never lived lavishly. . . . So let's let his legacy rest and let's stop invoking his name as though you've got something in common with him." Kilpatrick responded by accusing Hendrix of jealousy, saying his rival "hears people out here talking about that Kwame could be the next Coleman. And he doesn't like it."

Kilpatrick then said of Young: "He's my hero. He's an incredible figure in modern political history."[62]

FAT CATS AND DEMOCRATS

THE REAL "PARTY OF THE RICH"

"Turbulent, discontented men of quality, in proportion as they are puffed up with personal pride and arrogance, generally despise their own order. . . . If any bounds are set to the rapacious demands of that sort of people . . . revenge and envy soon fill up the craving void that is left in their avarice."

—EDMUND BURKE[1]

POLICE RAIDED THE FISHING VILLAGE JUST BEFORE DAWN. AMONG THE residents of Veldur, India, targeted in the raid was a twenty-year-old woman who was three months pregnant. "At around 5 in the morning when I was in the bathroom, several male police with batons in their hands forcibly entered the house and started beating members of [my] family who were asleep," Sugandha Vasudev Bhalekar later testified. Police broke through the bathroom door "and dragged me out of the house into the police van parked on the road." The officers "kept beating me on my back with batons," Bhalekar testified. "The humiliation meted out to the other members of my family was similar to the way I was humiliated. . . . My one and a half year old daughter held on to me but the police kicked her away."

Bhalekar was one of twenty-six women arrested in the raid on Veldur. Their crime? They had protested the construction of a nearby power plant being built by an American company, Enron.[2]

The White House was deeply involved with Enron, the Texas-based energy firm with worldwide ambitions. Enron officials were welcomed at the White House and traveled abroad with top administration officials who pushed the company's interests with foreign governments. Cabinet officers pressured foreign leaders to approve Enron's deals, which were funded in part by federal taxpayers. The Secretary of Commerce wrote a letter on Enron's behalf to the Indonesian government: "Enron power, a world renowned private power developer, is in the final stages of negotiating two combined cycle, gas turbine power projects. . . . I urge you to give full consideration to the proposals." The secretary of Energy met with Enron CEO Ken Lay to discuss proposed legislation, and the president praised Enron for being a good "corporate citizen." The administration gave similar backing for Enron projects in China, India, Bosnia, and elsewhere. Former administration officials were hired as Enron lobbyists, and a former Cabinet official took a job at a bank that loaned the company hundreds of millions of dollars.[3]

Needless to say, the cozy relationship between Enron and the White House involved campaign contributions—all told, Enron donated more than $1 million to the president and his party. But in early 2002, after Enron's collapse into bankruptcy generated massive reporting of accounting scams, insider trading, angry shareholders, and displaced employees, no one in the media seemed eager to blame the president implicated in all these dealings—Bill Clinton.[4]

This story of the extensive ties between Enron and the Clinton administration is one that the news media did their best to avoid reporting. Over a period of nearly two months (January 9–March 5) in 2002, the "Big Three" network evening newscasts on NBC, ABC, and CBS produced 198 stories about the Enron scandal, of which only six stories mentioned the Texas company's ties to the Clinton administration.[5] When *Time* magazine did a front-page story on Enron in January 2002, it omitted any reference to the relationship between Enron and the Clinton White House. Instead, *Time*'s Daniel Kadlec reported: "Enron

enjoyed considerable influence from the start of the Bush Administration.
. . . Lay and other Enron officials met six times with officials led by Vice
President Dick Cheney (a former oilman) to craft a new energy policy.
That policy, not surprisingly, was friendly to Enron and other energy
companies."[6]

Like much else during the Bush administration, the media's reporting
of the Enron debacle was full of distortions and omissions. Contrary to
what Kadlec reported in *Time*, for example, Dick Cheney is not "a former
oilman"; for five years, from 1995 to 2000, he was CEO of Halliburton,
whose chief business is providing engineering services to the petroleum
and natural gas industries. Halliburton doesn't own any oil fields or
tankers, nor does it own refineries or gas stations. The company's "broad
array of products and services," as it proclaims on its Web site, range
"from the manufacturing of drill bits . . . to pressure pumping services."[7]
Being the chief executive of an engineering firm is not the same as being
an "oilman," just like using word-processing software to write a book
doesn't make us part of the computer industry. And Enron's main business was natural gas, so what's the relevance of Cheney being an "oilman"?
Yet this kind of misleading half-truth—conspiratorial smears about Bush
and Cheney and "Big Oil"—found its way into *Time* magazine and
countless other news sources that sought to make the bankruptcy of
Enron a Republican scandal.

If political ties to Enron were the stuff of corruption and scandal,
however, Democrats were in it up to their eyeballs. A few highlights:

- The Clinton administration's relationship with Enron dated back at
  least as early as August 1993, when Ken Lay was invited to play golf
  with President Clinton in Vail, Colorado.[8]

- In 1994, when Deputy Energy Secretary Bill White returned from a
  trip to Mexico, he wrote to Ken Lay that there was "much
  opportunity" for natural gas development in that country.[9]

- In 1995, the administration sought Enron's comments on its energy plans and then directed staff to "rework the proposal to take into account the specific comments and suggestions you made," as White wrote to an Enron official.[10]

- Energy Secretary Hazel O'Leary brought along Enron officials on trade trips to India, China, Pakistan, and South Africa.[11]

- Enron donated generously to Democrats in Congress. From 1989 to 2001, seventy-one House Democrats and twenty-nine Senate Democrats collected a total of $367,653 in campaign contributions from Enron. The top two House members getting the most campaign cash from Enron's political action committee (PAC) during that twelve-year span were both Texas Democrats—Rep. Kent Bentsen, who got $42,750, and Rep. Sheila Jackson Lee, who got $38,000. Among the Senate Democrats who benefited from Enron's campaign funding were Sen. Charles E. Schumer of New York ($21,933) and Sen. Jeff Bingaman of New Mexico ($14,124). Before going bankrupt, the company even managed to give $950 to Hillary Rodham Clinton's 2000 Senate campaign.[12]

- In 1995, Enron beat out a South African company on a deal to build a pipeline from Mozambique's natural gas fields to South Africa. Clinton's National Security Adviser, Anthony Lake, and other administration officials were accused of pressuring the government of Mozambique to sign with Enron.[13]

- Commerce Secretary Ron Brown included Enron officials on at least seven trade trips, including the April 1996 trip to Croatia on which Brown was killed when his plane crashed into a mountain. Enron eventually landed a lucrative deal with Croatian dictator Franjo Tudjman—the company got a twenty-year contract to sell electricity in the Balkan country at above-market rates. This prompted accusations that the deal was part of an arrangement to gain U.S.

influence to support Croatia's bid for membership in the World Trade Organization, and to prevent Tudjman and his cronies from facing war crimes charges for atrocities committed during Yugoslavia's brutal civil war.[14]

- Secretary Brown showed a keen interest in Enron's effort to reach a deal with Indonesia's corrupt Suharto dictatorship to build two natural gas-powered electricity plants in that country. Beginning in 1994, Enron invested $25 million in this project, but had trouble getting the necessary approvals. In 1995, Brown wrote a letter to the Indonesian minister for trade and industry on behalf of Enron, urging the minister "to give full consideration to the proposals." In another letter to Indonesian officials, Brown wrote: "I would like to bring to your attention a number of projects involving American companies which seem to be stalled, including several independent power projects." Naming the two Enron plants among these stalled projects, Brown wrote: "Your support for prompt resolution of the remaining issues associated with each of these projects would be most appreciated." Enron's Indonesia deal finally fell apart in 1997, when the Suharto dictatorship was overthrown amid the Asian currency crisis.[15]

- The Clinton administration asked Enron to help get China and India to participate in the Kyoto global-warming treaty. Enron stood to profit two ways from the Kyoto protocols: first, the company's main business was natural gas, a relatively clean-burning fuel; second, Enron envisioned setting up a market in which countries could trade carbon-emissions credits under the treaty. In a December 1997 memo, Enron lobbyist John Palmisano called the Kyoto treaty a "victory" for the company: "This agreement will do more to promote Enron's business than will almost any other regulatory initiative. . . . Enron has immediate business opportunities which derive directly from this agreement."[16]

• It was while Ken Lay was on a January 1995 trade junket to India with Secretary Brown that two federal export-finance agencies, the Export-Import Bank and the Overseas Private Investment Corporation, announced a $400 million loan to Enron to build a power plant in Dabhol, India. This project—which grew into a $2.9 billion deal—merited President Clinton's personal intervention. On November 22, 1995, the president sent an "FYI" note to White House advisor Thomas "Mack" McLarty, enclosing a newspaper article about problems with the Dabhol project, which had run into opposition from both the World Bank and local villagers. (Among other objections, the deal called for Enron to sell electricity at nearly twice the going rate, with Indian taxpayers subsidizing the difference.) McLarty and Frank Wisner, the Clinton-appointed U.S. Ambassador to India, pushed the Indian government to approve the project.

In June 1996, Enron gave $100,000 to the Democratic National Committee. Four days later, India approved the deal.

But villagers around Dabhol kept protesting, saying pollution from the Enron plant would destroy the local fishing economy. The June 1997 raid on Veldur—in which pregnant Sugandha Vasudev Bhalekar was dragged from her bathroom—was part of a crackdown by Indian officials against the protesters.[17]

The Dabhol project brokered by the Clinton administration was one of several trouble spots in Enron's shady business practices that led to the company's spectacular collapse in December 2001. Bills at the project went unpaid, and banks were threatening to seize the plant in India unless Enron paid up. A clear sign that Enron was desperate for cash came when the company offered to sell its 65-percent share of the Dabhol project for $1 billion—a 50-percent discount off the plant's estimated value. In the fall of 2001, as the company's financial crisis deepened, Enron sought a merger with a rival firm, Dynergy. But there was a problem: Wall Street had gotten the scent of Enron's problems, and Moody's Investors Services was getting ready to downgrade the company's credit rating. Enron then called on the services of one of its old Democratic friends, Robert Rubin. Former secretary of the Treasury in the Clinton administration, Rubin had gone on to become chairman of Citigroup. Enron owed Citigroup $1 billion, and Rubin's bank faced huge losses if the Dynergy merger fell through. So on November 8, 2001, Rubin called Peter Fisher, undersecretary of the treasury in the Bush administration, and asked Fisher to put pressure on Moody's and other credit agencies to delay publication of the Enron downgrade. Meanwhile, Lay was calling on Commerce Secretary Donald Evans and Treasury Secretary Paul O'Neill, begging for their help.

But the Clinton administration era of crony capitalism was over. Fisher refused Rubin's request, Evans and O'Neill turned down Lay's pleas, and when Enron's lower credit rating was announced, the Dynergy deal fell apart. Within a month, Enron filed for bankruptcy. Hundreds of the company's employees were laid off, but not before top Enron executives cashed out their stock options.[18]

Perversely, Democrats looked to blame Republicans for the Enron disaster. California Rep. Henry Waxman, the top Democrat on the House committee investigating the scandal, huffed: "I am deeply troubled that the White House stood by and let this happen to thousands of families."[19] A Democratic National Committee spokeswoman insisted that "disclosures" about Enron were affecting public perceptions of the Bush administration: "When the constant drip, drip, drip of an investigation hits this close to people in the White House and in the administration, it is going to be a real liability to them."[20] But one former Bush adviser noted that Enron's corrupt practices dated back to the years when the company was cozy with the Clinton administration: "The partnerships that hid billions of dollars in Enron's debts from investors and that brought the company down occurred between 1997 and 2000. The government's regulators in those years were Clinton appointees."[21]

It might seem strange that the collapse of Enron—a company that poured hundreds of thousands of dollars into Democratic campaign cof-fers—could ever have been painted as a Republican scandal. Strange, per-haps, but not surprising. After all, Enron was a Texas company, and George W. Bush was a Texas president. Enron gave plenty of money to Republicans—more than $3 million between 1989 and 2001—and was a major contributor to the Bush campaign in 2000.[22] But the haste of the media to blame the Bush administration for the Enron scandal was largely a product of the decades-long propaganda effort by Democrats to convince Americans that Republicans are the "party of the rich." Much evidence, however, contradicts this stereotype.

Democrat Dollars

Democrats have certainly shown no aversion to filling their campaign coffers with contributions from Corporate America. One needs to look no further than Federal Election Commission (FEC) records for the 2006 campaign season. Through the FEC reporting period ending September 30, 2005, *seven of the top ten U.S. Senate candidates in terms of fundraising were Democrats*:

1. Hillary Clinton, New York, $15.4 million
4. Bill Nelson, Florida, $5.4 million
5. Maria Cantwell, Washington, $5.1 million
7. Edward M. Kennedy, Massachusetts, $5.0 million
8. Bob Casey, Pennsylvania, $4.1 million
9. John F. Kerry, Massachusetts, $4.1 million
10. Debbie Stabenow, Michigan, $3.7 million[23]

Meanwhile, a list of top corporate political action committee (PAC) donors to Democrats for the 2006 campaign season, through November 30, 2005, featured most of the same blue-chip companies that were giving to Republicans: United Parcel Service ($226,173), AT&T ($199,000), defense contractor Northrop Grumman ($198,500), insurance giant AFLAC ($193,500), General Electric ($193,350), General Dynamics, another big Pentagon contractor ($168,500), BellSouth ($166,100), defense contractors Boeing ($166,000) and Raytheon ($161,250), and Comcast ($153,950).[24]

Consider, for example, PACs that contributed to the Democrats' top fund raiser, Hillary Clinton. While the biggest chunks of her PAC money (through September 30, 2005) came from organized labor ($141,170), law groups ($71,087), and various single-issue advocates ($66,918), Hillary also collected substantial sums from the health-care industry ($62,900), finance and insurance interests ($59,000), the communications industry ($42,687), retail and service industries ($39,000), real estate and construction ($24,840), and the defense industry ($19,000).[25]

Reformers who promise to rid politics of the corrupting influence of big money have had little success in keeping wealthy donors from spending millions to elect Democrats. The Enron scandal helped boost the issue of campaign-finance reform, and in March 2002, President Bush signed the Bipartisan Campaign Reform Act (BCRA) into law. The new law's key provision was to limit the previously unregulated "soft money" that the political parties had collected from big contributors.[26] When it looked like Democrats might suffer from the shutoff of the "soft money" pipeline, rich Democrats soon found a loophole in non-profit "issue advocacy" organizations, called "527s" for the IRS code that regulates their operations. During the ensuing 2004 election cycle, a small group of wealthy liberals donated more than $80 million to 527s supporting Democrats. The top 527 donors in 2004—financier George Soros (who gave $23.4 million), insurance mogul Peter Lewis ($23 million), Hollywood playboy Stephen Bing ($13.9 million), and mortgage bankers Herb and Marion Sandler ($13 million)—were all Democrats. Gateway computer founder Ted Waitt gave $5 million to Democratic 527s, and venture capitalists Andy and Deborah Rappaport gave $4.3 million.[27]

Democrats who smear Republicans as the party of the greedy rich have to overlook more than just a few big-money Democratic donors. There's also the so-called "red state-blue state" divide. The "blue" states that voted for John Kerry in 2004 are far richer than the "red" states that voted for Bush. Summarizing research by the Bureau of Economic Analysis, Jerry Bowyer reported: "States with the highest per capita income trend Democrat; the states with the lowest per capita income trend Republican. The top ten 'blue states' . . . had an average per capita personal income of $36,327, which is 20 percent higher than the top ten 'red states,' which had an average of $30,275." Moreover, Bowyer found another difference. The Republican red states, despite their lower average incomes, had substantially higher rates of economic growth than the pro-Democrat blue states. In other words, while the rich people in Democratic states are "old money," Republican voters in the red states are "immune to class guilt because they didn't inherit their wealth." Bowyer concluded: "The notion that the GOP is the party of the rich simply doesn't match the economic reality."[28]

If Republicans were really the party of the rich, it might be expected that all the fat cats and high rollers would be happy to donate generously to President George W. Bush, whom Democrats so often denounced as favoring "tax cuts for the rich." Certainly, Bush had no shortage of campaign funds in 2004—all told, he collected nearly $375 million for his reelection bid. That was some $26 million more than was collected by his Democratic challenger, John Kerry. (In other words, Kerry raised about 97 percent as much as Bush.) But wait a minute. While Bush had no real rivals for the 2004 Republican nomination, Kerry got the Democratic nomination only after defeating a large pack of contenders. And each of those candidates raised substantial sums for their primary campaigns: Howard Dean of Vermont raised almost $53 million and North Carolina's John Edwards—who ended up as Kerry's running mate—raked in nearly $34 million. Even Ohio Rep. Dennis Kucinich, who ran as a socialist in all but name, managed an impressive haul of more than $13 million in contributions. If we combine together the campaign coffers of the top seven Democratic candidates (Kerry, Dean, Edwards, retired Gen. Wesley Clark, Rep. Dick Gephardt, Sen. Joe Lieberman, and Kucinich), we find that the total amount raised comes to $518 million. *Which means that the 2004 Democratic presidential candidates raised $144 million more than the Republican incumbent!*[29]

If Republicans are the "party of the rich," how could they be outspent by the party of the poor? It's not just presidential elections, either. In 2004, Tom Daschle of South Dakota was defeated in his bid for reelection to the Senate, despite having raised $3.1 million more than John Thune, the Republican who beat him. And in the 2004 Senate race in North Carolina, Democrat Erskine Bowles raised $13.4 million—nearly half a million more than Richard Burr, the Republican who beat him.[30]

Democrats claim to protect the downtrodden proletarian masses against the oppressive schemes of the wealthy few. Amazing, then, that Democrats can raise more money than the Republicans—and still lose on Election Day.

Heights of Hypocrisy

It's not just their donors who are rolling in cash. Democratic politicians themselves are, in many cases, stupendously wealthy. Nothing wrong with that (we're Republicans, remember), but rich Democrats sometimes get their money, and protect it from taxes, in ways that directly contradict their political rhetoric. This pattern is so widespread, Peter Schweizer of the Hoover Institution was able to write an entire book on the subject, *Do As I Say (Not As I Do): Profiles in Liberal Hypocrisy.*[31] Among other things, Scwheizer discovered:

John Kerry campaigned for president in 2004 saying that the "super-rich" should pay more taxes. But the Massachusetts senator and his heiress wife, with "a net worth exceeding $700 million . . . were paying only 15 percent of their income in taxes." Kerry had called for raising the taxes of Americans earning $200,000 a year—people who, according to the IRS, were already paying 25 percent of their income in taxes.[32]

House Democratic leader Nancy Pelosi supports organized labor and "affordable housing" for the poor and says that "the environment is a core value." Pelosi and her husband, a California real-estate magnate, have built a $50 million fortune by ignoring those values. They don't invest in "affordable housing," but in upscale projects like a private golf development that damaged the environment in Santa Clara County, California. While Pelosi frequently celebrates farm-labor hero Caesar Chavez, the grapes at the Pelosis' own Napa Valley wineries aren't picked by Chavez's United Farm Workers, but by underpaid migrants. (It would be interesting to check their green cards.) Nor is union labor welcomed at the ritzy hotels and restaurants—like the exclusive Auberge du Soleil resort and the Piatti restaurant chain—in which the Pelosis have invested their fortune.[33]

Ted Kennedy recently proposed repealing President Bush's tax cuts for any family earning over $130,000 a year and condemned Republican efforts to eliminate the estate tax. But the Kennedy family (with an estimated net worth of $500 million) derives substantial income from tax-protected trust funds, including an offshore trust on the remote Pacific island of Fiji. When patriarch Joe Kennedy died, his fortune was so sheltered from taxes that his heirs paid less than $140,000 (about .04 percent) in estate tax. The Kennedys' biggest investment, the Chicago Merchandise Mart, managed to underpay property taxes by $4 million a year thanks to its below-market-value assessment—the local tax assessor was a Kennedy family ally.[34]

"We're not about money," says Hillary Clinton.[35] But in 2000 she solicited $160,000 in gifts for her new home in Chappaqua, New York. While she decries the "ethos of selfishness" and opposes tax cuts, she and her husband have, over the years, been remarkably successful at avoiding taxes. The couple "appear to have repeatedly overstated their charitable contributions" to the IRS.[36] And then there was Whitewater. One of the little-reported aspects of that scandal was that fine print in the contracts for those buying Whitewater lots stipulated that, until the properties were paid off, payments would be counted as rent. Buyers who missed a couple of payments lost their equity and the lot went back to the development company, which could then resell it. This practice, illegal in many states, wasn't a rare thing at Whitewater—it happened to more than half of those who bought lots there, including one fellow who made payments totaling more than $11,000 for a $14,000 lot. After falling ill with diabetes, he missed a couple of payments and lost his property. Since those days, Schweizer observes, Hillary Clinton has gone on to crusade against "predatory mortgage lending practices."[37] She should know.

"Share, Share, Share"

Given the example set by star Democrats, it is hardly surprising that lesser lights in the Democratic constellation try to emulate them—though not always so successfully. Consider the case of the Inzunza family of San Diego. Ralph Inzunza Sr. was a popular Democratic politician in San Diego and passed on his love of politics to his sons, Ralph Jr. and Nick. Their entire family seemed to be involved in politics: both parents had served on the school board, their uncles served on the water board, and their aunt founded the Chicano Democratic Association. There was talk of which of the two brothers would be the first to run for California governor, and one San Diego publisher observed that "there is something Kennedyesque . . . about the Inzunzas."[38] And perhaps he was right.

Ralph Inzunza Jr. got himself elected to the San Diego City Council and immediately became involved in a project to expand citizen's rights to "free expression"—in the form of lap dances. A Las Vegas strip club owner, Mike Galardi, had a club in San Diego called Cheetahs. Galardi felt he was being deprived of revenue because of the city's "no touch" policy, forbidding physical contact between strippers and their clientele. Eleven days after taking office, Inzunza talked with a lobbyist for the California Cabaret Association, a group of strip club owners. Three months later, he received more than $5,000 in campaign contributions from Galardi's associates. Over the course of two years in office, Inzuna regularly met with Galardi's representatives, and also met with city attorneys and police officials involved in supervising the city's strip clubs. In May 2003 the FBI raided the offices of Inzunza and two of his city council colleagues, and in August, he was indicted on charges of wire fraud, extortion, and conspiracy. In 2005, he was found guilty of thirteen federal felony charges and sentenced to twenty-one months in prison.[39]

Nick Inzunza, seen as "the most political savvy of the Inzunzas," is also an example of the hypocrisy of the wealthy Democrat. In 2002, at age thirty-two, he was elected mayor of National City, a blue-collar suburb of San Diego, and in 2005, he declared himself a candidate for a seat in the California Assembly. Inzunza was also something of a real-estate mogul, boasting to a local magazine that he had spent a little over $3 million to buy property that, at the time of a 2003 interview, was worth more than $9 million. This, Inzunza explained, was part of his effort to "create affordable housing in the inner city." Which, as it turned out, was a nice way of saying that Nick Inzunza was essentially a slumlord. His rental properties were the subjects of lawsuits and complaints from tenants about "excessive rats" and "cockroaches." The *San Diego Union-Tribune*, in December 2005, described the problems faced by Inzunza's tenants: "No heat, no hot water . . . no smoke detectors. Broken windows, broken stove, broken shower, broken toilet."[40]

When tenants complained about these conditions, they were evicted. One of those tenants was William Cuesta, an AIDS victim who was on disability. His monthly disability check was $733. His rent was $695, and the conditions were horrible. So in March 2001, he wrote two letters to his landlady, Nick Inzunza's wife, Olga. "Where I come from in Texas, people who own property like 3720 Myrtle Ave. are called slumlords." Three days later, the Inzunzas filed suit to have Cuesta evicted. In a letter to the court, Cuesta said he had nowhere to go: "I will literally be on the street." But the Inzunzas' attorneys pressed the eviction proceedings and got a court order compelling Cuesta to pay the couple $2,122. What became of Cuesta after he was evicted is a mystery; as of December 2005, his family said they didn't know where he was.[41]

When reporters confronted National City's mayor with what they'd learned about his real-estate practices, Nick Inzunza blamed his wife. Claiming he hadn't "stepped foot on [the rental properties] in years," Inzunza told reporters: "Do I have control . . . over what my wife does? No, I don't." He explained: "My wife is very concerned in keeping the rents low." In an apparent effort to hide his role, the mayor transferred some of his rental units to his wife, who went to court and changed her name back to her maiden name.[42]

There's no law against being a cruel, greedy slumlord—though San Diego inspectors found some of the Inzunzas' properties were in violation of the city's housing code—and with his powerful Democratic connections, Nick Inzunza may yet go on to political glory. But is this the kind of behavior that Americans expect from a party that promises, in the words of Al Gore, "to fight for the people, not the powerful"?[43]

Herb Sandler is head of Golden West Financial, a California-based mortgage company, and a major contributor to Democratic 527 groups. In a 2004 interview, when asked to explain his political views, Sandler described what he called the "extreme radical right" philosophy of Republicans: "Take, take, take. Cut taxes, cut government, screw poor people." Blaming "this anti-tax thing" on Ronald Reagan and "wealthy right-wing funders," Sandler proclaimed: "I'm proud to pay taxes. . . . Why is it take, take, take all the time? Why can't we share, share, share?"[44] Given this attitude, one wonders what Sandler would think of fellow Democrat Nick Inzunza's path to real-estate riches. And what might Sandler say about Dorothy Rivers? As head of the Chicago Mental Health Foundation, her job was to share, share, share. Instead, Rivers decided to take, take, take. In 1997, she was indicted on twenty-two counts of mail and wire fraud, four counts of theft, seven counts of making false statements, three counts of tax evasion, three counts of failing to file tax returns, and one count of obstruction of a federal audit. Rivers was accused of defrauding the federal department of Housing and Urban Development, as well as state and local agencies, of $5 million. Among other things, she used the money stolen from these taxpayer-funded grants (part of which were designated to help homeless children and pregnant teens) to buy a $35,000 fur coat, hire a chauffeur, buy a Mercedes for her son, and throw extravagant parties, including one featuring a six-foot bubbling champagne glass. She used taxpayer money to make mortgage payments on a luxury apartment and a lakefront home.[45]

Herb Sandler surely would have nothing but scorn for a "take, take, take" scoundrel like Dorothy Rivers. Facing up to ten years in prison, she entered a plea bargain, pleading guilty in 1997 to stealing $1.2 million, and was sentenced to serve more than five years in federal prison. Prosecutors noted that she "never showed any remorse"[46] for her crimes, but Rivers served only three years of her sentence. Why? Well, part of the money she stole from taxpayers was spent on *political contributions to Democrats*. Share, share, share. In fact, Dorothy Rivers was an alternate delegate to the 1992 Democratic National Convention. As Rep. Bobby L. Rush, an Illinois Democrat, wrote in a letter, "Dorothy has been a loyal and hardworking member of the Democratic Party." The congressman's letter was addressed to Bill Clinton, who commuted Rivers's sentence before he left the White House in January 2001.[47]

Considering Herb Sandler's loathing of "this anti-tax thing," what would he think about one of the biggest tax cheats in U.S. history? What would such a loyal Democrat think about a billionaire who made a fortune doing business with theocrats in Iran and the old apartheid regime in South Africa? And what would Sandler think of a man who, when charged with massive tax evasion and fraud, fled the country and renounced his citizenship rather than face the charges?

We can only speculate how Herb Sandler would react to the "take, take, take" attitude of such a man. But there is one Democrat whose views of this sleazy tax cheat we don't have to wonder about.

Bill Clinton gave him a presidential pardon.

The Rich Party

Washington socialite Beth Dozoretz was on an Aspen ski vacation with a girlfriend when, on the morning of January 10, 2001, she got a phone call from her friend, the president of the United States.[48]

Wife of a wealthy health-care executive, Beth Dozoretz was more than a stylish Georgetown hostess. In March 1999, she'd been named finance chairwoman of the Democratic National Committee. A former fashion retailer, Dozoretz wasn't particularly political until 1992, when her third husband, Ron Dozoretz—head of Virginia-based FHC Health Systems, with an estimated net worth of $250 million—took her to the Democratic Convention in New York. As she watched Hillary Clinton ascend the podium at Madison Square Garden, Dozoretz later said, they made eye contact. "There was a connection there. . . . I'm an extremely spiritual person. I think there are no accidents in life."[49] With this moment of kismet began Dozoretz's career as a Democratic Party fundraiser, one that would lead to her being dubbed "Doyenne of the Dollars" by *Time* magazine. A photo from those days shows her smiling giddily, seated next to a laughing Bill Clinton, as they enjoyed a comedy routine by Robin Williams.[50]

When the president called her in January 2001, Beth Dozoretz was a guest at the Aspen chalet of songwriter Denise Rich. Dozoretz's songwriting friend was a wealthy divorcee "well-known in Manhattan social circles for her lavish, star-studded fundraising soirees," who had turned to songwriting "as a method of addressing her troubled marriage."[51] Denise was also a good friend of the Clintons. A very good friend indeed—Denise Rich had given $1 million to Democrats, including $70,000 to help elect Hillary Clinton to the Senate, and had also donated $450,000 for the Clinton presidential library. And in one of those amazing non-accidents that informed Dozoretz's spirituality, it just so happened that President Clinton was calling her in Aspen to discuss Denise's ex-husband.[52]

Denise's ex-husband wasn't in Aspen when the president called. Marc Rich was in Switzerland, living in a mansion known as Villa Rosa on the scenic shores of Lake Lucerne. Rich had been in Switzerland for nearly twenty years, ever since federal authorities accused him of swindling the U.S. government out of $48 million and indicted him on fifty-one counts, including racketeering and fraud.[53] (Not accidentally, Rich was indicted in 1983, during the administration of that notorious "anti-tax" right-winger, Ronald Reagan.)

U.S. authorities had reasons other than income taxes to be interested in Rich's activities. Rich specialized in trading commodities, including oil, from countries with governments that other people wouldn't do business with. He traded with Iran during the 1979–80 hostage crisis. He traded with South Africa during apartheid. And he did business with Cuba and Libya while those countries were under U.S. trade embargoes. In August 1983, Rich tried to smuggle to Switzerland two steamer trunks full of sub-poenaed documents. But federal agents got wind of the scam, seized the evidence, and Rich was charged with crimes ranging from wire fraud to racketeering. (It was perhaps no accident that the charges were brought by a federal prosecutor named Rudolph W. Giuliani.) When Switzerland refused to extradite the fugitive, Rich was named to the FBI's Ten Most Wanted List.[54]

Why then, in January 2001, was the president of the United States calling his good friend Beth Dozoretz in Aspen to discuss a tax-cheating, sanctions-defying, billionaire fugitive from justice? Well, it just so happened—remember, there are no accidents—that Marc Rich wanted a presidential pardon. Rich was in kind of a hurry, because Bill Clinton had less than two weeks remaining in his presidency before those extreme radical right-wing Republicans took over the White House. (Take, take, take.)

In 1999, not long after Dozoretz became the DNC finance chair-woman, Marc Rich hired a New York law firm to negotiate with Janet Reno's Justice Department. After November 2000, when it began to look as if Al Gore would lose the election to George Bush—Denise Rich gave $25,000 to fund Gore's Florida recount effort—Marc Rich's team of high-priced lawyers pulled out all the stops in a desperate bid to win a pardon for their client. Rich, whose Belgian Jewish parents brought him to American when they fled Hitler in 1942, was a benefactor to charities in Israel. His lawyers weren't afraid to play the Holocaust card with Clinton, trying (without apparent success) to get Nazi-hunter Elie Weisel to speak with the president about Marc Rich's philanthropic endeavors. Rich's lawyers did, however, succeed in getting former Israeli Prime Minister Shimon Perez to speak with the president about their client. Just after Christmas 2000, Rich's lawyers brainstormed how they might get more pressure from "the Jewish community" behind the Rich pardon campaign, with the team's New York public relations agent asking "who is close enough to lean on" New York Sen. Charles E. Schumer and wondering "who the top contributors are."[55]

Despite all these efforts, however, the Justice Department and the president's legal advisors were steadfastly opposed to a pardon for such a notorious scofflaw. White House counsel Beth Nolan opposed the Rich pardon, as did her predecessor, Bruce Lindsey. Clinton's chief of staff, Jon Podesta, said that "it was the unanimous view of the counsel's office that the appropriate remedy was not a presidential pardon."[56]

What did Bill tell his good friend Beth when he called her in Aspen that January morning? Dozoretz would later refuse to discuss it with congressional investigators, but Marc Rich's lawyers learned about it immediately. At 10:59 a.m., one of Rich's representatives sent an e-mail to his lawyer, Jack Quinn, describing the conversation between Clinton and Dozoretz. As if further proof were needed of Dozoretz's belief that there are no accidents, Quinn had formerly been Clinton's White House counsel and had also served as Al Gore's chief of staff. The e-mail he got that morning reported that Dozoretz "got a call today from [President Clinton] who said he was impressed by [Quinn's] last letter and that he wants to do it and is doing all possible to turn around the [White House] counsels. [Denise Rich] thinks he sounded very positive."[57]

Just how positively Clinton viewed the Marc Rich case was made clear six days later, when the president met with top staffers to discuss other possible pardons. The president himself brought up the Rich case, discussing it in such detail that Podesta concluded that Clinton "clearly had digested the legal arguments presented by Mr. Quinn." Still, the president's aides opposed the pardon. As Nolan recalled, "I didn't think it was going anywhere."[58]

Then, on Friday, January 19—the day before George Bush was to be inaugurated as president—two more things happened that were not accidents. First, in a phone conversation, Israeli Prime Minister Ehud Barak urged Clinton to pardon Rich. And then Cheryl Mills showed up at the White House. Mills was a Clinton administration veteran, having spent nearly seven years as deputy White House counsel before leaving in 1999. Mills was there to talk about the Rich pardon and met with the president and his staff. Nolan, who was in the meeting, later testified that while Mills didn't exactly urge Clinton to pardon Rich, "she was pushing everyone in the room to think hard about the issues." Nolan would later testify that she was unaware that Mills was a trustee of the Clinton library, to which Denise Rich had donated $450,000.[59]

Mills went to Nolan's office, and both of them talked on the phone to Jack Quinn. Mills told Nolan that deputy attorney general Eric Holder was in favor of the Rich pardon (earlier, however, Holder had indicated that he was against the pardon). So, at 6:38 on that Friday evening, Nolan called Holder to check. He said he was "neutral" on the pardon but, when pressed, said that he was "neutral, leaning favorable."[60]

Later that night—Nolan was getting only two or three hours a sleep nightly, trying to cope with the flood of last-minute pardon requests—the White House counsel decided to check the Justice Department's National Crime Information Center files on Marc Rich. She was alarmed to learn that not only did the FBI still consider Rich a fugitive (Quinn had told her otherwise), but that he was accused of dealing arms in violation of the Trading with the Enemy Act. It was after midnight when she called Jack Quinn, who assured her the NCIC information was inaccurate. Such was her concern, however, that Nolan then called the president at 2:30 a.m. Clinton took the call. Nolan told him about the arms trading and Rich's fugitive status, and reported her conversation with Quinn, telling him, "You know, what we have is Jack Quinn's word, that's all we have at this hour."

"Take Jack's word," Clinton said.[61]

Of all the criminals who escaped justice in Clinton's eleventh-hour orgy of pardons (see Chapter Eleven), none garnered more headlines than Marc Rich, because no other pardon seemed so evidently tainted by outright corruption. Of all the scandals associated with Clinton's administration, no other seemed so clearly to fit the classic definition of bribery, quid pro quo—a Latin phrase meaning simply, "this for that."

The *quid* was obvious in the staggering amounts that Rich's ex-wife had contributed to Democrats and to Clinton's presidential library. And the unjustifiable pardon of a notorious fugitive, over the objections of the White House counsel, was an equally obvious *quo*. All that was needed was the *pro*, the most devilishly difficult part of any bribery case, the proof that the contributions and the favor were connected. At first glance, this might have seemed simple enough. There was evidence of Clinton's conversations with Quinn and Dozoretz, and of Dozoretz's association with Denise Rich, plus the suspicious involvement of Clinton library trustee Cheryl Mills. But it was with good reason that the 42nd president was known as "Slick Willie."

A month after leaving the White House, with a congressional investigation underway, Clinton went on the offensive and published an op-ed in the *New York Times* listing eight reasons why he had granted the Rich pardon. The ex-president's arguments sounded as if they had been written by Jack Quinn, and so badly did Clinton distort the facts that the column was "in almost every important way a lie," observed *Washington Post* columnist Michael Kelly, who concluded: "Eight reasons, four lies. Not bad, even for the old master himself."[62]

If Clinton's lies couldn't save him, he could count on silence from the witnesses to his corruption, especially Beth Dozoretz and Denise Rich. The scandal that became known as Pardongate gave this duo of doyennes the opportunity to celebrate every Democrat's favorite part of the Constitution: the Fifth Amendment. Denise Rich—who has written songs for such artists as Aretha Franklin, Celine Dion, and Diana Ross—wasn't singing for congressional investigators. She was a no-show at the hearings. But on March 1, 2001, the rich divorcee's ski buddy Beth Dozoretz appeared before the House Committee on Government Reform, where Connecticut Republican Rep. Christopher Shays referred her to the e-mail about her Aspen phone conversation with President Clinton.[63]

> **Shays:** My question is, at any time while you were discussing the Marc Rich pardon with President Clinton, did either you or the president mention Denise Rich's contribution to the Clinton Library or the Democratic National Committee?
>
> **Dozoretz:** Upon the advice of my counsel, I respectfully decline to answer that question based on the protection afforded me under the United States Constitution.
>
> **Shays:** Let me ask you this: would that be your response to all our questions or are . . . there specific subjects or persons you will not discuss and others you are willing to discuss with us?
>
> **Dozoretz:** Sir, that will be my response to all questions.[64]

Keep in mind that the Fifth Amendment doesn't cover those who merely don't want to testify. You can't invoke the Fifth Amendment to protect your friends—it only protects witnesses from being required to give testimony that might implicate *themselves* in crimes. By pleading the Fifth in response to any question in the Marc Rich pardon investigation, the former finance chairwoman of the Democratic National Committee was in effect saying that *anything* she said about her pardon-related conversations with the president of the United States might be used as evidence against her.

With two key witnesses pleading the Fifth, we may never know whether the unusual events that led to Marc Rich's pardon constituted a crime—though, as Beth Dozoretz might say, the pardon was certainly no accident.

Dozoretz is still giving generously to Democrats. From 2001 through November 2005, according to FEC records, she and her multimillionaire husband gave more than $140,000 to Democrats, including $35,000 to the Democratic National Committee. Among the beneficiaries of Dozoretz dollars were the campaigns of California Sen. Diane Feinstein, Connecticut Sen. Christopher Dodd, New York Sen. Chuck Shumer, Illinois Sen. Barack Obama, Michigan Sen. John Dingell, New Jersey Sen. Robert Torricelli, South Dakota Sen. Tom Daschle, Michigan Sen. Debbie Stabenow, Louisiana Sen. Mary Landrieu, Montana Sen. Max Baucus, Dick Gephardt, John Kerry, and, of course, Hillary Clinton. None have returned their donations from this woman who refused to cooperate with a congressional investigation.[65] (Share, share, share!)

Marc Rich hasn't returned to the United States. Despite his presidential pardon for any criminal acts he committed, Rich is not immune to lawsuits in civil court, a serious financial consideration for a billionaire. Then there is the problem of his business with Saddam Hussein. That's right. Just because he'd eluded justice for seventeen years until getting pardoned, did not mean that Marc Rich stopped dealing with America's enemies. In 2004, when investigators started looking into the corruption of the United Nations "oil-for-food" program in Iraq, they say they discovered that one of the players in that rotten scam—along with the son of UN chief Kofi Annan—was the fugitive billionaire who still resides in that lakeside villa in Switzerland.[66]

Curiously, however, the tax dodger's ex-wife, Denise, is no longer a major political donor. Except for a single $2,000 contribution to the short-lived 2004 presidential primary campaign of Wesley Clark, FEC records indicate that Denise Rich hasn't given a dime to Democrats since her husband was pardoned by Bill Clinton.[67] Maybe the jet-setting songwriter simply got what she paid for and decided—as Democrats so often urged their fellow Americans during the Clinton years—it was time to move on.

10

PRESIDENTIAL PREDATORS

FONDLING THE BODY POLITIC

"Every president . . . every president we have ever had has always had
lovers because the pressure of the job is just too much."
—MONICA LEWINSKY TO LINDA TRIPP[1]

PRESIDENT JOHN F. KENNEDY KNEW ALL ABOUT THE LOYALTY OF
Democratic sheriffs. In 1960, he'd purchased a truckload of them in a
legalized bribery scheme that helped him trounce Hubert Humphrey in
the West Virginia primary. So no one in the presidential entourage was
surprised when, in 1961, a local Democratic sheriff and several policemen
waltzed up to JFK's suite at the Olympic Hotel in Seattle, escorting a pair
of hookers.[2] No one except Larry Newman. Promoted to the presidential
detail in 1961, the Secret Service agent was on his first major assignment,
providing security for Kennedy during a presidential speech. He hadn't
known about Kennedy's . . . extracurricular activities. The floor of the
hotel was supposed to have been sealed, with access limited to people with
special clearance. But the sheriff's party simply spilled out of the elevator
and headed blithely down the corridor with the sheriff "loudly proclaim-
ing that the two girls were for the president's suite."[3]

Personable but serious, with a chiseled face and air of authority,
Newman stopped the group before they could enter. Soon, Kennedy's

personal aide, Dave Powers, came out of the suite, thanked the sheriff for bringing the girls, took the hookers through the door, and shut it. Miffed that he hadn't been able to deliver the prostitutes to the president personally, the sheriff warned the hookers, who were already inside the suite: "If any word of this night gets out, I'll see that you both go to Stillicoom [a state mental hospital] and never get out."[4]

"I couldn't believe he said this, but he did," Newman told Pulitzer-winning journalist Seymour Hersh, author of *The Dark Side of Camelot,* a book that recounts seamier aspects of Kennedy's presidency. "One of the policemen, a lieutenant, asked me, 'Does this go on all the time?' I just didn't know what to say and said, 'Well, we travel during the day. This only happens at night.'"[5]

That night, in what he calls "my baptism by fire," Newman learned that Kennedy's appetites put his own security—and therefore the nation's—at risk. His promiscuity also set the tone for others. Later that evening, Newman would discover that at least six Seattle police officers, assigned to guard the fire escape exits on the floor, had abandoned their posts. He discovered them huddled together in a fire escape well, using binoculars to take turns watching Kennedy Chief of Staff Kenny O'Donnell banging two women in a hotel room across the way.[6]

At engagements across the country, Powers and other men acting as presidential pimps brought a steady parade of prostitutes to Kennedy's door. Secret Service agents weren't allowed to search or screen any of them. For the men assigned to protect him, Kennedy's rampant adultery wasn't a moral question, Newman said in an interview for this book from his home in Ft. Collins, Colorado. "Our concern, with the leader of the free world, was domestic, economic, and national security. If somebody went in [with Kennedy] who wasn't vetted and the president didn't come out the next day, or pictures were published in a Soviet paper, we would be sitting in front of a House subcommittee explaining why we let the situation develop. There was a lot of foreign intrigue in those days . . . the trench coat kind."[7]

The Dark Side of Camelot caused a furor when it was published in 1997. The press, Kennedy family, and Kennedy-philes challenged various aspects of it, with some success. Critics have cited Hersh's failure to reconcile minor inconsistencies, as well as his reliance on single sources. However, in telephone interviews for this book, Newman verified the accuracy of information Hersh attributed to him. In a separate interview, Joseph Paolella, a secret service agent who served Kennedy with Newman, confirmed that lax security procedures surrounding Kennedy's womanizing also sparked his concerns over espionage.[8]

When Newman, a registered Republican, learned we were writing a book about Democrats with a chapter on sexual indiscretion, he was quick to point out that during his tenure in the Capitol, "neither party had cornered the market on morality." Washington, D.C., he said, was an "equal opportunity playground."[9]

It still is, no doubt. But three decades after Newman left Washington, as reporters churned out way more than we wanted to know about the presidential appendage Bill Clinton called "Willard," Americans seemed to have drawn the inaccurate conclusion that adultery is part and parcel of the presidency. During the Monica Lewinsky scandal, *The Hill*, a D.C. weekly, sent a reporter to Peoria, Illinois, to see what heartlanders thought about Clinton's sexual shenanigans.[10]

"If you look back in history, a lot of our presidents have not been perfect," said Marguerite Hedges, sixty-three, who worked at the Peoria Public Library and voted for Clinton in 1996. Other Peorians cited Kennedy's string of affairs, including his liaison with Marilyn Monroe. Clinton supporter Bill Nichols, age sixty-five, a retired Caterpillar employee, said, "How many other presidents up there have not had affairs?"[11]

Great question, Bill. Here's the answer: A lot of them—mainly Republicans of late.

Not a single verifiable instance exists of a Republican president committing adultery over the past fifty years. Yes, yes, we know about Gen.

Dwight D. Eisenhower's wartime affair with Kay Sommersby, his English military driver. But that was *General* Eisenhower. Once Ike arrived at the White House, history shows he behaved like a grown-up. Then there was the gossipy snippet about a Bush 41 affair that Kitty Kelly threw into *The Family: The Real Story of the Bush Dynasty*, a book with such credibility problems that *Newsweek* refused to excerpt it. (The woman in question, Jennifer Fitzgerald, who was sixty-two at the time she and George were supposed to have been red-hot lovers, denied any affair.)[12]

Among GOP presidents, as far as is known, you have to travel all the way back to Warren G. Harding, whose term lasted from 1921–1923, to find a chief executive doing the wild thing in the White House with someone other than his wife. By contrast, among Democratic presidents since World War II, only Jimmy Carter was a faithful husband. Meanwhile, three of the last four Democrats to occupy the Oval Office were serial adulterers—all of them to pathological proportions. In his biography of Kennedy, *An Unfinished Life,* historian Robert Dallek records Kennedy declaring in 1961 that if he did not have a woman every three days, he would have a "terrible headache."[13]

Lyndon Johnson cuckolded one of his biggest political supporters, Charles E. Marsh, the immensely wealthy publisher of the *Austin American-Statesmen.* Johnson carried on a long-term, passionate affair with the beautiful and erudite Alice Glass, Marsh's consort and the mistress of Longlea, his eight hundred-acre estate in the Virginia hunt country. But neither that, nor his marriage to the relentlessly upbeat Lady Bird, was enough to stop Johnson's notorious womanizing. While in the Senate, he kept a "nooky room" for his illicit sexual indulgences. Dallek, who also wrote a Johnson biography, records the Texan's bristling machismo: once, upon hearing of Kennedy's sexual exploits, Johnson angrily exclaimed, "Why, I had more women by accident than he ever had by design."[14]

Then, of course, there was Bill Clinton. Of the three lascivious postwar Oval Office Democrats, Clinton's transgressions seemed, as *Time's*

Lance Morrow observed, the most "sordidly silly," the product of a man whose character, "at least in this compartment of his life, seems a hybrid of Arkansas horndog and the Runaway Bunny. . . . [T]he psychiatrist in us suspects that the President of the United States may have a little trouble being a grownup."[15]

Therein may lie the difference between Democrats and Republicans who aspire to the presidency. Republicans seem to take seriously the honor of the office, their inescapable position as role model, and their responsibility to govern. Democrats, on the other hand, are like zit-faced teenagers starting up a rock band—only in it for the chicks.

What accounts for the difference? More importantly, what difference does the difference make?

The first question may have its roots both in faith and conservatism. Four post-war Republican presidents—Eisenhower, Reagan, and both Bushes—expressed strong belief in a Judeo-Christian morality that values women and, in doing so, places great stock in marital fidelity. That worldview brings with it an adherence to moral standards that, unpopular as they may be, don't change with the times. (That's why they're called "standards.") And though Clintonista Democrats would like us to believe that "everybody does it" and "everybody lies about it," times have not changed the fact that adultery devastates families and demoralizes both men and women.

Perhaps modern GOP presidents, realizing this, have sought to model what they preach: the overarching importance of the family unit, cemented by marital faithfulness. Democrats, meanwhile, cherry-pick the portions of the Judeo-Christian ethic that prop up their social agenda, but jettison any tenet that calls for honor and personal restraint. (Example: John Kerry, in an October 2004 campaign speech on social justice, quoted Matthew 25:40, "Whatever you do to the least of these, you do unto me," but in weaving tales of his Vietnam heroics, apparently forgot about the biblical admonition against lying.)[16]

Conservatism also emphasizes the rule of law, and when a public figure commits adultery, the law tends to bend and ultimately break. With the world as his witness, Clinton broke the law, committing perjury and obstructing justice, and was impeached by the House on both counts. While some of his fellow Democrats called for his resignation, others decried the impeachment trial as—all together now—"a partisan witch hunt!" It is interesting to note that the last Republican president to obstruct justice resigned under a *bipartisan* threat of impeachment. Clinton, the last Democrat to do so, finished out his term and remains his party's MVP. The dichotomy underscores Democratic lawlessness, its adherence to a malleable morality that can be molded to suit the moment.[17]

In addition to its emphasis on unchanging moral standards and the rule of law, conservatism—the bedrock philosophy of modern Republicanism—also places great stock in personal responsibility and restraint. Republican presidents appear to realize what Democratic presidents do not: that the leader of the free world is responsible to more than just his Willard.

Post-war Democratic presidents (save Jimmy Carter, God love him) have embraced a rock-star entitlement mentality: the world is their oyster. Women are groupies, to be exploited and cast aside. Yet amazingly, feminists were among Clinton's most rabid apologists.

Star-struck female admirers of Camelot, though, would not learn of Kennedy's wanton betrayal of their beloved Jackie until much later. In that era, the boundaries of journalism prevented reportorial prying into the private lives of public officials. That in itself is another check in the Democratic hypocrisy box: in Kennedy's day and prior, most reporters were men, as were most politicians. The understanding was, boys will be boys.

"The newspaper business in those days . . . was a hell of a lot more fun," said Roosevelt-era reporter Bob Donovan of journalists' reason for keeping mum about FDR's long-running affair with Lucy Mercer Rutherford, who once served as Eleanor Roosevelt's social secretary. "We didn't think we were angels; we knew all the things we were doing; so to point our hand at someone else wouldn't seem sporting!"[18]

Roosevelt's relationship with Lucy Rutherford, like Eisenhower's with Kay Sommersby, was discreet. Though both represented failures of character, the characters of good men sometimes fail them, and the affairs of Ike and FDR were entirely unlike those of post-war Democratic presidents whose favorite pastime seems to have been wading naked into the secretarial pool. And while Bob Donovan's point seems exactly the kind of retrograde chauvinist comment that sparked the modern feminist movement, feminists didn't bat an eyelash when Clinton-era male journalists pined for the good old days.

On February 23, 1998, with the Lewinsky affair just a few weeks old, *New York Times* syndicated columnist Anthony Lewis pulled out all the stops, invoking racism, civil liberties, and paranoid G-men in a lofty missive that attempted to demonstrate that we shouldn't really want to know about the marital treachery of public figures: "Straying from the straight and narrow does not disable one as a statesman, a general or a civil rights leader."[19]

"Thirty-five years ago J. Edgar Hoover, obsessed by racist fears, began wiretapping and bugging Dr. Martin Luther King Jr.," Lewis wrote. "The eavesdropping caught King in apparent marital infidelity. The FBI director had a tape sent to him with an anonymous letter suggesting that Dr. King commit suicide or his 'filthy, abnormal self' would be exposed."[20]

"Would this country," Lewis wanted to know, "be better off if allegations about Dr. King's behavior had been published then? If [J. Edgar Hoover] had succeeded in destroying one of the few authentic American heroes of this century?" What Lewis didn't mention—or didn't know—was that it was Kennedy's affair with Hollywood socialite Judith Campbell Exner that enabled Hoover to coerce the president into allowing him to wiretap and bug King.[21]

Scripps-Howard journalist Dan Thomasson, his partner Dan Wyngaard, and later *New York Times* columnist William Safire would be among the first to dig into the Exner-Kennedy link, particularly with respect to mobster Sam Giancana. It was a brief footnote in the 1974

Church Committee Report on intelligence activities that sparked the reporters' interest. The notation summarized Kennedy's links to the mob, making several references to a "friend of the president" who acted as a courier between the two.[22]

The "friend" was Judith Exner. While a senator on the presidential campaign trail, Kennedy met the Elizabeth Taylor look-alike through his friend, Frank Sinatra. Kennedy, either horny or smitten, pursued Exner enthusiastically. The two launched a passionate affair that Kennedy, once elected, managed to work in between hookers and noonday trysts in the White House pool with a pair of healthy young secretaries known as "Fiddle" and "Faddle."[23]

Sinatra also introduced Exner to Mafia don Sam Giancana, who, as we've shown, was already a good friend to the Kennedy clan. One evening, according to several accounts, Kennedy showed Exner a large satchel containing about $250,000 in hundred-dollar bills and asked her to take it to Giancana. Exner said she would—then continued to carry money and messages between the mobster and the president.[24]

The affair ended in 1962 after Hoover, a Kennedy antagonist, confronted him with a top secret agency memo depicting a politically lethal triangle: a president, his lover, and the mob. "Hoover got pretty much what he wanted after that," Dan Thomasson wrote after Exner's death in 1999, "including authorization to eavesdrop on Martin Luther King, Jr., whom he claimed had communist connections."[25]

The story illustrates a point unpopular with Democrats: marital fidelity matters. Kennedy's indiscretion caused him to offer up, as columnist Anthony Lewis put it, "one of the few authentic American heroes of this century" as a price for Hoover's silence. This perfidy must have seared the conscience of Kennedy's brother Robert, who as attorney general had to authorize Hoover's surveillance of King: RFK had fought passionately for black civil rights, while JFK was merely sympathetic.[26]

Presidential blackmail was only one among a number of serious national security risks foreseen by Larry Newman and other agents assigned to protect Kennedy. Another was espionage. Any one of the women Dave Powers and others delivered to the president "could have been a spy," said Joseph Paolella, who corroborated for us Newman's assertion that the men assigned to protect Kennedy weren't allowed to search his visitors—or conduct background checks.[27] That last security breach might have brought Camelot crashing down, had Kennedy lived.

In March 1963, Kennedy developed a keen interest in a high-level sex scandal that was threatening the careers of British Prime Minister Harold Macmillan and his war minister John Profumo. Though married to a glamorous woman, Profumo had been conducting an affair with Christine Keeler, twenty-one, a call girl who was also the mistress of a Soviet deputy naval attaché. Coincidentally, Kennedy was also married to a glamorous woman—and conducting an affair with a call girl with Communist ties.[28]

JFK met Ellen Rometsch, twenty-seven, through Lyndon Johnson's protégé Bobby Baker, the powerful Senate Secretary who notched favors among members by pimping for them on the side. Rometsch, a dark-haired beauty, had grown up in East Germany, where she belonged to Communist groups and worked as a secretary for the Communist leader Walter Ulbricht. She later fled to the West with her family, married a West German official, and moved to Washington, D.C. While her hubby conducted affairs of state, Rometsch conducted affairs of another sort: sex for money. In the spring and summer of 1963, she visited the White House repeatedly and, writes historian Dallek, "attended naked pool parties and had sex with Kennedy."[29] As the Profumo scandal heated up, Hoover notified Bobby Kennedy that the FBI knew about Rometsch. An informant had told the Bureau that the woman, who had also sold her favors on Capitol Hill, had been sent to the United States to gather information. The attorney general knew well the danger of revelations of the president's involvement with a beautiful and naked suspected East German spy. So, in keeping with the counter-espionage strategy of twentieth-century Democrats, he attempted to cover up the problem.

Bobby hastily arranged for Rometsch to be deported—and also well paid for her silence. But the Kennedy money alone couldn't make this particular problem go away. At that inconvenient moment, Republicans on the Senate rules committee began investigating Bobby Baker for influence-peddling and other ethics violations, a probe that would inevitably lead to Baker's call girls, including Ellen Rometsch. Then, in October 1963, a story by investigative reporter Clark Mollenhoff appeared in the *Des Moines Register*. The article raised questions about Rometsch's abrupt deportation and her liaison with "several high executive branch officials."[30] Bobby Kennedy immediately sent word to Hoover, asking him to keep the Senate off Rometsch's trail. The attorney general said he was "greatly concerned, as was the president, with the possible harm which will come to the United States if irresponsible action is taken with the Ellen Rometsch allegations."[31] Hoover played ball: in a meeting with Sen. Mike Mansfield, a Democrat, and Sen. Everett Dirksen, a Republican, Hoover said that he'd turned up no evidence that Rometsch was a spy, or even that she'd visited the White House. He had, however, learned that Baker's girls had serviced a number of senators on Capitol Hill. Mansfield and Dirksen took Hoover's hint—and carried his half-truth back to the rules committee, which then steered its inquiry clear of Rometsch.

Despite his selling out Martin Luther King Jr., using a paramour as a mobster mule, and cooperating in the obstruction of a major senate investigation, it has been popular among historians to imagine that JFK's womanizing didn't affect his ability to lead. This is a typically Democratic notion. To wink at lawlessness is of a piece with the party's *by any means necessary* ethos. And, philosophizing aside, it doesn't even comport with the laws of physics to suggest that Kennedy could carry on multiple long-term affairs, a kind of revolving-door adultery in which Exner, Rometsch, Marilyn Monroe, and others could be seen simultaneously at various times, and meanwhile frolic with Fiddle and Faddle, bed hookers at night, all the while keeping Hoover and the Republicans from finding out—and yet be undiminished as a president. One wonders what he might have achieved if he'd set aside more time to govern.[32]

As any liar or cheat will tell you, serial deception is enormously time consuming. Clinton's deception, *borne of infidelity,* ultimately consumed his presidency, shackling him to a vicious, 24/7 public relations grind designed to fool the public into letting him keep his job. Even when the Senate failed to hand him his pink slip, Clinton's presidency was effectively over. Some of his most ardent supporters "couldn't wait to get him out of sight," observed former *Rolling Stone* senior editor Joe Eszterhas.[33] With eighteen months left in Clinton's term, people like Eszterhas, 1960s celebrants who had welcomed Clinton as the "first rock and roll president in American history," wanted him gone.[34]

"He was supposed to tell the truth—finally—after all the White House liars we'd grown up and grown older and grown more cynical with," Eszterhas wrote. "He made us feel queasy now."[35]

11

LOGICAL LEGACY

THE CLINTON YEARS

"What did the president know and when did he know it?"
—SEN. HOWARD BAKER, REPUBLICAN
WATERGATE HEARINGS, 1973

TWO KINDS OF PEOPLE BELLY UP TO THE 40-FOOT MAHOGANY bar at Stetson's Famous Bar and Restaurant: locals and Democrats. Built in the early twentieth century, the two-story neighborhood watering hole on U Street in D.C. boasts bullet holes in the ceiling, mementos left by the first owner, a retired cop who used to party with his police buddies after closing time. Every now and then, when the boys were feeling festive, they'd fire their service revolvers into the air like cowboys at an Old West saloon. Once, during a recent remodel, bar manager Tommy Osborne found a .38 caliber slug parked in the ceiling.[1]

On Friday, March 2, 2001, John Podesta was parked in Stetson's, firing back drinks with friends. Angular and tough, with the heart of a former trial lawyer, Podesta had only weeks prior finished a roller coaster term as Bill Clinton's chief of staff. Bush 43 had already taken office, but hearings on Pardongate, Clinton's eleventh-hour clemency spree, were still under way. Podesta had, the day before, testified before Congress about the 42nd president's decision to pardon international fugitive and rogue-nation oil profiteer Marc Rich. Now it was time to unwind, according to the *Washington Post's* seen-about-town column, "The Reliable Source," and Podesta did so at Stetson's, where about a dozen Clintonistas pressed him with cocktails commemorating his damage control work on various White House scandals: tequila for Travelgate, Jack Daniel's for Whitewater, Sex on the Beach for Monica Lewinsky, and Kamikaze for Pardongate.[2]

Apart from the contemptuous gall of Democrats toasting each other over serial escapes from justice, the most remarkable element of "The Reliable Source" report was the absence of any Shanghais or Singapore Slings. Surely the Podesta party hoisted a glass or two in honor of the mother of all Clinton cover-ups: Chinagate. An Asian-themed libation would have seemed the logical choice.

Podesta and others in the Clinton White House, along with congressional Democrats, and the DNC, worked overtime to achieve what history may well view as the most successful political cover-up of the twentieth century. In Chinagate, the White House spin machine operated at full tilt, transforming an *exclusively Democratic* scandal involving conspiracy, espionage, money laundering, bribery, and influence peddling into a bipartisan inquiry into campaign finance reform.[3]

During Chinagate hearings in 1997 focusing on illegal campaign contributions from foreign donors to Clinton-Gore and the DNC, the White House damage control crew met every morning in Podesta's West Wing office to sift through the bullets and bombshells likely to hit the press that day. "There was always the possibility to detonate an incoming story," Podesta said.[4]

And it was important to do so. "It was clear from the outset that this wasn't just another investigation," Sen. Richard Durbin, Democrat from Illinois, told veteran Washington journalist Elizabeth Drew. "It concerned the future of the Democratic Party."[5]

But not only for the reasons Durbin claimed—that campaign finance rules might be changed to Democrats' disadvantage. Though it has gone down in the public memory as a high-dollar campaign finance scandal involving influence peddling and tacky party favors such as Lincoln bedroom sleepovers, Chinagate was in reality a Watergate-sized scandal that reached into forty states and at least four continents, one that should have brought down the Clinton presidency and, as Durbin obliquely noted, dealt a mortal blow to the Democratic Party itself.[6]

The scandal broke in October 1996 much as the Monica Lewinsky case would fourteen months later, with "one stumble leading into a minefield," *Insight* magazine reporter Jennifer Hickey wrote.[7] During the 1996 presidential campaign, the *Los Angeles Times* initially reported a $250,000 contribution to the Clinton-Gore campaign by a South Korean company. Federal campaign contributions by foreign nationals are highly illegal; after Clinton won a second term, reports of dozens of illegal donations by Asian nationals to Clinton-Gore and the DNC exploded into the news. Featured prominently in the stories were Clinton associates James Riady (the billionaire owner of Lippo Bank California); businessman Ted Sieong; and John Huang, former DNC vice chairman, a one-time Commerce Department employee and, many suspected, an agent for the Communist Chinese.[8]

In a show of transparency, the DNC hired an outside firm to review its 1996 contributions and returned $3.2 million in illegal campaign funds, including $1,298,800 raised by Huang. That might have closed the matter had signs not emerged that Democrats both knew about and actively solicited the foreign cash. They howled about their innocence anyway, like collared bank robbers who return the loot then whine that they shouldn't go to jail.[9]

Then, on February 17, 1997, the *Washington Post's* Bob Woodward and Brian Duffy broke the story of an alleged plot by the Red Chinese government to "direct contributions from foreign sources to the Democratic National Committee before the 1996 presidential campaign."[10] Congress convened hearings, led in the House by Rep. Dan Burton (R-Indiana) and in the Senate by the imposing Sen. Fred Thompson of Tennessee, a tough-minded, good-natured Republican who had, to universal acclaim, acted as minority counsel in the Watergate hearings in 1973. Thompson, an honorable man, found himself fighting dishonorable people, as will be seen. Still, by fits and starts, evidence emerged of millions of dollars in primarily Asian, but also Middle Eastern and South American, cash flowing into Democratic coffers in direct exchange for presidential access, willful blindness to arms-trading dangerous to U.S. interests, and American policy concessions on human rights, trade, and defense.[11]

Ever a vigilant steward of the law, Attorney General Janet Reno in 1996 and 1997 steadfastly refused to authorize independent counsel Ken Starr, who was already investigating the Clintons' involvement in the smelly Whitewater land deal, to investigate Clinton and the DNC on these more serious matters.[12] But in January 1998, as inquiries into the president's sexual excesses in the Paula Jones and Monica Lewinsky cases boiled over into allegations of perjury and obstruction of justice, Reno gave Starr the green light to investigate *that*.[13] Her gnat-straining selectivity caught the attention of Admiral Thomas H. Moorer, former chairman of the Joint Chiefs of Staff. Later, as the House prepared for impeachment proceedings against Clinton in conjunction with his conduct in the Jones-Lewinsky affair, Moorer wrote a letter to Tom DeLay, then Majority Whip.[14]

Moorer urged Congress to probe Chinagate and the role Clinton played in the "betrayal of our security." Noting that the House leadership had allowed Clinton to define the terms of his own impeachment inquiry, Moorer wrote of Chinagate, "If there is corrupt foreign influence at the highest levels, is it likely that the investigation of it would have been assigned to the independent counsel? Indeed, is there not the possibility that what was assigned to the independent counsel was originally intended as a diversion from just those improprieties which the President knew the public would not tolerate?"[15]

Moorer, in wondering whether Reno used the Jones-Lewinsky investigation as a red herring, knew that the American people would not tolerate improprieties like these:

- In May 1998, well after the Thompson hearings had concluded, but as the nation was riveted on the salacious details of the Lewinsky affair, a Taiwan-born American businessman named Johnny Chung spoke with investigators. He revealed that of $366,000 he had given to the DNC, $100,000 had come from Liu Chaoying, a Chinese aerospace executive who also happened to be a lieutenant in the People's Liberation Army. Later, Chung told prosecutors that a total of $300,000 had been ordered into his bank account by the head of Chinese military intelligence, who Chung said he had met through Liu. Meanwhile, Liu's parent company, China Aerospace, provided equipment for the missiles in China's nuclear arsenal and had in 1991 and 1993 been sanctioned by the United States for selling missiles to Pakistan. Before these revelations, Chung had cheerfully told the Thompson committee that the Clinton White House "is like a subway. You have to put in coins to open the gates." Investigators learned that Chung had visited the White House forty-nine times between February 1994 and February 1995, and particularly liked to "hang around" Hillary Clinton's office, something, as journalist Elizabeth Drew noted, "no ordinary citizen could do."[16]

- In early 1996, Clinton overrode Secretary of State Warren Christopher, the Defense Department, and U.S. intelligence agencies, and relaxed controls on the export to China of sensitive satellites packed with technological secrets that could threaten "significant military and intelligence interests." To achieve this, the president shifted control of communications satellite export licensing from the State Department to the Commerce Department, then headed by Ron Brown, former DNC chairman and a key party fundraising strategist. By then, the conservative watchdog group Judicial Watch had filed suit against Commerce, charging that Brown was selling seats on trade missions to China and other countries in return for campaign donations to Democrats. Brown had indeed, in 1994, made room for Atlantic Richfield and Occidential Petroleum executives after six-figure donations to Democrats. And Bernard Schwartz, chairman of space technology innovator Loral Corporation, was included on Brown's September 1994 trip to China shortly after he gave $100,000 to the party. Loral and Hughes Electronics, another major Democratic donor, were both involved in a breach of security in transferring missile technology to China.[17]

- In a convenient bit of dual patronage, a man named Yah Lin "Charlie" Trie laundered hundreds of thousands of dollars into both the Clinton-Gore campaign and the Clinton's legal defense fund. Trie, a member of a Red Chinese-linked criminal syndicate, made donations to buy access to the president for Chinese benefactors such as Wang Jun, a Beijing arms dealer. The *New American* reported that "following a $460,000 donation to the legal defense trust, Trie—acting as a courier on behalf of China—placed 'a strategic memo in front of the President at a time of international crisis, resulting in a reply that changed a long-established element of foreign policy.'" The reply indicated to China that, despite its previous assurances to the free Chinese of Taiwan, the U.S. government would not intervene to stop escalating Chinese military aggression toward them. While Trie was handing over the legal defense-fund cash, Clinton national security advisor Sandy Berger, who in 2004 would go on to distinguish himself as a document thief, was delivering to the Beijing government America's broken promise to the people of Taiwan, written on White House letterhead.[18]

- Clinton, on dozens of occasions, refused to sanction Beijing for exporting weapons technology to terrorist states. In 1994, after a Russian spy was discovered in the CIA, he issued Presidential Decision Directive 24 (PDD 24), according to a *FrontPageMagazine* report. The order put intelligence gathering under the direct control of the president's National Security Council and, ultimately, the White House. The move created a top-down, four-tier, White House–controlled system, and walled off information sharing between the FBI and CIA "at a time when both agencies were working separate ends of investigations that would eventually implicate China in technology transfers and the Democratic Party in a Chinese campaign cash grab." PDD 24 enabled the administration to conceal its dealings with China by requiring investigators to negotiate labyrinthine procedures to obtain permission for search warrants, wiretaps, and other intelligence collection activities. Had agents, unfettered by Clinton's obstructionist bureaucracy, been able to confirm Chinese transfer of weapons technology to rogue nations like Iran and Syria, "Clinton would have been forced by law and international treaty to act." Instead, procedural walls, erected between the FBI and the Justice Department's Criminal Division by presidential fiat, deprived investigative agencies of information critical in espionage and terrorist cases. This not only enabled the Communist Chinese to build military strength using American innovation, but also contributed heavily to the balkanized U.S. intelligence-sharing system that would later enable Muslim terrorists to kill nearly three thousand Americans on September 11, 2001.[19]

Admiral Moorer's analysis of Janet Reno's decision to keep the Chinagate investigation in-house, but to unleash Ken Starr on a chubby-cheeked intern, has merit. The appointment of an independent counsel makes headlines and lends heft to allegations. It would be no surprise if the spin-obsessed Clinton administration had deemed it better to distract the nation and lemming press with a titillating sex scandal—a rap Clinton had already proven he could beat—than to leave a news hole waiting to be filled with tales of a presidency for sale.

Or money laundering. Chinagate also involved a woman named Maria Hsia, who organized the infamous Hsi Lai temple fundraiser attended by

Vice President Al Gore in Los Angeles in 1996. Temple organizers had charged $5,000 per couple to attend the luncheon, raising $45,000 before the event. But a woman named Man Ho, the temple's chief administrative officer, told the Thompson committee that DNC vice chair and fundraiser John Huang "thought that the temple could contribute more." So temple funds in the amount of $55,000 were given to resident nuns, who barely touched the cash before coughing it up for Clinton-Gore. This, in fact and effect, laundered the tax-exempt funds of a religious group by passing it through straw donors. Man Ho also testified that Hsia told her "the event was approved at the White House."[20]

In *The Corruption of American Politics*, journalist Drew wrote that information obtained, but not published, by the Thompson committee alleged that Maria Hsia, who had escorted Gore to Taiwan in 1989 and arranged the temple fundraiser, had "recruited someone in the California State government to be an agent for China." This information also alleged that when another U.S.-based Chinese agent was fleeing authorities in France, "Hsia had obtained phony papers to get him out of that country."[21]

How did Chinagate morph in the national memory from espionage, bribery, and money laundering into a tale of bipartisan campaign finance abuse? Through what Larry Klayman, founder of Judicial Watch, said "may be the largest incidence of obstruction of justice in U.S. history."[22]

By the time of the Thompson hearings, Drew wrote, the Clinton White House had already "perfected the art of wrecking potentially troublesome hearings—by offering as little information as possible, as slowly as possible, and by casting the hearing as 'partisan.' To the Clinton White House, there was no such thing as a legitimate hearing into their activities; it therefore set forth to delegitimize any inquiry it considered adversarial. Every hearing was a war zone. This approach hadn't been taken ever before in such a systematic way."[23]

Sensing in Chinagate a party-wrecking scandal, Democrats caught on quickly. When Thompson, in his opening statement, mentioned that

Chinese money might have affected the 1996 presidential election, they set out to discredit Thompson and paint the hearings as a baseless "partisan witch hunt." They largely succeeded, making the Tennessee senator, who played square when he could have played dirty, look like a red-baiting conspiracy theorist. Meanwhile, though no Republican candidate was implicated in Chinagate, Democrats jabbed fingers at the GOP, claiming that the problem wasn't Democrats' criminal behavior, but the campaign finance *system*. Reform was needed . . . reform! Revelations from Thompson-hearing witnesses that revealed Chinagate as an exclusively Democratic scandal did not deter media outlets from participating in this fiction. For example, *Newsweek's* October 28, 1996, cover showed pictures of *both* presidential candidates, Bill Clinton and Bob Dole, with the cover line, "Candidates for Sale."[24]

Meanwhile, the White House did its part. The scandal broke just before the 1996 election largely because of John Huang's extraordinary fundraising prowess, which resulted in a $4 million injection into DNC coffers. As *American Spectator* investigative reporter James Ring Adams observed, "Only later, and as slowly as the White House could manage, did it emerge how closely Huang worked with Clinton's people. Secret Service logs . . . revealed that Huang visited the Executive Mansion fifty or so times during the first nine months of 1996. . . . The White House has refused to divulge who authorized the visits."[25]

As Adams noted, Huang's level of access suggested that White House aides were his willing abettors in the violation of federal election law and "the extent of this complicity showed starkly in attempts to shield Huang from the press."[26] Then DNC cochair Christopher Dodd, who still represents Connecticut in the Senate, refused to make Huang available for interviews. When Judge Royce Lamberth ordered Huang to give a deposition in the Judicial Watch case against Commerce, the DNC refused to give out his address. Meanwhile, Huang's lawyer, John C. Keeney Jr., went underground. It wasn't until Judge Lamberth told Keeney to make his client available within twenty-three hours—then ordered U.S. marshals to search the DNC headquarters for Huang—that the lawyer finally produced Huang.[27]

Meanwhile, in an unprecedented orgy of lawlessness, Thompson-hearing witnesses ignored subpoenas. Eighteen witnesses fled the country to avoid testifying, twenty-three who lived outside the country refused to testify, and seventy-nine potential witnesses invoked their Fifth Amendment right against self-incrimination. As Drew observed, "Never before had a congressional hearing been treated with such disregard."[28]

The Justice Department chipped in with its own brand of obstruction. On July 2, 1997, the day after the Thompson hearings began, FBI agents conducting surveillance on the Arkansas home of Charlie Trie watched helplessly as Trie's secretary, Maria Mapili, and her lawyer loaded four boxes of documents into a white Lexus. Earlier, mixed in with fish heads and other detritus in Trie's garbage cans, investigators had found shreds of paper that turned out to be DNC donors lists and checks from Asian donors to Clinton's legal defense fund, as well as other evidence, including a FedEx receipt showing that the White House had in May mailed two pounds of documents to Trie. The stakeout agents had thought they had Justice's okay to search Trie's home to prevent further destruction of evidence. But at the last minute, Justice officials denied the search warrant. As the white Lexus sped away, FBI special agent Daniel Wehr requested permission to stop the car. Justice said no, enabling Mapili and her lawyer to make off with the four boxes, which agents later confirmed held documents under subpoena by both a federal grand jury and the Senate.[29]

Wehr later testified before the Senate that the Justice Department blocked FBI agents from following any leads that led back to Clinton. "I was told by [supervisor] Laura Ingersoll that we would not pursue any matter relating to the solicitation or payment of funds for access to the presidency," Wehr told the Senate on September 22, 1999. When Wehr asked why, he said Ingersoll told him, because "that's the way the American political process works."[30]

"I was scandalized by that answer," Wehr said.[31]

In a 2001 interview, I. C. Smith, FBI special agent in charge of Arkansas during the early part of the Chinagate probe, told *WorldNetDaily* reporter Paul Sperry that "there's no doubt" Janet Reno and top Justice Department official Lee Radek fixed the Chinagate probe in favor of Clinton. Justice and White House lawyers worked "hand and glove" to bury the investigation, he said. The cover-up so disgusted Smith that he retired from the FBI in 1998.[32]

He wasn't Justice's only casualty. Charles LaBella, a U.S. attorney from San Diego who worked as chief prosecutor on Justice's Chinagate task force, quit in protest over Reno's obstructionist tactics. Before leaving, he wrote the attorney general a memo: "Senior White House officials, working with senior DNC and Clinton-Gore personnel, were the architects of a contributions-for-access-and-perks system." In his memo, LaBella noted that there was ample evidence to suggest Clinton and his advisors knew foreign funds were pouring into the DNC and his reelection effort.[33]

In the end, Justice prosecuted only donors, including James Riady, Johnny Chung, Man Ho, Maria Hsia, and Charlie Trie. No member of the Clinton White House, no Democratic candidate, and no official of the DNC was prosecuted. Don Simon, an attorney for Common Cause, the government watchdog group that originally filed complaints with the Justice Department in 1996, said prosecutors completely ignored portions of federal law that would have applied to officials like Clinton, Gore, Harold Ickes, and then DNC chair Terry McAuliffe.[34]

The Chinagate cover-up highlights Democrats' hypocrisy: When Republican President Richard Nixon spied on the Democrats, took huge donations from individual donors, operated a slush fund, sold ambassadorships, and engaged in a smear campaign against his political opponents, Democrats stood ready to impeach him. When Bill Clinton, in return for huge donations, sold out national security to an emerging Communist superpower, altered or ignored U.S. policy in favor of enemy nations, and granted presidential access and favors to foreign agents, Democrats lied, spun, and obstructed justice to protect their president and party.

Chinagate's burial has enabled liberals to continue to warm their hands by the fires of Watergate, to continue to hold up the Nixon administration as the now-spurious measuring rod against which all modern presidential scandal should still be gauged. Surely a public relations coup of this magnitude was one among those that John Podesta and Clinton loyalists celebrated that March night at Stetson's.

The Stain

Still, drinking to successful damage control may be a fitting bookend to a presidency that oozed onto the national stage in the form of a damage-control interview on *60 Minutes*, hastily arranged to extinguish Clinton's first "bimbo eruption," Gennifer Flowers, a former lounge singer. The married governor and then presidential candidate had been bedding other women since at least 1977, once in the back seat of a turquoise Cadillac El Dorado during a midday break from his duties as Arkansas attorney general.[35]

In the end, though, "it was the stain that got him," wrote *Basic Instinct* screenwriter and former *Rolling Stone* senior editor Joe Eszterhas in *American Rhapsody*, a jiggling, lipstick-smeared, and socially astute history of the Clinton sex scandals.[36] He was speaking, of course, of the semen-stained blue dress that belonged to Monica Lewinsky, who serviced the president of the United States in a corridor off the Oval Office, sometimes while he hashed out foreign policy on the phone. In a weird sartorial odyssey, the blue dress became perhaps the world's most famous frock, floating first from an Oval Office tryst to the back of the intern's closet. From there, upon the advice of her friend and enemy Linda Tripp, Monica, by then under Ken Starr's spotlight, retrieved the dress, ziplocked it, and hung it in the closet of her mother's New York apartment like an off-the-rack noose.[37]

By the summer of 1998, when news of the dress's existence splashed down in the press, Monica-gate had split the nation into two camps. On one side, many Democratic voters—blissfully unaware that their president had helped China better aim its weapons at their children—protested that the Republicans were invading Clinton's privacy. Allied feminists shrieked, "Sexual McCarthyism!" A married president, they fumed—and the French agreed—ought to be able to have a little fun on the side, and if he had to lie to the American people after he zipped up his pants, then it was *Ken Starr's* fault for poking his right-wing nose where it didn't belong. And well, who cared about perjury and obstruction of justice?

In the other camp: Republican voters (and many disgusted Democratic ones) who believed that when a president strays, he ought not to be able to lie to the American people, to the U.S. Justice Department, and to Congress. That's what criminals do, the thinking went. And, like so many criminals now caught dead to rights by the bull's-eye accuracy of DNA technology, Bill Clinton was nailed by two whitish dots on a blue dress that cost $49.95 at the Gap. Its existence and significance told the nation that, finger-waggling presidential denials notwithstanding, "there was a skunky odor in the air," Eszterhas wrote. "America felt like it needed a psychic disinfectant. We were Grossed Out, Pissed Off, and Ready to Throw Up."[38]

Which is precisely why Bill is lucky he had Monica. Even with its budget-draining investigation, charges of perjury and obstruction of justice, and, ultimately, presidential impeachment, Monica-gate is what many Americans—including our children, we're sad to say—remember about the presidency of Mr. and Mrs. William Jefferson Clinton. When Clinton's myopic memoir, *My Life*, hit stores in June 2004, the national media focused on his adolescent sexual behavior, his confessional pillow talk with Hillary, and his retrofit remorse. For the Clintons, reporters' obsession with the prurient was fortuitous, shifting attention away from eight years of corruption that didn't involve intriguing new uses for cigars.

By then, Hillary Clinton, capitalizing on her Wronged Wife status and lugging a heavy war chest—full of *legal* donations, no doubt—had gotten herself elected as the junior senator from New York. Since then, she's advocated for the poor by looting the White House, raising three times as much campaign cash as any other senator, and pocketing an $8 million book advance for her ghostwritten memoir, *Living History*. Hillary, who had been elected to the Senate the month before news of the advance broke, kept the money, unlike Newt Gingrich, who in 1995 had to return a $4.5 million advance after House Democrats questioned his ethics. A Clinton spokeswoman said she would give an undisclosed amount to charity.[39]

While still First Lady, Hillary was "the consistent, stable, and reliable guiding organizational hand for the entire Clinton presidency," observed *New York Times* best-selling author Barbara Olson. But not in a good way. In *The Final Days: The Last, Desperate Abuses of Power by the Clinton White House*, Olson wrote that her research "found Hillary involved, in one form or another, in virtually every White House scandal—even if just masterminding the defense and counterattacks as in the Lewinsky affair."[40]

Some thoughtful Democrats, such as former Sen. Zell Miller of Georgia, have repudiated the corruption of Hillary and her husband in particular, as well as lamenting generally their party's wholesale and immoral slide to the left. In his 2003 book, *A National Party No More: The Conscience of a Conservative Democrat*, Miller wrote, "The Democratic Party is no longer a national party in the sense of seeking to represent the common good as it may be implicated in national questions involving all sections of our country."[41] In 2004, he endorsed George W. Bush and became the first member of an opposition party to make a major address at a party nominating convention. Though Democrats branded Miller a "Zellout," they like to forget that he once was an enthusiastic Clinton supporter and keynoted the Democratic National Convention in 1992.[42]

By 1998, with two years left to go on Clinton's second term, at least 439 Democratic officeholders had switched to the GOP. (Only three Republicans leapt the fence in the other direction.) Such defections raise questions: Are the Clintons an anomaly? Or do formerly loyal Democrats now see the handwriting on the wall—that the Clintons are the logical legacy of the modern Democratic ethos and that their brand of corruption is the party's future?[43]

Bill Clinton, of course, became the only president ever impeached on the grounds of personal malfeasance and the first accused of rape.[44] More Clinton friends and associates were convicted or pleaded guilty than friends and associates of any other president. More cabinet officials came under criminal investigation. More witnesses fled the country or refused to testify, and more suddenly and mysteriously died.[45]

Before his first term was out, both Bill and Hillary Clinton had weathered multiple scandals.

A special prosecutor investigated the roles of both Clintons in the Whitewater Development Corporation, a business they'd launched with their friends Jim and Susan McDougal in 1978. After Clinton attorney Vince Foster died, suspiciously, of suicide in July 1993, three Hillary Clinton aides removed documents from his office. An ensuing investigation unearthed evidence of illegal loans in connection with Whitewater and a land deal known as Castle Grande; missing billing records from the Rose Law Firm; and a savings and loan scandal that cost taxpayers $69 million. On January 26, 1996, Hillary appeared before the grand jury probing her Whitewater investments. As part of a pattern of obstructionism that floated the Clintons over many scandals, she peppered her testimony liberally with such responses as "I don't know anything about this," "I have absolutely no recollection," and "I have no information whatsoever."[46]

In the end, fifteen people were convicted of federal charges, including the McDougals, White House counsel Webster Hubbell, and Arkansas Governor Jim Guy Tucker. In the final hours of his presidency, Bill Clinton pardoned four of the felons, including his ex-girlfriend Susan McDougal, whose husband didn't make the cut since he had already died in prison.[47]

Other first-term scandals included Travelgate, in which Hillary Clinton ordered the firing of the entire White House travel office on the pretext of financial mismanagement, allegedly to make room for Clinton travel-business cronies from Arkansas. Independent counsel Robert Ray found that Hillary made "factually false" statements in the case, but declined to prosecute since, he said, there was no evidence that she knew she was lying.[48]

Then there was Filegate, in which hundreds of FBI files on prominent Republicans somehow made their way into the possession of Anthony Marceca, a temporary White House worker, and White House security chief Craig Livingstone. Bill Clinton argued that the files had arrived at the White House through a bureaucratic blunder. But in June 1996, Marceca repeatedly invoked the Fifth Amendment when questioned in a closed-door session of the Senate Judiciary Committee.[49]

The following month, *Newsweek* reported on an interesting strategy adopted by the Clinton White House in both Travelgate and Filegate: When asked who was responsible for hiring ex-bar-bouncer and political prankster Craig Livingstone, Clinton aides answered: Vince Foster. When asked how she first became aware of problems in the White House Travel Office, Hillary Clinton answered: Vince Foster. A Capitol Hill staffer interviewed by *Newsweek* explained this as the "blame-the-dead-guy defense."[50]

Independent counsel Robert Ray closed the Filegate investigation in March 2000, finding "no credible evidence" that Hillary or any senior White House officials were involved in seeking the FBI files.[51]

But while Hillary Clinton seemed bulletproof, her husband became the first president to establish a legal defense fund, the first to be hauled before a grand jury, the first to have to surrender a blood sample as evidence, and the first to be held in contempt of court for lying to a federal judge. He was also the first to surrender his law license. On January 19, 2001, as president-elect George W. Bush was making the rounds of preinaugural events in the Capitol, Bill Clinton was signing a plea deal that may well have kept him out of prison.[52]

The Arkansas Bar Association wanted to permanently disbar the outgoing chief executive. On January 10, David Kendall, Clinton's personal lawyer, had flown to Little Rock to take on Marie-Bernarde Miller, whom the state bar association had appointed to prosecute the case. Unintimidated by Kendall's client, Miller kept him waiting for hours. Then she laid out the bar's terms: To avoid prosecution for perjury in the Paula Jones case, Clinton had to accept a five-year suspension of his law license and pay $25,000 in legal fees. Also, he would have to admit that he knowingly violated a judge's order to tell the truth.[53]

That, wrote Barbara Olson in *The Final Days*, was "a duty the President of the United States and Yale Law School Graduate should not have needed a special judicial decree to remember."[54] When Kendall put the ABA's plea deal on the table, Clinton was furious. He was also trapped. Failure to sign would mean disbarment, which, short of jail, would have been the ultimate Nixonian disgrace. And so Bill Clinton signed an admission of guilt packed with more pirouettes and two-steps than a Branson, Missouri, stage show. He had, he certified, "tried to walk a fine line between acting lawfully and testifying falsely, but I now recognize that I did not fully accomplish this goal, and that certain of my responses . . . were false."[55]

Translation for ordinary Americans: "I committed perjury."

As we've shown, the seeds for the Clinton corruption had been sown throughout Democratic history, taking root in the twentieth century. Roosevelt and Truman coddled foreign agents; Clinton sold himself to them outright. JFK, Clinton's idol, was a serial adulterer, as was his successor, Johnson; Clinton followed in their footsteps, even using state troopers to procure women for him while he was Arkansas governor. One woman, the indomitable Paula Jones, who declined Clinton's advances and later sued him for sexual harassment, proved his undoing.

Clinton even emulated his Democratic predecessors Roosevelt, Truman, and Kennedy in consorting with the mob.

On November 4, 1994, the president sat down to write a note to his close friend, Arthur A. Coia, head of the Laborer's International Union of North America (LIUNA), the same union whose corruption Ron Fino would detail for federal investigators two years later. "I just heard you've become a grandfather," Clinton scribbled on White House stationery.

"Congratulations!" Coia, a frequent White House visitor, had recently gifted the president with an expensive golf club, a persimmon driver engraved with Clinton's signature and the presidential seal. The week before, Clinton had given Coia a Callaway "Divine Nine" wood.[56]

It was the least he could do. According to FEC records, Coia's union PAC had poured nearly $1.5 million into Democratic campaign coffers in the 1993–94 election cycle. By 1996, that figure would more than triple. Which is perhaps why Clinton continued associating with Coia, even after Justice Department officials sent the LIUNA president a draft racketeering complaint that said Coia had "associated with, and been controlled and influenced by, organized crime figures."[57] The RICO complaint specifically accused Coia of participating in a mob kickback scheme to loot LIUNA health and welfare funds and split the proceeds with the late New England Mafia boss Raymond Patriarca. Moreover, Justice accused Coia of stealing from upstate New York union locals to share the cash with Joseph Todaro, head of the Buffalo crime syndicate.

Though Justice informed the White House of the RICO complaint, none of this was apparently troubling to the Clintons. Bill and Hillary continued inviting Coia to White House dinners and state affairs and consulting him on Democratic political strategy. In February 1995, Hillary even keynoted LIUNA's annual leadership meeting at the swank Fontainebleau Hotel in Miami. Perhaps that was because they knew the RICO complaint was going nowhere. Though it had taken Justice a year to compile the case against Coia and other conspirators, it took them only three months to drop it—and allow Coia to remain head of the LIUNA as long as he promised to kick out those dirty mobsters. Three former LIUNA officials who lost their jobs in Coia's subsequent purge told *American Spectator* investigative reporter Byron York that Coia, in a strategy meeting held while the RICO complaint was still pending, said that Bill Clinton had fixed the problem.[58]

Coia "said he talked to Clinton and Clinton assured him that everything would be okay," said John Serpico, a longtime Coia rival who headed

LIUNA's powerful Chicago local. "Clinton was going to help him out and take care of this thing." In separate interviews, former LIUNA New York/New Jersey vice president Samuel Caivano and his son David, who administered the union's New York PAC, substantiated Serpico's account.[59]

If Clinton indeed fixed fed troubles for his mob-linked pal, it was only, as his former advisor Dick Morris put it, "because he could."[60] Which may also have been why, in his final days in office, the outgoing president made himself messiah, judge, and king, unleashing a torrent of executive orders and presidential pardons. Among the most shocking orders was the one he signed at one minute to midnight, on December 31, 2001: an agreement that would allow U.S. servicemen—or any U.S. citizen—to be hauled before the International Criminal Court, a body driven both by anti-U.S. sentiment and by the desire to subvert the authority of nation-states to the will of international institutions.[61] Clinton's action is particularly ironic in light of the Democratic frenzy over the alleged incursion on civil rights by presidential wiretaps, a story that hit the news in late 2005. In that party's skewed messianic philosophy, civil rights are what Democrats say they are. Sodomy and the killing of the unborn, for example, are civil rights secured by liberal courts and worth marching over. But U.S. sovereignty over the judicial fate of its own citizens, and the hard-copy constitutional right of a jury trial by peers, can be sacrificed on the altar of the liberal Democratic vision of the global village.

The scores of pardons Clinton doled out to friends, family, and unrepentant felons during his last weeks in office were rooted not in vision, but in venality. In the final days of his presidency, the White House became "a palace of favors, with a memorable mélange of characters coming and going at all hours," Olson wrote. "Think of a suburban swap meet combined with an open house at a bail bondsman's office."[62]

On his last *day* in office, Clinton issued an astonishing 140 pardons, often skirting such pesky protocols as Justice Department vetting and criminal background checks. Just in time to still be president, Clinton pardoned his brother, Roger, who had done time on cocaine charges.

Roger had tried unsuccessfully to sell presidential pardons to some of his former prison buddies, but Hillary Clinton's brother, Hugh Rodham, had better luck. He got Bill to pardon high-volume cocaine trafficker Carlos Vignali and charged the Vignali family a mere $200,000 for the service.[63]

Clinton also pardoned friends of friends, such as a pair of Arkansas tax cheats who happened to be friends of Clinton's friend Harry Thomason, the big-shot television producer. He pardoned terrorists, bank robbers, and con men; money-launderers, arms dealers, and assorted thugs. He forgave former members of Congress, friends of Jesse Jackson, and a few members of his own cabinet. Some Clinton pardons were properly vetted and cleared. But he also rammed through forty-seven pardons with no Justice Department review.[64]

Clinton apologists and critics tried to make sense of his manic burst of last-ditch mercy. President Jimmy Carter said flatly that the Marc Rich pardon (see Chapter Nine) was a financial quid pro quo. Left-wing *New York Times* columnist Bob Herbert blamed Democrats' willingness to overlook the "ethical red flags" to elect him.[65]

Red flags? By the time Democrats nominated Bill Clinton in 1992, the warning signs looked more like a phalanx of scarlet bed sheets flapping madly over Arkansas:

- A 1990 federal drug probe had already yielded testimony that Gov. Clinton was an enthusiastic user of cocaine;[66]

- Clinton had attended parties "at which cocaine would be served like hors d'oeuvres and sex was rampant";

- Arkansas state trooper Larry Patterson testified about large "quantities of drugs flown into Mena [Arkansas] airport, large quantities of money, large quantities of guns" and that the matter was repeatedly discussed in front of Clinton by his bodyguards;

- Arkansas State Police investigator Russell Welch, who had been investigating drug running and money laundering at Mena, was mysteriously infected with military-grade anthrax;

- and on January 23, 1992, the *Star* tabloid broke a story alleging that Clinton had had affairs with five Arkansas women, including former lounge singer Gennifer Flowers, who claimed her liaison went on for twelve years.[67]

Some Arkansas journalists warned Democrats about the politician their state was about to foist on the country. "His word is dirt," wrote Meredith Oakley of the *Arkansas Democrat-Gazette*. The *Pine Bluff Commercial* noted: "It's very difficult to catch Bill Clinton in a flat lie. His specialty is a lengthy disingenuousness."[68]

But kingmaker journalists, apparently regarding local reporters as rubes, told the Clintons immediately and out loud that they were willing to help bury scandal in order to get them elected. The Flowers story broke just as the Clinton campaign was gathering steam. Though the *Star* was a Michael-Jackson-pregnant-with-alien-baby type of tabloid, the Flowers story had enough specific detail to be at least partially credible. The television newsmagazine *60 Minutes* invited the candidate to address the charges on the air on Sunday, January 26, right after the Super Bowl.[69]

The *60 Minutes* crew hauled its reporting and camera team, including veteran producer Don Hewitt, to the Ritz-Carlton in Boston. Twice during the now-famous interview in which Hillary stood lovingly by her man, Hewitt called a break. "He told the Clintons how he'd made John Kennedy president by the producing the debates in 1960, and he could do the same for them," wrote George Stephanopolous in *All Too Human,* a memoir of his time as one of Clinton's closest advisors. "Like a director coaxing his leading couple, he crouched down in front of the couch and whispered, 'Just say yes or no. Yes or no, and we'll move on to other things.'"[70]

During the interview with journalist Steve Croft, Clinton denied

Flowers's story and would not admit adultery. What American viewers saw, wrote Stephanopolous, "was a talented and idealistic couple who were committed to their marriage and the country's future." At the time, Stephanopolous himself believed Clinton and thought Flowers was lying. The next day he found out otherwise: the woman had tapes, "scratchy but apparently authentic recordings of Clinton and Gennifer talking in intimate tones about their personal relationship and the presidential race . . . ," Stephanopolous wrote. "My whole torso tightened as I was hit by a wave of nausea, doubt, embarrassment, and anger."[71]

In Stephanopolous's 443-page memoir, he first learns that Bill Clinton is a liar on page 68. By page 74—two weeks after the *60 Minutes* interview in real time—Clinton had lied again, this time about dodging the draft.

Of course, all of this became public prior to the Democrats' nominating this man for president. The *St. Louis Post-Dispatch* on July 1, 1992, ran an account of humorist Mark Russell's address to the American Association of Retired Persons (AARP). "This just in!" Russell quipped to his senior-citizen audience. "Bill Clinton has just denied dodging the draft while smoking marijuana at a white country club after a one-night stand before doing business with a savings and loan whose lawyer was his wife, Hillary." Fifteen days later, the Democrats tapped the object of this ridicule—whom the *Post-Dispatch*, in a tidy summation of our entire argument, referred to as "scandal-plagued" and having "locked up the Democratic nomination" in the same sentence—to lead the free world.[72]

This was not, as Bob Herbert wrote, a mere overlooking of ethical red flags. Instead, it was Democrats' *overt willingness* to tolerate scandal, crime, and corruption—to advance their agenda *by any means necessary*— that bred Bill and Hillary Clinton and elevated them to power. In the Clintons, the party had succeeded in producing that which it had been incubating throughout its history. The question now is, does the Clintons' brand of lawless mendacity herald what Americans can expect under future Democratic rule?

Clues lie in the character of the post-Clinton presidential candidates trotted out by the DNC. It is notable that both of Clinton's would-be successors—Al Gore in 2000 and John Kerry in 2004—proved to have their own problems with corruption and dishonesty. Gore, who scarily declared that "no controlling legal authority"[73] prohibited his illegal fundraising, also tried to engineer a selective recount in heavily Democratic Florida counties during the aftermath of the 2000 presidential election. When Kerry ran, Vietnam veterans charged that he had both embellished his war record and falsely accused American GIs of atrocities against civilians. Also, Kerry staffer Sandy Berger, Clinton's former national security advisor, was caught during the campaign stuffing National Archives documents down his pants.[74] For now, it appears the Democratic Party is content to give America more of the same—especially since many observers consider Hillary Clinton a shoo-in as her party's presidential standard-bearer in 2008.

At this writing, however, Hillary is busy with other matters. In early 2006, she scheduled trusty troubleshooter David Kendall to fly to Los Angeles to try and extricate her from a lawsuit in which a Hollywood entrepreneur is suing her and Bill for fraud, unfair business practices, and civil conspiracy.[75] Peter Paul is an entertainment executive and partner with Spider-Man creator Stan Lee in Stan Lee Entertainment. In a lawsuit filed on February 25, 2004, in the Superior Court of California in Los Angeles County, Paul alleged he contributed $1.2 million to elect Hillary Clinton to the Senate in return for an agreement that Bill Clinton would act as a goodwill ambassador for Stan Lee Entertainment upon leaving the Oval Office.[76] Paul charged, unsurprisingly, that the president reneged on the deal, and that Hillary's election committee, meanwhile, did not report the lion's share of Paul's contributions.

Media have looked askance at Paul's claims because he was, decades ago, convicted of three felonies, including drug and fraud charges. But the Clintons claim they didn't know Paul had a record when Bill allegedly agreed to accept $16 million in cash and stock, the promised payment for his future role stumping for Stan Lee.[77] Or when Hillary attended the swank Hollywood events Paul underwrote (at a cost of $1.2 million) to promote her senate campaign, and at which Hillary was repeatedly photographed with Paul. Ex-felon or not, the Federal Election Commission in December 2005 agreed with Paul on Hillary's campaign finance misdeeds. Her treasurer, Andrew Grossman, signed a conciliation agreement in which he admitted to filing three false campaign finance reports, which omitted $721,895 in in-kind contributions from Paul.[78] At least one of the false reports was filed after Paul notified Hillary Clinton of her campaign's failure to accurately report his donations.[79]

With the pay-to-play charges still pending, it looks like business as usual for David Kendall who seems to be making a career of horsetrading for the Clintons and mucking out their stalls to keep his famous clients in office and out of jail.

HONOR AMONG THIEVES

HIP-DEEP IN THE "CULTURE OF CORRUPTION"

"Liberals simply can't grasp the problem Lexis-Nexis
poses to their incessant lying."

—ANN COULTER[1]

TOM DELAY WAS SMILING. IN HIS COAT, TIE, AND DRESS SHIRT, DeLay was wearing his biggest, most cheerful grin as he posed for the picture that looked for all the world like a campaign photo. The Texas Republican appeared, as one reporter observed, "like a proud member of Congress who might just have won the lottery, not one indicted on charges of money laundering."[2]

Yet when he mugged for the cameras on October 20, 2005, he really mugged—having just been booked and fingerprinted at the Harris County, Texas, sheriff's office. In a moment that warmed the cockles of Democrats' hearts, Travis County district attorney Ronnie Earle had charged DeLay with money laundering and conspiracy.[3]

But DeLay's smile angered a lot of Democrats, who had apparently thought the former House Majority Leader would show up for his police photo shoot looking like Nick Nolte after a three-day bender. One group, funded by left-wing billionaire George Soros, had already begun taking orders for T-shirts, at $15 a pop, featuring the mug shot of the second-highest Republican in the House. The picture of a smiling DeLay—with "no ID markings, no booking numbers," one disappointed Democrat commented—wasn't what his enemies had hoped to buy.[4]

Foiling a Democratic propaganda campaign wasn't the only reason for DeLay's smile, however. He was also supremely confident that he'd beat the rap. Texas law grants power for investigating misconduct by state public officials to the district attorney of Travis County, home of the state capital Austin—a Democrat-dominated city in an increasingly Republican state. And the Travis County D.A. since 1976 has been Ronnie Earle, a passionately partisan Democrat with a history of bringing trumped-up charges. When Sen. Kay Bailey Hutchison was preparing to run for her 1994 reelection campaign, Earle indicted her on official misconduct charges. But when the case went to court, Earle "threw a snit . . . and refused to put on the state's case," resulting in acquittal for the Republican senator.[5]

If his indictment in Texas didn't worry Tom DeLay, there was another scandal that might have caused him concern. It had the makings of a classic Democratic scandal: gamblers, shady business dealings, and reputed New York gangsters with colorful nicknames: "Big Tony" Moscatiello and "Little Tony" Ferrari.

But the man at the center of this scandal wasn't a Democrat. Jack Abramoff is a former chairman of the College Republicans and a veteran conservative activist with connections to the most powerful men in the GOP, including DeLay. And while the scandal featured some of the usual Capitol Hill influence peddling, it was much more serious than the exchange of political favors for campaign cash that Americans have come to expect from crooked Beltway wheeler-dealers. No, this scandal was infinitely worse than that, because it involved a Florida man named Konstantinos Boulis.[6]

A Greek immigrant who made his fortune in the restaurant business, "Gus" Boulis had developed a lucrative casino cruise line and sold it to a partnership organized by Abramoff and Adam Kidan, a New York native who met Abramoff as a College Republican during the Reagan era. It is not known whether Boulis was himself a Republican or a Democrat—and not really relevant now, because Boulis has been dead since February 2001.[7]

Gus Boulis was murdered. Police in Florida say "Big Tony" told them that "Pudgy" Fiorillo killed Boulis after "Little Tony" got a call from Kidan, ordering the hit.[8]

If that sounds like a plot from *The Sopranos*, it's a lot less complicated than the business transactions surrounding the SunCruz line that Boulis sold to Abramoff and Kidan, and infinitely simpler than the lobbying scams that Abramoff is accused of masterminding with another Republican operative, Michael Scanlon.[9]

Formerly the press secretary to DeLay, Scanlon set up a Beltway public relations firm that investigators say joined Abramoff in one of the more bizarre hustles in Washington history. Abramoff was a lobbyist for the Coushatta Indian tribe of Louisiana. The tribe operated casinos, and other tribes in neighboring Texas opened their own casinos, luring customers away the Coushattas. So, the Louisiana tribe paid Scanlon's firm to hire former Christian Coalition director Ralph Reed—an old Abramoff buddy from College Republican days—to lead a campaign that, as Reed said, would "get our pastors riled up," pressuring Texas Republicans to shut down the Indian casinos in that state. It worked. Abramoff and Scanlon then turned around and sold their services for $4.2 million to one of the Texas tribes, offering to get their casinos reopened.[10]

In November 2005, Scanlon pleaded guilty to federal bribery charges, agreeing to pay back nearly $20 million in kickbacks he received by defrauding his and Abramoff's clients.[11] He admitted giving "things of value" to an individual identified in court documents as "Representative 1," reported to be Rep. Bob Ney, an Ohio Republican who entered into the congressional record two speeches, provided to him by Scanlon and intended to influence Abramoff and Kidan's dealings with Gus Boulis— the guy who sold them the SunCruz casino line. The guy whom

Abramoff and Kidan are accused of ripping off by filing phony loan papers. The guy who ended up shot dead on the streets of Fort Lauderdale, Florida.[12]

So, let's add things up here:

- Greek casino-boat millionaire shot dead.

- Famous Christian conservative activist.

- Indian tribes played for dupes by powerful lobbyist.

- "Big Tony" and other colorfully nicknamed wise guys.

- Ohio congressman promoting a deal between the lobbyist and the dead Greek guy.

Confusing? Yeah, we'd say so, considering that this bizarre business implicates the same Republican Party that scored big in 2004—especially in the key state of Ohio—by attracting support from voters who said "moral values" were the most important issue in the election.[13]

What was probably more mystifying, however, was this: why was Tom DeLay still smiling?

Abramoff's Democrats

As 2005 ended, rumors were flying that Jack Abramoff was ready to cut his own deal with federal prosecutors, reportedly offering to testify against others involved in his schemes. And yet Tom DeLay was not only declaring his confidence that he would escape the scandal, but was maneuvering to regain his job as House Majority Leader.[14] Why? Because Democrats were hip-deep in money from Abramoff's clients.

Between 1997 and 2004, according to the National Republican Senatorial Committee (NRSC), "clients and associates of Jack Abramoff contributed over $3.1 million to Democrat Party interests." That amount is nearly three-quarters of the $4.3 million Abramoff and friends reportedly donated to Republicans. The nonpartisan Center for Responsive Politics (CRP) counted some $1.5 million of Abramoff-connect contributions to Democrats from 2000 through October 2005, compared to $2.9 million for Republicans.[15]

The NRSC provided a breakdown of the Democratic committees that got money from Abramoff and friends:

- Democratic Senatorial Campaign Committee: $430,000

- Democratic Congressional Campaign Committee: $629,000

- Democratic National Committee: $177,000

The NRSC reported that forty of forty-five Senate Democrats got money from Abramoff, his associates, and clients from 1997 through 2004,[16] while the CRP listed Abramoff-connected contributions to congressional Democrats (2000-2005) including:

- Rep. Patrick Kennedy, Rhode Island, $42,500

- Sen. Patty Murray, Washington, $40,980

- Rep. Charles Rangel, New York, $36,000

- Sen. Harry Reid, Nevada, $30,000

- Sen. Byron Dorgan, North Dakota, $28,000

- Sen. Tom Daschle, South Dakota, $26,500

- Rep. Brad Carson, Oklahoma, $20,600

- Rep. Dale Kildee, Michigan, $19,000

- Rep. Steny Hoyer, Maryland, $17,500

- Sen. Tom Harkin, Iowa, $15,500

- Rep. Chris John, Louisiana, $15,000[17]

According to the NRSC analysis, Abramoff's clients and associates between 1997 and 2005 gave $729,000 to Senate Democrats, including $98,550 to Massachusetts Sen. John Kerry, $28,830 to Connecticut Sen. Joe Lieberman, $20,00 to California Sen. Barbara Boxer, and $12,950 to New York Sen. Hillary Rodham Clinton.[18]

That's why Tom DeLay was smiling. It's sort of like an Enron rerun: if taking money from Abramoff and friends is a "culture of corruption," to borrow a phrase from Nancy Pelosi, then Democrats got their fair share—and Pelosi herself got $3,000 worth.[19]

So the Indian gambling lobbyist might go to prison, and maybe even take out a few members of Congress as he falls. But it's a decidedly bipartisan congressional scandal—the first in three decades during which Democrats nearly ran the table on dirty dealing. And still, even at their sleazy worst, Republicans just barely out-cheat the Democrats.

Even when voters are confronted with the ugly spectacle of an Abramoff scandal—millions of dollars in gambling money, "Big Tony" and "Little Tony," ripped-off Indian tribes and a dead man in Florida—can the Democrats win an election by campaigning against Republican on the issue of corruption? It's hard to see how. In a scandal swirling around the ex-College Republican lobbyist, Democrats still managed to scoop up something like 55 to 70 percent as much Abramoff-related loot as did their GOP counterparts. (Nancy Pelosi might want to focus-group this bumper-sticker slogan: "Vote Democrat: Only 60% as Corrupt as Republicans!")

Such arguments, of course, are an invitation to slide down the slippery slope of moral relativism. Republicans who swept into Congress in 1994 promising Americans a revolution of reform can't hold their heads high by running on an "everybody does it" platform. And even the sordid sleazy history of Democratic corruption is no defense of GOP leaders who seem to have cashed in their principles like chips at an Indian casino. True, voters who want to "clean up the mess in Washington" might find it hard to see the party of Chinagate as the solution to the problem. But the inability of Democrats to get political traction on the scandal issue doesn't make it any less of a scandal.

What the Abramoff gang did was doubly dirty because they're Republicans—supposedly the party of faith and family, representing folks who aren't offended by the Ten Commandments. OK, so what part of "Thou shalt not steal" is so hard to understand? And, somewhere off on the fringes of this scam, there's the nasty question of who "whacked" Gus Boulis and why. How many degrees of separation are there between some of Washington's most prominent pro-lifers and someone—perhaps someone known to "Big Tony"—who violated the part about "Thou shalt not kill?"

A Party That "Stands for Something"

Like we said two hundred pages ago, we didn't sign a contract to write a book about Republican scandals. We plunged you into this immoral muck of gambling, lobbying, and double-dealing to make a completely different point: Even at such a shameful ebb, the Grand Old Party is still grand. That's because it's still basically the party that our old friend Senator Hoar praised so confidently more than a century ago. George Hoar suffered through the worst abuses of the Grant administration and never lost faith:

> It never occurred to me that the Republican party could not and would not cure these evils when once its attention should be called to them. It never occurred to me . . . that the wrong-doings of the party that loved liberty were to be remedied by putting the country in the power of those who hated it. . . .[20]

He never doubted, and the reader might well imagine that flinty old man from Maine smiling as he beholds how his "party that loved liberty" reacted to the Abramoff scandal.

To start with, unlike the Democratic crook Marc Rich, no suspects fled to Switzerland. Kidan, Scanlon, Abramoff—all of them surrendered, pleaded guilty and began cooperating with federal prosecutors. Unlike the "nuns on the run" of Chinagate, witnesses didn't hop a flight to destinations unknown. And, unlike the Clinton-era Justice Department under Janet Reno, the Bush administration's prosecutors didn't seem to be dragging their feet. By January 11, 2006, Justice officials were saying their investigators had already zeroed in on a "first tier" of Congress members (three Republicans, two Democrats), and certain staffers were described as "persons of interest."[21]

We keep our ears pretty close to the keyhole of the Vast Right-Wing Conspiracy, and as the Bush administration prosecutors began casting suspicion on GOP power players in early 2006, the most remarkable noise was the one we *didn't* hear: no Republicans were whining about a "partisan witch hunt." Quite the opposite. Some of the toughest reporting on the Abramoff scandal was done by the "neoconservative" journal *Weekly Standard,* calling it a tale of "the black depths of human avarice and greed."[22] When that article was posted as a "must read" at FreeRepublic.com, a free-for-all right-wing Internet forum, the reaction from grassroots Republicans was generally harsh, with the member known as "Edison" posting a widely-shared sentiment: "If Delay, Ney or anyone in the congress has any taint from these guys they need to go. . . . I will be glad to see anyone with dirty ties to this group tossed and jailed."[23]

In Congress, meanwhile, the Republicans started acting like grownups. DeLay renounced his bid to regain his House leadership position, and there was talk of hotly contested battles for the top spots.[24] A liberal New England Republican (Rep. Charles Bass of New Hampshire) joined with a right-wing Mormon Republican (Arizona Rep. Jeff Flake) calling for wide-ranging reforms.[25] No ethical Band-Aids for the GOP—they were applying tourniquets. Congressmen on both sides of the aisle began donating their Abramoff-connected campaign funds to charity (but not Democratic Senate Leader Harry Reid of Nevada, who vowed to keep every dime he got from the Abramoff crowd, ridiculously insisting, "This is a Republican scandal.").[26]

The clearest evidence that Hoar's "party that loved liberty" still held to its old standards was the implosion of Ralph Reed's political future. He'd been aiming at the lieutenant governorship of Georgia, as a potential first step toward a possible national career in office. But news of his implication in the Abramoff affair had two disastrous results: it dried up his fund-raising, and turned off his strongest supporters, young Republican idealists—"students, budding activists and campaign managers"—who now saw the former fair-haired boy as a political albatross, tainted by his gambling ties.[27]

Tom DeLay might still be smiling by the time this book rolls off the press, and Ohio's Bob Ney may be still clinging to office, but their long-term political prospects aren't good. Rank-and-file Republicans simply won't put up with such shenanigans, and they know some things are just plain wrong, even if they're not a crime.

Is there any hope for the Democrats? Oh, they might yet win some elections, but is there any hope they can be reformed? Can they turn over a new leaf, break their corrupt habits, and go legit? Probably not. They are who they are and—as Rush Limbaugh often says—they only win elections when they can convince voters they're something else. In that sense, they really are donkey *cons*—a bunch of fly-by-night con men, hustling the suckers too stupid to understand you can't get something for nothing. "We're going to raise taxes on the rich, give everybody all sorts of free government benefits, stop global warming, abolish racism, sexism, homo-phobia and greed. . . ." That old liberal snake oil isn't working, and it has-n't worked for a long time. Like Aaron Burr, today's Democrats can run, but they can't hide.

The Republicans' prospect is hopeful, just as it was in Senator Hoar's day, because it is *still* "the party that stands for something." Think of that dark day in 1974 when the elder George Bush told President Nixon it was time to resign. Such a public disgrace had never before befallen any American party. Yet it was scarcely six years later that the Republicans came roaring back, with Ronald Reagan scoring a landslide over Jimmy

Carter. Less than a decade later, the Berlin Wall had fallen and the "Evil Empire" of Soviet despotism followed soon into the ash heap of history. A good party is more than "the foibles and faults of individual leaders," as Senator Hoar saw so clearly in 1889:

> The future will have its great occasions, its great perils, its great trials, its great opportunities, its great interests. . . . The men who have forsaken us will return. The Mugwump and the Independent will come scurrying back. . . . The capitalist will know where to look for security to his property, the laborer for good wages for his labor, the patriot for safety and honor for his country. . . . For these reasons, if the Republican party be but true to its ideals, I believe the future of the party is as assured as the future of America.[28]

Acknowledgments

Thanks to: God, the Giver of Gifts, Jehovah Jireh. My husband and best friend Danny, along with our brilliant sons Christian and Jacob, plus Mom and Grandma, all of whom cheered me on, shouldered the extra housework, kid-sat, taxied, ordered pizza, patiently endured, and generally did without—I couldn't have done it without you. My coauthor, Stacy McCain, a walking encyclopedia whose sharp wit and insight made this book what it is. Nelson Current and Joel Miller, editor and coach extraordinaire (with nerves like yours, you shoulda been a fighter pilot). Alive Communications and Lee Hough, the Tony Dungy of literary agents. Chip MacGregor, who believed in me. Anita Palmer, who routinely saves my life and sanity. Janine Tomlin, fabulous friend and super-mom, who even sent me flowers to root me on. Cynthia Mahlberg, who is faithful to pray. Larry Warner, who saw my dreams and was always there. The entire *World Magazine* crew—especially Marvin Olasky, Joel Belz, Mindy Belz, Nick Eicher, Tim Lamer, and Gene Edward Veith—who made me a better writer and were behind me all the way. Bob and Kathy Case of the World Journalism Institute, who continue to give me a wonderful opportunity to pass on what I've learned. Hugh Hewitt, who helped me brainstorm the depths of political criminality. The *Washington Times* research staff—including "Sopko, the Nexis god." And, boldly representing Red State America, Thomas "Reader X" LaGrange.

—Lynn Vincent,
San Diego, California, January 12, 2006

Thanks to the talented folks at Nelson Current and Alive Communications, and to my colleagues at the *Washington Times*. I especially thank my bosses—editor-in-chief Wesley Pruden, managing editor

ACKNOWLEDGMENTS

Francis B. Coombs Jr., assistant managing editor Maria Stainer, national editor Ken Hanner, and deputy national editor Victor Morton—for pretending not to notice I've been doing even less work than usual lately. Thanks to the gang in the *Washington Times* research library (John Haydon, Clark Eberly, John Sopko, Amy Baskerville, and Dean Brown), and to work buddies Pete Parisi, Ralph Hallow, Greg Pierce, Jeff Kuhner, James Morrison, and Robert Morton. I am grateful to many friends in the newspaper business, including Burgett Mooney III, Mitch Talley, Pierre-Rene Noth, Mike Columbo, John Willis, and Christopher Barker. Thanks for friendship to some old buddies (Danny Holland, David Brook, Bert Spence, John McDaniel, and the Deltas) and to pastor Vladimir Corea. I cannot forget dear relatives like Aunt Pat, Aunt Barbara, Uncle Bobby, my loyal brothers Kirby and Rodney, my cousins the Shums, and my Bittner in-laws. For the past several months, my kids (Kennedy, Bobby, Jimmy, Jeff, Emerson, and Reagan) have put up with an extra-grumpy daddy. I am grateful to God for my Proverbs 31 wife, Lou Ann, who's been putting up with me for years. And I know Danny Vincent is blessed to have Lynn, whose generosity and patience have made her a pleasure to work with.

—Robert Stacy McCain,
Mount Aetna, Maryland, January 12, 2006

About the Authors

Lynn Vincent is features editor for *World Magazine,* where she covers current events, culture, and politics. Her third book, *Same Kind of Different as Me* (W Publishing), will be released in June 2006. A U.S. Navy Veteran, she lives with her husband, Danny, and their two sons in San Diego, where she frequents Little League baseball games and votes Republican.

Robert Stacy McCain is a twenty-year veteran of the newspaper business. An assistant national editor at the *Washington Times,* he has written for such publications as *The American Conservative, Chronicles, New York Press,* and *Ripon Forum.* In 1995, he was awarded the George Washington Medal by the Freedoms Foundation at Valley Forge. A native of Georgia, he lives in Maryland with his wife, Lou Ann, and their six children.

Notes

Prologue

1. This narrative of Burr's flight is based on Buckner F. Melton, Jr., *Aaron Burr: Conspiracy to Treason* (New York: John Wiley & Sons, 2002), pp. 156-61.

2. Willard Stern Randall, *Thomas Jefferson: A Life* (New York: Henry Holt and Company, 1993), pp. 507, 510, 544-47; The Reader's Digest, *Family Encyclopedia of American History* (Pleasantville, N.Y.: The Reader's Digest Association, 1975), pp. 162-63, 338, 1097-98.

3. Thomas E. Woods, Jr., *The Politically Incorrect Guide to American History* (Washington, D.C.: Regnery Publishing, 2004), pp. 31-42.

4. Both the monument's inscription and the original quote from Jefferson's autobiography can be found online at http://www.monticello.org/reports/quotes/memorial.html; for a brief history of the monument, see the National Park Service site, http://www.nps.gov/thje/memorial/memorial.htm#.

5. A Google search indicates that the false history on the DNC Web site (http://www.democrats.org/a/party/history.html) has been replicated on some four hundred other sites.

6. The Reader's Digest, *Family Encyclopedia of American History*, pp. 162-63, 282-83, 338; *Encyclopedia Americana*, Vol. 5 (New York: Americana Corp., 1957), pp. 63-64.

Chapter 1: Modus Operandi

1. Marcus Tullius Cicero, "First Oration Against Catiline," 62 B.C. The original Latin: *"Quo usque tandem abutere, Catilina, patientia nostra? . . . Patere tua consilia non sentis, constrictam iam horum omnium scientia teneri coniurationem tuam non vides?"* Defeated by Cicero in the election for the office of consul, Catiline hoped to capture the office by a seditious plot, which Cicero exposed in this famous speech to the Senate. Frederick Holland Dewey, ed., *Cicero's Selected Orations* (New York: Translation Publishing, 1961), p. 1.

2. Dinitia Smith, "No regrets for a love of explosives," *New York Times*, Sept. 11, 2001; Peter Collier and David Horowitz, *Destructive Generation: Second Thoughts About the '60s* (New York: Summit Books, 1989), pp. 80-81.

3. Smith, "No regrets for a love of explosives." Smith notes that Ayers in 2001 said he couldn't remember the "kill your parents" remark, but then called it "a joke about the distribution of wealth."

4. Collier and Horowitz, *Destructive Generation*, p. 68.

5. Smith, "No regrets for a love of explosives."

6. *New York Times*, Letter to the Editor, September 16, 2001. The *Times* reporter who had originally interviewed Ayers protested: "All I did was write what he told me." (Jonathan Katz, "Bringing the fight to the newsstand," *Daily Northwestern*, November 29, 2001.)

7. Robert Paul Wolff, Barrington Moore Jr., and Herbert Marcuse, *A Critique of Pure Tolerance* (Boston: Beacon Press, 1969), pp. 95-137; online at http://www.marcuse.org/herbert/pubs/60spubs/65repressivetolerance.htm.

8. Thomas Sowell, *The Vision of the Anointed: Self-Congratulation as a Basis for Social Policy* (New York: Basic Books, 1996), pp. 149-67.

9. John Stuart Mill, *Autobiography* (London: Longmans, Green, Reader & Dyer, 1873), online at http://www.utilitarianism.com/millauto/seven.html.

10. Bob Barr, "An Inquiry of Impeachment," press release November 5, 1997, online at http://www.inetresults.com/impeach/inquiry.html; David Plotz, "Rep. Bob Barr," Slate.com, February 22, 1998; "Managers: Evidence, law prove perjury, obstruction of justice," CNN.com, January 15, 1999; Lee May, "Ex-Rep. Swindall gets year for perjury," *Los Angeles Times*, August 29, 1989.

11. Onell R. Soto, "Rep. Cunningham resigns; took $2.4 million in bribes," *San Diego Union-Tribune*, November 29, 2005; Unbylined, "Bush nominates Judge Carol Chien-Hua Lam to be U.S. Attorney in San Diego," *Los Angeles Metropolitan News-Enterprise*, August 2, 2002; White House press release, August 1, 2002, online at http://www.whitehouse.gov/news/releases/2002/08/20020801-15.html.

12. Carroll Kilpatrick, "Nixon resigns," *Washington Post*, August 9, 1974. It was George H. W. Bush, then chairman of the Republican National Committee, who bluntly told Nixon, "Mr. President, you have to resign." ("Presidential Transitions: The Torch Is Passed," White House Historical Association, online at http://www.whitehousehistory.org/04/subs/04_a03_a03.html.)

13. "Livingston bows out of the speakership," CNN.com, December 19, 1998.

14. "Janklow to quit after manslaughter verdict," Associated Press, December 10, 2003.

15. "Remarks of Sen. John Edwards, 'Two Americas,' Des Moines, Iowa, December 29, 2003," online at http://www.gazetteonline.com/iowacaucus/candidate_news/edwards64.aspx

16. Al Gore, acceptance speech, Democratic National Convention, Los Angeles, August 17, 2000.

17. Paul Krugman, "The acid test," *New York Times*, May 2, 2003.

18. "Wellesley College, 1969 Student Commencement Speech, Hillary D. Rodham, May 31, 1969," online at http://www.wellesley.edu/PublicAffairs/Commencement/1969/053169hillary.html.

19. David Brock, *The Seduction of Hillary Rodham* (New York: The Free Press, 1996), pp. 22-23; Hillary Rodham Clinton, *Living History* (New York: Simon & Schuster, 2003), p. 42.

20. Collier and Horowitz, *Destructive Generation*, pp. 29-43; David Horowitz, *Radical Son: A Generational Odyssey* (New York: Touchstone, 1997), pp. 240-46, 264-68; William Manchester, *The Glory and the Dream* (New York: Little, Brown and Co., 1974), pp. 1471-76.

21. Edward Jay Epstein, "The Black Panthers and the police: A pattern of genocide?" *New Yorker*, February 13, 1971.

22. Ibid.; Alan Bisport, "The night of the Panthers," *Hartford Advocate*, November 30, 2003. The extent of surveillance of the New Haven Panthers was discovered in May 1977 (*Facts on File Yearbook 1977* [New York: Facts on File, 1978], pp. 422-33).

23. *Facts on File Yearbook 1969* (New York: Facts on File, 1970), pp. 345, 544. The shifting number of defendants seems to have made them somewhat difficult to sloganize. The Rackley murder defendants have been variously called the "New Haven Nine" (Joyce Milton, *The First Partner: Hillary Rodham Clinton* [New York: William Morrow and Company, 1999], p. 38), the "New Haven Seven" (Julius Lester, quoted in Horowitz, *Radical Son*, p. 377), and the "Connecticut Eight" (Bisport, "The Night of the Panthers").

24. *Facts on File Yearbook 1969*, pp. 544, 795; *Facts on File Yearbook 1970* (New York: Facts on File, 1971), p. 39.

25. Ibid., p. 166; Gail Sheehy, *Hillary's Choice* (New York: Random House, 1999), pp. 77-80; Donna Radcliffe, *Hillary Rodham Clinton: A First Lady for Our Time* (New York: Warner Books, 1993) p. 8; Brock, *The Seduction of Hillary Rodham*, pp. 31-32; Milton, *The First Partner: Hillary Rodham Clinton*, pp. 37-40; Barbara Olson, *Hell to Pay: The Unfolding Story of Hillary Rodham Clinton* (Washington, D.C.: Regnery Publishing, 1999), pp. 54-56.

26. *Facts on File Yearbook 1970*, pp. 266, 287.

27. Ibid., p. 308.

28. Ibid., pp. 630, 683; *Facts on File Yearbook 1971* (New York: Facts on File, 1972), p. 388; Milton, *The First Partner: Hillary Rodham Clinton*, p. 37.

29. *Facts on File Yearbook 1971*, p. 388, 495, 616; Unbylined, "Former Black Panthers Who Have Turned to Higher Education," *Journal of Blacks in Higher Education*, October 1998; Dan Hall, untitled article, Associated Press, October 13, 1977.

30. Richard Poe, "Hillary and the Panthers: The Real Story," NewsMax.com, August 19, 2003.

31. Mary Owen, "Sister of Texas dragging death victim attacks Bush," *Detroit Free Press*, October 23, 2000; T. J. Milling, Kathy Walt, and Ronnie Crocker, "Jasper suspect wrote of links to racist group," *Houston Chronicle*, June 11, 1998.

32. Biographers who describe Hillary's role in defending the Panthers include Radcliffe (*Hillary Rodham Clinton: A First Lady for Our Time*); Brock (*The Seduction of Hillary Rodham*); Milton (*The First Partner: Hillary Rodham Clinton*); and Olson (*Hell to Pay: The Unfolding Story of Hillary Rodham Clinton*). Sheehy's *Hillary's Choice* omits young Ms. Rodham's role in the New Haven trial, but includes extensive material about Hillary's involvement with the Panthers during her internship with Treuhaft (pp. 80-82). Hillary, of course, doesn't mention her Panther involvement in *Living History*. A Google search on December 31, 2005, produced more than 800 hits for the combination of terms "urban legend," "Hillary," and "Panthers." See for example, http://www.snopes.com/politics/clintons/panthers.asp.

33. Howard Kurtz, "Dick Morris, high on the critical list," *Washington Post*, February 3, 1999.

34. "Lewinsky goes public," BBC News, February 7, 1999, online at http://news.bbc.co.uk.

35. Rich Noyes, "The Liberal Media," Media Research Center, online at http://www.mediaresearch.org/SpecialReports/2004/pdf/liberal_media.pdf.

36. It appears that syndicated columnist Anthony Lewis was the first U.S. print journalist to employ the "everybody lies about sex" remark, attributing it originally to an English writer, Peregrine Worsthorne. Lewis compared Clinton's womanizing to Martin Luther King Jr. and the Duke of Wellington (Anthony Lewis, "One's sex life should be off limits," *New Orleans Times-Picayune*, February 25, 1998).

37. "Major statements by President Clinton on the Lewinsky affair," December 19, 1998, online at http://www.law.umkc.edu/faculty/projects/ftrials/clinton/clintonstatements.html.

38. Pornographer Larry Flynt reportedly spent $4 million to investigate and expose GOP sex scandals (Carol Lloyd, "Finally, the Flynt report," Salon.com, March 26, 1999). For various details of the Clinton-Lewinsky saga alluded to here, the authoritative source is still the so-called "Starr Report" (official title, "Referral to the United States House of Representatives pursuant to Title 28, United States Code, § 595(c)," Office of the Independent Counsel, September 9, 1998), online at http://www.time.com/time/daily/scandal/starr_report/files.

Chapter 2: Rap Sheet

1. "Two and Two Equal Not Guilty," *Time Magazine*, February 14, 1983.

2. Eric Felten, "Mr. Impeachment," *The Weekly Standard*, September 28, 1998.

3. Marjorie Williams, "The perplexing case of Judge Alcee Hastings," *Washington Post*, July 7, 1998.

4. Ibid; Unbylined, "Two and two equal not guilty: A federal judge beats the daylights out of a bribery prosecution." *Time Magazine*, February 14, 1983.

5. Scripps Howard News Service, "Judge lied 32 times on stand, report says," *Chicago Tribune*, October 8, 1987; Wire service report, "Senate convicts federal judge on 8 charges," *Chicago Tribune*, October 21, 1989; David Dahl, "Senate convicts Judge Hastings," *St. Petersburg Times*, October 21, 1989.

6. Felten, "Mr. Impeachment."

7. Political Graveyard, online at http://politicalgraveyard.com/special/trouble-disgrace.html.

8. Mr. Kestenbaum's bio is located at http://potifos.com/; P. J. O'Rourke quote from Brainy Quote, online at http://www.brainyquote.com/quotes/quotes/p/pjorour101111.html.

9. Stephen Hayes, "The Gentlewoman from Florida," *The Weekly Standard*, October 30, 2000.

10. Jack Sharp, "Corrine Brown: Running on a record of fraud," *Capitol Hill Blue*, August 17, 1999.

11. Hayes, *Weekly Standard*; Sharp, *Capitol Hill Blue*.

12. Ibid.

13. John Elvin, "Ann and Barney defend Clinton," *Insight on the News*, November 30, 1998.

14. Jack Sharp, "Virginia's bombastic Congressman Jim Moran: 'I like to hit people,'" *Capitol Hill Blue*, August 17, 1999.

15. Michelle Malkin, "Moran keeps on misbehaving," *Insight on the News*, July 15, 2002.

16. Don Wycliff, "Soul survivor," *Chicago Tribune Magazine*, November 16, 2003; Facts on File Yearbook 1969 (New York: Facts on File 1970), p. 510.

17. Facts on File Yearbook 1969, p. 794; Edward Jay Epstein, "The Black Panthers and the police: a pattern of genocide?" *The New Yorker*, February 13, 1971.

18. John McCormick, "Radical Chic: A Panther on the hill," *Newsweek*, November 2, 1992; Alex Tresniowski and Champ Clark, "Change of heart: Robby Rush hopes to honor his slain son by banning guns," *Time Magazine*, May 22, 2000; Kevin Chappell, "Where are the civil rights icons of the '60s?" *Ebony*, August 1996.

19. Marion Clark and Rudy Maxa, "Rep. Wayne Hays $14,000-a-year clerk says she's his mistress," *Washington Post*, May 23, 1976.

20. Historical Summary of Conduct Cases in the House of Representatives, Committee on Standards of Conduct, November 9, 2004; "Ex-Representative Diggs ordered to prison July 23," *Christian Science Monitor*, July 15, 1980; "Diggs opens funeral home," *Washington Post*, December 7, 1983.

21. Historical Summary of Conduct Cases; Leonard Buder, "Body found in Richmond's home is identified," *New York Times*, October 7, 1982.

22. Historical Summary of Conduct Cases; "Biaggi gets 8 years in Wedtech case," Associated Press, November 19, 1988.

23. National Brief, *The Hotline*, American Political Network, Inc., August 11, 1995; Dunstan McNichol, "Congress members' free rides home being scrutinized," *Wisconsin State Journal*, March 6, 1993.

24. William J. Eaton and Sara Fritz, "Wright in plea bargain to resign," *Los Angeles Times*, May 25, 1989.

25. Tim Graham, "Condit vs. Coelho," *National Review*, July 30, 2001; Brian Bloomquist, "Sickness, scandal sink Al's top aide," *New York Post*, June 16, 2000.

26. John Fund, "Phantom voters: Ballot-box fraud may have real impact at the polls," *Opinion Journal*, October 23, 2000.

27. Phil Rockdrohr, "Reynolds blasts Jackson, media," *The Times (Northwest Indiana)*, December 12, 2003.

28. "California Representative Tucker resigns," United Press International, December 12, 1995.

29. Tim Jones, "Lawmaker convicted of bribery," *Chicago Tribune*, April 12, 2002; John Caniglia, "Traficant again is on the offensive against FBI," *Cleveland Plain Dealer*, December 31, 2000.

30. "N.J. Sen. Torricelli cleared in federal probe," CNN.com, January 3, 2002; David Freddoso, "Torricelli made dubious excuse for diamonds," *Human Events*, August 26, 2002; Allison R. Hayward, "Passing the torch," National Review Online, September 30, 2002; Deroy Murdock, "Dem Jersey Games," National Review Online, October 2, 2002; "GOP anxious to use control of Senate," CNN.com, November 6, 2002.

31. Historical Summary of Conduct Cases.

32. "Former Rep. Joshua Eilberg Dies at 83," Associated Press, March 26, 2004.

33. Government and Politics: Herman Talmadge (1913–2002), *The New Georgia Encyclopedia*, online at http://www.georgiaencyclopedia.org/nge/Article.jsp?id=h-590; Talmadge's quote is fromAmerica's Anchorman: History of Scandals 1979-2005, online at www.rushlimbaugh.com/home/daily/ site_112905/content/anchorman_3.guest.html.

34. Historical Summary of Conduct Cases.

35. Ibid.

36. Ibid.

37. Political Graveyard, online at http://politicalgraveyard.com/special/trouble-disgrace.html.

38. Historical Summary of Conduct Cases.

39. Toni Locy, "Sad and sorry take of misdeeds: 3 years given ex-lawmaker," *Houston Chronicle*, November 10, 1994.

40. Kristan Metzler, "Fauntroy plead on bad report," *Washington Times*, August 10, 1995.

41. Historical Summary of Conduct Cases; Unbylined, "Finance violations bring rebuke for congressman," *Chicago Tribune*, June 22, 2001.

42. Historical Summary of Conduct Cases; Mike Feinsilber, "House whips Gingrich with desultory dispatch," *Fort Worth Star-Telegram*, January 22, 1997.

43. Historical Summary of Conduct Cases.

44. Political Graveyard. http://politicalgraveyard.com/special/trouble-disgrace.html.

45. Peter Mantius, "Swindall must report to prison on February 11," *Atlanta Journal Constitution*, February 5, 1994.

46. Unbylined, "Lukens gets 30 months in prison for corruption," *Columbus Dispatch (Ohio)*, June 20, 1996; Unbylined, "Rep. Lukens gets 30 days in jail: Ohio congressman also fined $500 for sex with teen," *Chicago Tribune*, July 1, 1989.

47. B. Drummond Ayres, "Judge assails GOP mailing in North Carolina," *New York Times*, November 6, 1990; Kay Daly, "Vote early, vote often," *WorldNetDaily*, November 13, 2000.

48. Mary Kay Quinn, "Ex-Congressman fined for false election claim," *Akron Beacon Journal*, March 19, 1997; Doug Thompson, "Congressional den of thieves," *The Federal Observer*, March 27, 2005.

49. Greg Krikorian and Jodi Wilgoren, "Rep. Kim sentenced to serve home detention," *Los Angeles Times*, March 10, 1998; David Rosenzweig, "Rep. Kim offered S. Korea TV job, urges judge to end probation," *Los Angeles Times*, October 8, 1998.

50. "Former senator fined, given probation," *Milwaukee Journal Sentinel*, November 30, 1995; John Elvin, "After long battle, Durenberger deals," *Insight on the News*, September 18, 1995. McLaughlin, "From Stalinist fellow traveler to servant of big business."

51. "Diaries' sex attract agents," *New York Times*, September 9, 1995; "The Packwood Case: Statement from Senate Ethics Committee," *New York Times*, September 7, 1995.

52. Editorial, "Shuster's rebuke: The congressman was reckless and unrepentant," *Pittsburgh Post-Gazette*, October 12, 2000; Richard E. Cohen, "Ethics Committee Sanctions Shuster," *The National Journal*, October 7, 2000.

53. Historical Summary of Conduct Cases; "House Ethics Panel Slaps Delay," www.cbsnews.com, September 30, 2004.

54. Jerry Seper, "Cooperation key for Cunningham," *Washington Times*, November 30, 2005.

55. Amy Keller, "Members misbehaving: Congress' top scandals," *Roll Call*, June 14, 2005.

56. Ibid; Timothy J. Burger, "Kolter guilty plea close to shutting the books on House Post Office Scandal," *Roll Call*, May 9, 1996; Lloyd Grove, "Rostenkowski's old ways & means," *Washington Post*, April 11, 1996.

57. Keller, "Members misbehaving: Congress' top scandals"; Charles Babington, "Hawkish Democrat joins call for pullout," *Washington Post*, November 18, 2005; Jesse J. Holland, "House expels Ohio Rep. Traficant, only second sitting member removed since Civil War," Associated Press, July 24, 2002.

58. Keller, "Members misbehaving"; Editorial, "No immunity for Keating," *St. Petersburg Times*, October 29, 1990.

59. Keller, ""Members misbehaving"; Michael Dobbs, "Koreagate figure tied to Oil-for-food scandal," *Washington Post*, April 15, 2005.

60. Keller, "Members misbehaving."

61. Doug Thompson, "A congressional den of thieves," *The Federal Observer*, August 8, 2005.

62. Tracy Thompson and Elsa Walsh, "Jurors view videotape of Barry drug arrest," *Washington Post*, June 29, 1990.

63. Victoria Churchvill and Arthur S. Brisbane, "D.C. officials confirm Barry's visit to model," *Washington Post*, May 3, 1987.

64. Jane Ashley, "The Barry Years: Triumphs and Troubles," *Washington Post*, January 21, 1990; Michael York and Tracy Thompson, "Barry sentenced to 6 months in prison," *Washington Post*, October 27, 1990.

65. *Washington Post* archives: "Marion Barry: Making of a Mayor," updated May 21, 1998.

66. Leo Damore, *Senatorial Privilege: The Chappaquiddick Cover-Up* (Washington, D.C.: Regnery Gateway, 1988), p. 7; also see this book generally for a detailed account of the Chappaquiddick incident.

67. Damore, pp. 8, 382

68. Damore, p. 8.

69. Damore, pp. 77-86, jacket copy; also see Gargan's comments throughout.

70. Damore, pp.77-86; Adam Clymer, *Edward M. Kennedy, A Biography* (New York: William Morrow and Company, Inc., 1999), pp. 145-54.

71. Damore, p. 328.

72. Damore, pp. 77-86, Clymer, pp., 145-54.

73. Ibid.

74. Ibid.

75. Ibid.

76. Damore, pp. 3, 21, 77-86, 171, 215, 326, 331–32.
77. Damore, pp. 23-24. Farrar's diagram appears in photo section.
78. Damore, pp. 200-208, 335, 395.
79. T-shirt tale told in P. J. O'Rourke, *Parliament of Whores: A Lone Humorist Attempts to Explain the Entire U.S. Gov ernment* (New York: The Atlantic Monthly Press, 1991), p. 23.

Chapter 3: Roots of the Rot

1. Quoted in Theodore H. White, "The Making of the President 1960" (New York: Antheneum House, 1961), p. 429. Hoar's remark was in reply "to a European inquirer," White says. It was first published in the *North American Review*, November 1889. It appears that White slightly edited the remark for his readers, substituting "Ku Klux Klan" for Hoar's original "Kuklux." See Hoar's original "Are Republicans in to Stay," online at http://cdl.library.cornell.edu/cgi-bin/moa/moa-cgi?notisid=ABQ7578-0149-74.
2. Christopher Matthews, "Dead Men Voting," *San Francisco Examiner*, November 19, 2000.
3. David Greenberg, "Was Nixon robbed?" *Slate*, October 16, 2000, at http://www.slate.com/id/91350. Greenberg, a professor at Rutgers University, is among those who have sought to dismiss the 1960 vote fraud as a "legend" or "myth"; see also, for example, Gerald Posner, "The fallacy of Nixon's graceful exit," *Salon*, November 10, 2001, at http://www.salon.com/politics/feature/2000/11/10/nixon/.
4. See, for example, Amity Shlaes, "A surprising winner emerges in the US election," November 15, 2000, online at http://www.townhall.com/columnists/amityshlaes/printas20001115.shtml.
5. Earl Mazo and Stephen Hess, *Nixon: A Political Portrait* (New York: Harper & Row, 1968), p. 245.
6. Peter Carlson, "Another Race to the Finish," *Washington Post*, November 17, 2000.
7. Mazo and Hess, *Nixon: A Political Portrait*, p. 248.
8. Ibid.
9. Greenburg, "Was Nixon Robbed?"
10. Ibid.
11. Mazo and Hess, *Nixon: A Political Portrait*, p. 248.
12. Carlson, "Another Race to the Finish."
13. Mazo and Hess, *Nixon: A Political Portrait*, p. 246.
14. Carlson, "Another Race to the Finish."
15. Ibid.; Carlson notes that Kennedy appointed Judge Kluczynski to the federal bench in 1961.
16. Matthews, "Dead Men Voting."
17. Mazo and Hess, *Nixon: A Political Portrait*, pp. 245-46; Carlson, "Another Race to the Finish."
18. William L. Riordon, Plunkitt of Tammany Hall (New York: McClure, Philipps & Co., 1905), online at http://www.marxists.org/reference/archive/plunkett-george/tammany-hall/.

19. The Reader's Digest, *Family Encyclopedia of American History* (Pleasantville, N.Y.: The Reader's Digest Association, 1975), pp. 162-63.

20. Melton, *Aaron Burr: Conspiracy to Treason*, pp. 23-33; Randall, *Thomas Jefferson: A Life*, p. 507.

21. The Reader's Digest, *Family Encyclopedia of American History*, pp. 162-63; Randall, *Thomas Jefferson: A Life*, p. 523.

22. Randall, *Thomas Jefferson: A Life*, pp. 544-546; Melton, *Aaron Burr: Conspiracy to Treason*, pp. 35-37.

23. Melton, *Aaron Burr: Conspiracy to Treason*, pp. 46-49, 64-65; The Reader's Digest, *Family Encyclopedia of American History*, p. 163.

24. The Reader's Digest, *Family Encyclopedia of American History*, p. 163; Melton, *Aaron Burr: Conspiracy to Treason*, pp. 53-99.

25. Melton, *Aaron Burr: Conspiracy to Treason*, pp. 17-20.

26. Ibid., pp. 53-54

27. Ibid., pp. 53-99.

28. Ibid., pp. 74-77, 134-35.

29. Ibid., pp. 103-6, 119-24.

30. Ibid., pp.113-19, 165-66, 206-16. In scandal as in so much else, Burr prefigured his party's future habits. His disgrace did not end his influence in the Democratic Party, and the term "Burrites" became one synonym for his Tammany successors. After four years of exile in Europe, he returned to the United States, and eventually resumed his law practice in New York. (The Reader's Digest, *Family Encyclopedia of American History*, p. 163.) Historian Gustavus Myers points out that Burr "controlled Tammany Hall from 1797 until even after his fall. From then on to about 1835 his protégés either controlled it or were its influential men. The phrase, 'the old Burr faction still active,' is met with as late as 1832, and the Burrites were a considerable factor in politics for several years thereafter." (Gustavus Myers, *The History of Tammany Hall* [New York: Boni & Liveright, 1917], online at http://www.geocities.com/doswind/myers/tammany_02.html.)

31. Randall, *Thomas Jefferson: A Life*, pp. 550-52.

32. The Reader's Digest, *Family Encyclopedia of American History*, pp. 1196-99.

33. Ibid., pp. 1200-2.

34. William Lee Miller, *Arguing About Slavery: The Great Battle in the United States Congress* (New York: Alfred A. Knopf, 1995), pp. 479-81.

35. Unbylined, *The American Presidents* (Danbury, Conn.: Grolier, 1992), p. 50.

36. Melton, *Aaron Burr: Conspiracy to Treason*, pp. 109-10.

37. Myers, *The History of Tammany Hall*, Foreword and Chapter 20, online at http://www.geocities.com/doswind/myers/tammany_00.html and http://www.geocities.com/doswind/myers/tammany_20.html.

38. Ibid.

39. "Dead Rabbits," Wikipedia, online at http://en.wikipedia.org/wiki/Dead_Rabbits); William Bryk, "Mr. Wood Is Mayor," *New York Press*, online at http://www.nypress.com/print.cfm?content_id=3400; Myers, *The History of Tammany Hall*, Chapter 21, online at http://www.geocities.com/doswind/myers/tammany_21.html.

40. The Reader's Digest, *Family Encyclopedia of American History*, p. 1051, 1257; Myers, *The History of Tammany Hall*, Chapter 22, online at http://www.geocities.com/doswind/myers/tammany_22.html.

41. Albon P. Man Jr., "Labor Competition and the New York Draft Riots of 1863," *Journal of Negro History*, October 1951.

42. Shelby Foote, *The Civil War: A Narrative, Vol. 2, Fredericksburg to Meridian* (New York: Vintage Books, 1986), p. 637; The Reader's Digest, *Family Encyclopedia of American History*, pp. 356-57; Myers, *The History of Tammany Hall*, Chapter 22: "In the Supreme Court and the Court of Common Pleas, citizens were turned out at the rate, often, of about 1,000 a day. The State census of 1865 gave the city 51,500 native and 77,475 naturalized voters. The figures were doubtless false, probably having been swelled to allow fraudulent totals at the polls to come within the limits of an officially declared total of eligible voters." http://www.geocities.com/doswind/myers/tammany_22.html

43. The Reader's Digest, *Family Encyclopedia of American History*, pp. 1145-46, 1097-98.

44. Hoar, "Are Republicans in to Stay."

45. The Reader's Digest, *Family Encyclopedia of American History*, pp. 121, 117.

Chapter 4: The Gang's All Here

1. *The Godfather* (1972).

2. Gus Russo, *The Outfit: The Role of Chicago's Underworld in the Shaping of Modern America* (New York: Bloomsbury, 2001), pp. 57, 89-90.

3. Russo, *The Outfit*, pp. 17-18; "The Five Points & Eastman Gangs," online at http://glasgowcrew.tripod.com/fivepoints.html; "John Torrio," online at http://www.carpenoctem.tv/mafia/torrio.html; for Luciano's boast, see http://www.drugwar.com/assassination.shtm.

4. David Pietruzsa, *Rothstein: The Life, Times, and Murder of the Criminal Genius Who Fixed the 1919 World Series* (New York: Carroll & Graf Publishers, 2003), pp. 53-54, 73, 82-83; "Sullivan, Timothy Daniel," online at http://bioguide.congress.gov/scripts/biodisplay.pl?index=S001061.

5. Pietruzsa, *Rothstein*, pp. 1-3, 196-97, 272.

6. Ibid., pp. 8-14; "Frank Costello (1891-1983): Prime Minister of the Underworld," online at http://www.carpenoctem.tv/mafia/costello.htm.

7. Pietruzsa, *Rothstein*, 337-341; Russo, *The Outfit*, pp. 90-91. Luciano's version of events clashes with the standard history of the 1932 convention. Compare, for instance, William Manchester, *The Glory and the Dream*, pp. 56-57.

8. Russo, *The Outfit*, pp. 90-91.

9. "Frank Costello (1891-1983): Prime Minister of the Underworld."

10. Unbylined, "Carmine de Sapio," *London Daily Telegraph*, February 8, 2004.

11. Manchester, *The Glory and the Dream*, pp. 134-36.

12. Ibid., p. 138.

13. Ibid., pp. 138-39.

14. Russo, *The Outfit*, p. 215.

15. Allan May, "The History of the Kansas City Family," online at http://crimemagazine.com/kcfamily.htm.
16. Russo, *The Outfit*, p. 216
17. Manchester, *The Glory and the Dream*, p. 390; Russo, *The Outfit*, pp. 218-19, 223.
18. Pietrusza, *Rothstein*, pp. 216-18, 359; Russo, *The Outfit*, pp. 220-21; Allan May, "The Last Days of Lepke Buchalter," online at http://crimemagazine.com/buchalter.htm.
19. Russo, *The Outfit*, p. 222; Michael Barone, "Conventions Held During Wartime Can Be Gloomy," *Wall Street Journal*, August 30, 2004. An FBI memorandum, dated July 25, 1936, cites a report by a trucker that Hillman's union "amounted to a strong arm racket" which had "forced him entirely out of business," online at http://foia.fbi.gov/lbuchalter/buchalter_louis_lepke_pt01.pdf.
20. Russo, *The Outfit*, pp. 174-75.
21. Ibid., p. 232.
22. Ibid., pp. 229-32, 237-42.
23. Ibid., pp. 241-42.
24. Ibid., p. 304.
25. Ibid., pp. 303-34. During Capone's heyday, Chicago mobsters were more bipartisan in their politics. Republican William Thompson was Chicago's mayor during Capone's rise to power, but was defeated by Democratic reformer William Dever in the 1923 election. Dever's crackdown on bootleggers prompted Capone to move his headquarters to suburban Ciccro, Illinois, where Republican Mayor Joseph Klenha went along with the gangsters. Democratic Mayor Anton "10 Percent Tony" Cermak, recognized as "the father of Chicago's powerful Democratic political machine," was elected mayor in 1931. Cermak was supported by gangster Roger Tuohy, a Capone rival. Capone's gang blamed Cermak when a police detective shot Capone henchman Frank Nitti in December 1932, and Cermak was assassinated two months later by Guiseppe Zangara—reportedly on orders from the Chicago mob. (Russo, *The Outfit*, pp. 19, 26, 38, 85-95; "Anton Cermak," Wikipedia, online at http://en.wikipedia.org/wiki/Anton_Cermak.)
26. Russo, *The Outfit*, pp. 360-61.
27. Ibid., pp. 369-72.
28. Ibid., pp. 405-10, 451-53.

Chapter 5: The Union Label

1. Linda Chavez and Daniel Gray, *Betrayal* (New York: Crown Forum, 2004), p. 3.
2. Philip Dine, "Union leaders laugh at Republicans old-style labor-mob probe," *St. Louis Post Dispatch*, July 26, 1996.
3. Eugene Methvin, "A Corrupt Union and the Mob," *Weekly Standard*, August 31, 1998.
4. Dine, "Union leaders laugh at Republicans old-style labor-mob probe."
5. Methvin, "A corrupt union and the mob"; Dan Herbeck, "Justice dept. claims union as been dominated by mob," *Buffalo News*, January 31, 1996.

6. Ibid.
7. Methvin, "A corrupt union and the mob."
8. Dine, "Union leaders laugh at Republicans old-style labor-mob probe.";
Douglas Turner, " Fino links president of labor union to mafia in testimony,"
Buffalo News, July 25, 1996.
9. Methvin, "A corrupt union and the mob."
10. Chavez and Gray, p. 78-79.
11. Center for Responsive Politics, 2004 Election Cycle filings with the Federal
Election Commission.
12. Ibid.
13. Ibid.
14. Linda Chavez and Daniel Gray, p. 3; William McGurn, "Teacher's pets," *Wall
Street Journal,* August 2, 2001.
15. Ibid.; "Top All-Time Donor Profiles," 1989–2004 Cycles.
16. McGurn, "Teacher's pets."
17. Chavez and Gray, p. 4.
18. Center for Responsive Politics, 2003-2004 Election Cycle filings with the
Federal Election Commission.
19. Ibid.
20. Stefan Gleason, "Clinton's labor board must go," National Review Online,
December 10, 2001.
21. National Legal and Policy Center, *Union Corruption Update,* January–October
2005.
22. "Two Teachers' Union Officials Convicted of 23 Counts of Federal
Conspiracy, Fraud, and Money Laundering," State New Service, Washington,
September 2, 2005.
23. Justin Blum, "Audit Says Union Lost $5 Million in Theft; Teachers Groups
Sues Eight from D.C. Local," *Washington Post,* January 17, 2003.
24. "Union Scandal is Abrupt Turn for D.C. Insider," *Washington Post,* January 19,
2003.
25. "Two Teachers' Union Officials Convicted of 23 Counts of Federal
Conspiracy, Fraud, and Money Laundering."
26. Unbylined, "Teachers Union Scandal: An Inside Look; FBI Lists Items
Confiscated in Probe," *Washington Post,* January 16, 2003.
27. Blum, "Audit Says Union Lost $5 Million in Theft; Teachers Groups Sues
Eight from D.C. Local"; Chavez and Gray, p. 164.
28. Timberg, "Union Scandal is Abrupt Turn for D.C. Insider."
29. Craig Timberg and Allan Lengel, "Union Paid For Party for Mayoral Aide,"
Washington Post, February 9, 2003.
30. Chavez and Gray, *Betrayal,* p. 163.
31. Timberg and Lengel, "Union paid for party for mayoral aide."
32. Yolanda Woodlee, "Union's Treasurer violated D.C. Code," *Washington Post,*
January 26, 2003.
33. Chavez and Gray, p. 67.
34. Indictment filed by U.S. Attorney for the Southern District of New York

against former International Brotherhood of Teamsters President Ron Carey, January 25, 2001.

35. Jimmy Hoffa," online at http://www.reference.com/browse/ wiki/Jimmy_Hoffa; "James Hoffa," online at http://www.britannica.com/ebc/article-9367187? query=Hoffa&ct=; "Jimmy Hoffa," online at http://en.wikipedia.org/wiki/ Jimmy_Hoffa.Wikipedia.

36. Ron Carey Indictment, January 25, 2001.

37. Michael Ledeen and Mike Maroney, "The White House Joins the Teamsters," *American Spectator*, November 1998.

38. Micah Morrison, "Who is Harold Ickes?" *Wall Street Journal*, October 26, 2000; Ledeen and Maroney, "The White House Joins the Teamsters."

39. Ibid.

40. Center for Responsive Politics, PAC Donations, 1992–1996.

41. Decision of Teamsters Election Officer Kenneth Conboy to Disqualify Int'l Brotherhood of Teamsters President Ron Carey, November 17, 1997.

42. Ron Carey Indictment, January 25, 2001.

43. Ibid.

44. Ibid

45. Steve Greenhouse, "Link to teamsters inquiry forces advocacy group to cut back," *New York Times*, October 30, 1997.

46. Ron Carey Indictment, January 25, 2001.

47. Decision of Teamsters Election Officer Kenneth Conboy.

48. Ibid.

49. Ibid.

50. Ibid.

51. Chavez and Gray, *Betrayal*, p. 86.

52. Decision of Teamsters Election Officer Kenneth Conboy.

53. Ibid.

54. Ibid.

55. Commentary, *Washington Times*, September 1, 2001.

56. Ibid.

57. Ibid.

58. Chavez and Gray, *Betrayal*, p. 88.

Chapter 6: International Criminals

1. Mona Charen, *Useful Idiots: How Liberals Got It Wrong in the Cold War and Still Blame America First* (Washington, D.C.: Regnery Publishing, 2003), pp. 187-89.

2. Tom Cooper, "Grenada, 1983: Operation 'Urgent Fury,'" *Air Combat Information Group Journal*, September 1, 2003.

3. Unbylined, "Grenada invasion quick, deadly," *Victoria Advocate*, July 22, 2003; "Armed invasion of Grenada 1983," Wars of the World, online at www.onwar.com/aced/data/golf/grenada1983.htm.

4. Charen, *Useful Idiots*, p. 188.

5. "Court allows prisoners from Grenada's 1983 coup to appeal to Privy Council," Associated Press, June 29, 2005.

6. Ibid.
7. Charen, *Useful Idiots*, p. 189.
8. Ibid., p. 190
9. Ibid., p. 190. Cooper, "Grenada, 1983: Operation 'Urgent Fury.'"
10. Richard Cohen, "War and peace," *Washington Post*, November 1, 1983.
11. "Operation Urgent Fury," globalsecurity.org, online at http://www.globalsecurity.org/military/ops/urgent_fury.htm; Chapman Pincher, *Traitors: The Anatomy of Treason* (New York: St. Martin's Press, 1987), p. 154.
12. David Horowitz, "An Enemy Within," FrontPageMagazine.com, September 19, 2001; John Fund, "Who is Barbara Lee?" *Opinion Journal*, online at www.opinionjournal.com/diary/?id=95001156, September 17, 2001.
13. Ibid.
14. Ibid.
15. Horowitz, "An Enemy Within."
16. Ibid.
17. Ibid.
18. Ibid; Jim Herron Zamora, "Dellums to run for election as Oakland mayor," *San Francisco Chronicle*, October 7, 2005.
19. Horowitz, "An Enemy Within"; Lisa Vorderbrueggen, "Rep. Lee in peace prize group," *Contra Costa Times*, June 30, 2005.
20. Robert W. Lee, "Totally Radical!" *The New American*, March 29, 1999; Web site of Rep. Bernie Sanders, online at http://bernie.house.gov/pc/.
21. Ibid.
22. Democratic Socialists of America Web site (www.dsausa.org), online at http://www.dsausa.org/about/where.html.
23. Lee, "Totally Radical!"
24. Democratic Socialists of America Web site (www.dsausa.org), online at http://www.dsausa.org/about/where.html.
25. Democratic Socialists of America Web site (www.dsausa.org), online at http://www.dsusa.org/about/newlit.html.
26. Charen, *Useful Idiots*, p. 205-10.
27. Hugh Hewitt, "One Weekend in April, a Long Time Ago," *The Weekly Standard*, September 9, 2004.
28. Charen, *Useful Idiots*, pp. 218-20.
29. Web site of the Congressional Progressive Caucus, online at www.house.gov/lee/CongressionalProgressiveCaucus.
30. Ann Coulter, *Treason: Liberal Treachery from the Cold War to the War on Terror,* (New York: Crown Forum, 2003), pp. 17-34.
31. See generally, David Horowitz, *Radical Son: A Generational Odyssey* (New York: Simon and Schuster, 1997), pp. 1-95.
32. Mona Charen, *Useful Idiots*, p. 15.
33. Whittaker Chambers, *Witness* (New York: Random House, 1952), p. 444.
34. Sam Tanenhaus, *Whittaker Chambers: A Biography* (New York: Random House, 1997), p. 108-10.

35. "Whittaker Chambers," Wikipedia, online at http://en.wikipedia.org/wiki/Whittaker_Chambers.

36. Coulter, *Treason,* pp. 18-19.

37. Ibid, pp. 19-22.

38. Ibid.

39. Ibid.

40. Ibid, pp. 41-43.

41. Tanenhaus, pp. 189-90.

42. National Security Agency, online at http://www.nsa.gov/venona/index.cfm.

43. Stephane Courtois, et al, *Black Book of Communism* (Boston: Harvard University Press, 1999).

44. Unbylined, "Congressman flies U.N. flag: Stance on global body contrasts with colleagues seeking pullout," WorldNetDaily, May 27, 2003.

45. Democratic Socialists of America Web site, online at http://www.dsausa.org/about/where.html.

46. Testimony of Khidir Hamza, Senate Foreign Relations Committee, July 31, 2002.

47. John H. Cushman Jr., "Democratic congressman asserts Bush would mislead U.S. on Iraq," *New York Times,* September 30, 2002.

48. George Will, "Baghdad Bonior," Townhall.com, October 3, 2002, online at http://www.townhall.com/opinion/columns/georgewill/2002/10/01/164393.html.

49. Ibid.

50. Ibid.

51. Cushman, "Democratic congressman asserts Bush would mislead U.S. on Iraq."

52. Mindy Belz, "Waterlogged," *WORLD Magazine,* November 12, 2005.

53. Norman Podhoretz, "Who is Lying About Iraq?" *Commentary Magazine,* December 2005.

54. Ibid.

55. Ibid.

56. Ibid.

57. Jim Burns, "Do Democrats Just Want to Fight Democrat Wars?" *Human Events,* Dec 23, 2005, online at http://www.humaneventsonline.com/article.php?id=11073.

58. Ibid.

59. "Kennedy's Texas Remark Stirs GOP Reaction," CNN.com/Inside Politics, Thursday, September 18, 2003.

60. Linton Weeks and Peter Baker, "Bush Spars with Critics of Iraq War," *Washington Post,* November 12, 2005.

61. Senate Report on the U.S. Intelligence Community's Pre-War Intelligence Assessments on Iraq, 2004, pp. 9-14.

62. David Corn, "Senate Report Whacks CIA, not Bush," *The Nation,* July 9, 2004.

63. Testimony of Khidir Hamza, Senate Foreign Relations Committee, July 31, 2002.

64. Burns, "Do Democrats Just Want to Fight Democrat Wars?"

Chapter 7: Aiding and Abetting

1. Lowell Ponte, "Jesse Jackson: A Real Con Man," FrontPageMag.com, July 18, 2003; Ponte attributes this quote to George Bernard Shaw, but it appears more likely that Shaw, a socialist, actually said: "A government policy to rob Peter to pay Paul can be assured of the support of Paul."

2. Mike Saewitz, "Alert issued for missing girl," *Sarasota Herald-Tribune*, February 3, 2004. The story of Carlie Brucia's kidnapping that follows is based on several news accounts, including: "Police certain they have car used in girl's abduction," CNN.com, February 5, 2004; Robert Eckhart and Mike Saewitz, "Suspect held in abduction," *Sarasota Herald-Tribune*, February 5, 2004; "Key evidence missing in Carlie's killing," CNN.com, February 6, 2004; "Housemmate tips police to Smith after seeing video," CNN.com, February 6, 2004; "Timeline of events," *Sarasota Herald-Tribune*, February 5, 2004.

3. "Police certain they have car used in girl's abduction," CNN.com, February 5, 2004.

4. Unbylined, "Carlie mourned," TBO.com, February 8, 2004.

5. Mike Saewitz, "Crisis for a tough-talking judge," *Sarasota Herald-Tribune*, February 15, 2004; Chris Davis, Matthew Doig, and Robert Eckhart, "One chance too many?" *Sarasota Herald-Tribune*, February 15, 2004.

6. Davis, et al., "One chance too many?"

7. Ibid.

8. Ibid.

9. Ibid.

10. Saewitz, "Crisis for a tough-talking judge."

11. Ibid.; FEC records online at www.fecinfo.com; "Robert B. Bennett Jr.," online at http://www.12circuit.state.fl.us/bios/bennett.htm.

12. Davis, et al., "One chance too many?"

13. "Carlie mourned," TBO.com.

14. Saewitz, "Crisis for a tough-talking judge."

15. Ibid.

16. Ibid.

17. Ibid.

18. Ibid.

19. Mike Saewitz, "O'Reilly rails on at retiring Rapkin," *Sarasota Herald-Tribune*, December 10, 2004.

20. Davis, et al., "One chance too many?"

21. Ibid.

22. Robert Stacy McCain, "The Racial Profiling Myth," *The American Conservative*, May 19, 2003 (review of Heather Mac Donald, *Are Cops Racist?* [New York: Ivan R. Dee, 2003]); Dorothy Rabinowitz, "The Other War," OpinionJournal.com, August 11, 2005.

23. "Girl's family wants to know why suspect was free," Associated Press, February 8, 2004.

24. Thomas Sowell, *The Vision of the Anointed: Self-Congratulation as a Basis for Social Policy* (New York: Basic Books, 1996), pp. 149-67.

25. Robert Stacy McCain, "Most-Wanted TV," *Washington Times*, August 6, 2003.

26. Willard Gaylin, *The Killing of Bonnie Garland: A Question of Justice* (New York: Penguin 1995), quoted in Steve Cooley, et al., "Los Angeles District Attorney's Response to Stanley Williams's Petition for Executive Clemency," online at http://da.co.la.ca.us/pdf/swilliams.pdf.

27. "Jurors prayed before, after death deliberations," Associated Press, December 3, 2005.

28. Saewitz, "Crisis for a tough-talking judge."

29. Jennifer Gollan, "Woolsey's pitch for rapist questioned," *Marin Independent Journal*, February 7, 2004.

30. Ibid.

31. Ibid.

32. Jennifer Gollan, "Woolsey apologizes for letter," *Marin Independent Journal*, February 10, 2004.

33. Michelle Malkin, "Shame on you, Lynn Woolsey," Townhall.com, February 18, 2004.

34. Jennifer Gollan, "Woolsey apologizes for letter."

35. Jennifer Gollan, "Teen victim rejects Woolsey's apology," *Marin Independent Journal*, February 11, 2004.

36. Califorina Institute for Federal Policy Research, "California Results from General Election held on November 2, 2004," online at http://www.calinst.org/pubs/vote2004.pdf.

37. Dan Flynn, "Cop Killer: How Mumia Abu-Jamal Conned Million Into Believing He Was Framed" (Washington, D.C.: Accuracy in Academia, 1999), pp. 3-4.

38. Ibid.; Steve Lopez, "Wrong Guy, Good Cause," *Time*, July 23, 2000.

39. Robert Stacy McCain, "'Cop Killer' author says Mumia's guilt is certain," *Washington Times*, October 4, 2000.

40. Greg Butterfield, "Garden Rocks for Mumia," online at http://www.mumia2000.org/May7.

41. Robert Stacy McCain, "The Dictator's Defender," *Washington Times*, December 9, 2005.

42. Butterfield, "Garden Rocks for Mumia"; C. Clark Kissinger, "Briefing Paper on the Case of Mumia Abu-Jamal," *Refuse & Resist*, January 2000, online at http://www.refuseandresist.org/mumia/2000/011900briefing.html; Chaka Fattah, "Congressional Black Caucus Questions Due Process for Mumia Abu-Jamal," press release, October 13, 1999; Jeff Mackler, "5000 in LA Protest 'Republocrat' Attacks on Mumia Abu-Jamal," *Socialist Action*, September 2000 (www.socialist action.org)

43. "Consider the Facts That Convicted Mumia Abu Jamal," online at http://www.danielfaulkner.com/Pages/considerfacts.html.

44. Lopez, "Wrong Guy, Good Cause"; C. Clark Kissinger, "Philadelphia: The

Power Structure and the Railroad of Mumia Abu-Jamal," *Revolutionary Worker*, July 30, 2000.

45. Stuart Taylor Jr., "Guilty and Framed," *The American Lawyer*, December 1995.

46. Maureen Faulkner, "Letters," *The Village Voice*, December 8–14, 1999.

47. Unbylined, "Desmond Tutu and Wole Soyinka Oppose Execution of Mumia Abu-Jamal," *Revolutionary Worker*, January 17, 1999.

48. John Price, "Victory or Trickery?" SeeingBlack.com, December 21, 2000; Maryclaire Dale, "Judge dismisses Abu-Jamal's death sentence," Associated Press, December 18, 2000.

49. Taylor, "Guilty and Framed."

50. Petition online at http://cm-p.com/pdf/nobel_laureate_list.pdf.

51. Cooley, et al., "Los Angeles District Attorney's Response to Stanley Williams's Petition for Executive Clemency"; Leslie Fulbright, "Measure of a Man's Life," *San Francisco Chronicle*, December 4, 2005.

52. Cooley, et al., "Los Angeles District Attorney's Response to Stanley Williams's Petition for Executive Clemency."

53. Mark Leno, "Avoiding ultimate mistake in applying ultimate punishment," *San Francisco Chronicle*, November 14, 2005.

54. Josh Kleinbaum, "Tookie's time running out," *Los Angeles Daily News*, December 4, 2005; Leslie Fulbright, "Williams: Redemption or Unrepentant Criminal?" *San Francisco Chronicle*, December 4, 2005.

55. Street Gangs Resource Center, online at http://www.streetgangs.com/homicides/ and http:///www.streetgangs.com/homicides/homicidetable.html; Barbara Becnel, "The Crips co-founder now realizes violence does not solve anything," *Los Angeles Times*, August 22, 1993.

56. Dan Morain, "Death Row violence part of gang power struggle, San Quentin officials say," *Los Angeles Times*, June 11, 1989; Kimberley Sevcik, "Has Stanley Williams Left the Gang?" *New York Times Magazine*, August 10, 2003; Becnel, "The Crips co-founder now realizes violence does not solve anything"; Cooley, et al., "Los Angeles District Attorney's Response to Stanley Williams's Petition for Executive Clemency."

57. Becnel, "The Crips co-founder now realizes violence does not solve anything"; Sevcik, "Has Stanley Williams Left the Gang?" *New York Times Magazine*, August 10, 2003.

58. Becnel, "The Crips co-founder now realizes violence does not solve anything."

59. Dr. Hunter "Patch" Adams, et al., letter to Governor Arnold Schwarzenegger, November 23, 2005, online at http://cm-p.com/pdf/nobel_laureate_list.pdf. See also, "Nobel Laureates, Faith Leaders, Join Growing Chorus Requesting Clemency for Stanley Tookie Williams," press release, Curtis, Mallet-Prevost, Colt & Mosle, LLP, online at http://www.cm-p.com/pdf/pressrelease_112305.pdf.

60. Cooley, et al., "Los Angeles District Attorney's Response to Stanley Williams's Petition for Executive Clemency.

61. Adams, et al., letter to Governor Arnold Schwarzenegger.

62. John Fund, "My Felon Americans," OpinionJournal.com, March 7, 2005.

63. "Rally focuses on felon voting rights," Associated Press, April 18, 2004.

64. Thomas Beaumont and Jonathan Roos, "Felon plan seen as political," *Des Moines Register*, June 29, 2005.

65. Margie Hyslop, "Right to vote?" *Washington Times*, July 14, 2002; Afefe Tyehimba, "Unlock the vote," *Baltimore City Paper*, April 10, 2002.

66. Christina Bellantoni, "Warner first in America in restoring felons' rights," *Washington Times*, April 29, 2005.

67. Christopher Uggen and Jeff Manza, "They've paid their debt; let them vote," *Los Angeles Times*, July 18, 2003; "If Felons Could Have Voted, National Election Outcomes Would Have Been Different," American Sociological Association, January 9, 2003, press release online at http://www2.asanet.org/media/felons.htm.l.

68. Ibid.

69. Steve Bousquet, "Court Passes on Felon Voters Law," *St. Petersburg Times*, November 15, 2005.

70. David Kidwell, Phil Long, and Geoff Dougherty, "Hundreds of felons cast votes illegally," *Miami Herald*, December 1, 2000.

71. Uggen and Manza, "They've paid their debt; let them vote."

72. Fund, "My Felon Americans"; Lesley Clark and Gary Fineout, "State's ban on felons voting stands," *Miami Herald*, November 15, 2005.

73. The Reader's Digest, *Family Encyclopedia of American History* (Pleasantville, N.Y.: The Reader's Digest Association, 1975), pp. 930-32.

74. Fund, "My Felon Americans." In the interest of being "fair and balanced," we'll point out that three non-Democrats voted in favor of the Reid amendment: Pennsylvania Sens. Arlen Specter and Rick Santorum, and Ohio Sen. Mike DeWine. The roll call vote on Reid's amendment (S.2879) to the bill (S.565) is online at www.senate.gov.

75. Hyslop, "Right to vote?"; "Population trend good for city, O'Malley," *The Baltimore Sun*, November 17, 2005; "FBI: Baltimore Ranks High For Violent Crime, Homicide," WBAL-TV (www.thewbalchannel.com), November 3, 2003.

76. Hyslop, "Right to vote?"

77. Uggen and Manza, "They've Paid Their Debt; Let Them Vote"; Peter Kirsanow, "The Felon Franchise," NationalReview.com, January 8, 2004; Dan Kennedy, "Muzzle Awards," *Boston Phoenix*, June 28-July 5, 2001.

78. Ponte, "Jesse Jackson: A Real Con Man."

Chapter 8: Scene of the Crime

1. Fred Siegel, *The Future Once Happened Here* (San Francisco: Encounter Books, 2000), p. 281.

2. Matthew Cella, "Homicide rate up again," *Washington Times*, June 17, 2003; Cheryl W. Thompson, Ira Chinoy, and Barbara Vobejda, "Unsolved killings plague district," *Washington Post*, December 3, 2000; Del Quentin Wilber, "Unsolved killings haunt D.C. detectives," *Washington Post*, February 14, 2005.

3. Howard Kurtz, "Media defend fascination with story of missing intern," *Washington Post*, July 10, 2001. Levy's disappearance was not front-page news in Washington until nearly six weeks after she was reported missing (Arthur Santana, "D.C. keeps little data on missing," *Washington Post*, June 10, 2001).

4. Michelle Malkin, "The media's immigration blinders," *Jewish World Review* (www.jewishworldreview.com), June 5, 2002.

5. Michael Doyle, "Investigators try to tie suspect to Levy's death," *Modesto Bee*, October 5, 2002.

6. "Chandra Levy's remains found in D.C. park," CNN.com, May 22, 2002; Matthew Cella and Jim Keary, "Levy's body found in Rock Creek Park," *Washington Times*, May 23, 2002; "Private eyes find leg bone in Rock Creek Park," CNN.com, June 6, 2002; "Levy Probe Again Focuses On Inmate," Associated Press, September 29, 2002.

7. Barry was directly involved in policy decisions that contributed to skyrocketing crime in the nation's capital. The *Washington Post* attributed the decline of D.C. police department to "two decades of political interference by Mayor Marion Barry" (Michael Powell, Sari Horwitz, and Cheryl W. Thompson, "D.C. Police Problems Festered," *Washington Post*, October 12, 1997). Fred Siegel also discusses at length Barry's role in the District's crime problem (*The Future Once Happened Here*, pp. 104-5, 110-15).

8. John Shiffman, "Kemp gets 10 years for corruption," *Philadelphia Inquirer*, July 20, 2005; "Philadelphia corruption trial at a glance," Associated Press, May 9, 2005; John Shiffman, "Jail terms for trio end City Hall case," *Philadelphia Inquirer*, October 7, 2005; John Shiffman, "Mariano surrenders to FBI," *Philadelphia Inquirer*, October 27, 2005.

9. Fran Spielman, "Daley defends fired Hired Truck chief," *Chicago Sun-Times*, February 12, 2004; Steve Warmbir and Tim Novak, "Mob ties run throughout city truck program," *Chicago Sun-Times*, January 25, 2004; Matt O'Connor and Dan Mihalopoulos, "Key figure pleads guilty to Hired Truck Charges," *Chicago Tribune*, July 29, 2005; Fran Spielman, "Emanuel defends scandal-scarred Daley," *Chicago Sun-Times*, August 25, 2005; Karen Mellen, "Democrats revel in countywide gains," *Chicago Tribune*, November 4, 2004; The federal prosecutor in the Chicago corruption probe, U.S. Attorney Patrick Fitzgerald, was appointed to head up the investigation of accusations that Bush administration officials had leaked the name of a CIA employee (Abdon M. Pallasch, "Prosecutor goes where others fear to tread," *Chicago Sun-Times*, October 30, 2005).

10. "Former Mayor Campbell Indicted on Corruption and Tax Charges," U.S. Department of Justice press release, August 30, 2004; "Former Atlanta Chief Operating Officer Wallace Pleads Guilty to Federal Corruption and Tax Charges," U.S. Department of Justice press release, September 5, 2002; "Georgia: Atlanta and Fulton County Guilty of Corrupt Racial Set Aside Program," Adversity.net.

11. "Six Defendants Charged in Wide-Ranging Racketeering and Extortion Scheme," U.S. Department of Justice press release, January 18, 2005; "Former

City Official Convicted of Corruption," Department of Justice press release, May 16, 2005; Pete Kotz, "City for sale," *Cleveland Scene*, July 20, 2005; Mike Tobin, "Another official tied to bribery," *Cleveland Plain Dealer*, June 14, 2005; Steve Luttner, "Jury convicts Gray in second trial," *Cleveland Plain Dealer*, August 18, 2005. Onunwor, elected and reelected as a Democrat, changed his affiliation to the GOP in 2002, shortly before he was arrested for corruption that began immediately after he was first elected in 1997. East Cleveland has never elected a Republican mayor. (Leila Atassi and Joseph L. Wagner, "Brewer pulls vote upset in E. Cleveland," *Cleveland Plain Dealer*, October 5, 2005; "Federal indictment charges against Nate Gray unsealed," Cleveland.com, January 18, 2005; "Africa-born mayor hits streets," Associated Press, August 19, 2001.)

12. Rich Lowry, "The Big Sleazy," National Review Online, November 2, 2004.
13. Ibid; Josh Levin, "Assessment: Ray Nagin," Slate.com, September 2, 2005; Nicole Gelinas, "Who's Killing New Orleans?" *City Journal*, Autumn 2005; Steve Ritea, "Morial's uncle faces federal theft, fraud charges," *New Orleans Times-Picayune*, August 6, 2005; John Maginnis, "Louisiana is on corruption watch again," August 10, 2005; Adam Nossiter, "New Orleans corruption: narrative versus facts," Associated Press, July 3, 2005.
14. Michael Grunwald and Susan B. Glasser, "The Slow Drowning of New Orleans," *Washington Post*, October 9, 2005; Lise Olsen, "City had evacuation plan but strayed from strategy," *Houston Chronicle*, September 8, 2005; Jennifer Harper, "Inside Politics," *Washington Times*, September 5, 2005; Wesley Pruden, "When the flood empties the ATM," *Washington Times*, September 13, 2005; John Hill, "Police Officers investigated for alleged misconduct after storm," Gannett News Service, September 30, 2005; Lee Hancock, "Storm tossed what was left of New Orleans' police image," *Dallas Morning News*, October 26, 2005.
15. Jake Tapper, "Amid Katrina Chaos, Congressman Used National Guard to Visit Home," ABC News (www.abcnews.go.com), September 13, 2005; Allan Lengel, "FBI Searches Louisiana Congressman's Homes," *Washington Post*, August 4, 2005.
16. Siegel, *The Future Once Happened Here*, pp. 25-27, 78-79, 153-56.
17. Julia Vitullo-Martin, "Detroit Fights Back," *City Journal*, Summer 1995.
18. Details of Messerlian's life and death, along with other facts about the 1967 riot can be found in Michigan American Local History Network, "1967 Detroit Riot Victims," online at http://www.geocities.com/michdetroit/riot1967.html. Other sources for this account of the Detroit riot include: James Neuchterlein, "Remembering the Riots," *First Things*, October 1997; "12th Street Riots," Wikipedia, online at http://en.wikipedia.org/wiki/12th_Street_Riot; "Detroit Riots 1967," Rutgers University, online at http://www.67riots.rutgers.edu/d_index.htm; William Manchester, *The Glory and the Dream* (Boston: Little, Brown and Company, 1974), pp. 1323-24.
19. Quoted in "The Kerner Commission Report and the Failed Legacy of Liberal Social Policy," Heritage Foundation Lectures No. 619, June 24, 1998.

20. Stephan Thernstrom, "The Kerner Commission Report Lacks Credibility," lecture at the Heritage Foundation, March 13, 1998.

21. Thomas Sowell, *Basic Economics: A Citizen's Guide to the Economy* (New York: Basic Books, 2000), pp. 158-59; Thomas Sowell, *Applied Economics: Thinking Beyond Stage One* (New York, Basic Books, 2003), pp. 161-91; Stephan Thernstrom and Abigail Thernstrom, *America in Black and White; One Nation Indivisible* (New York: Simon & Shuster, 1997), pp. 184-88; Myron Magnet, *The Dream and the Nightmare: The Sixties' Legacy to the Underclass* (San Francisco: Encounter Books, 2000), pp. 175-77.

22. "Jerome Cavanagh," Wikipedia, online at http//en.wikipedia.org/ wiki/Jerome_Cavanagh; Siegel, *The Future Once Happened Here*, pp. 3-4.

23. "Detroit, Michigan," Wikipedia, online at http://en.wikipedia.org/ wiki/Detroit,_Michigan.

24. Manchester, *The Glory and the Dream*, pp. 490-96.

25. George C. Leef, *Free Choice for Workers: A History of the Right to Work Movement* (Ottawa, Ill.: Jameson Books, 2005), pp. 28-30.

26. Jack Lessenberry, "Now for the future," *Metro Times Detroit*, November 7, 2001.

27. "Jerome Cavanagh," Wikipedia, online at http//en.wikipedia.org/ wiki/ Jerome_Cavanagh; "1967 Detroit Riot Victims," online at http://www.geoci- ties.com/michdetroit/riot1967.html; "Detroit Riots 1967," online at http://www.67riots.rutgers.edu/d_index.htm. Between 1950 and 1970, while Detroit's total population declined by more than 300,000, its black population actually increased by 360,000, from 16.2 percent of the total in 1950 to 44.5 percent in 1970. See Thomas J. Sugrue, *The Origins of the Urban Crisis: Race and Inequality in Postwar Detroit* (Princeton, N.J.: Princeton University Press, 1996), p. 23.

28. Tamar Jacoby, *Someone Else's House: America's Unfinished Struggle for Integration* (New York: Free Press, 1998), pp. 236-38.

29. Thernstrom, "The Kerner Commission Report Lacks Credibility"; Manchester, *The Glory and the Dream*, pp. 1306-11.

30. Manchester, *The Glory and the Dream*, p. 1310.

31. "Detroit Riots 1967"; Manchester, *The Glory and the Dream*, p. 1319; H. Rap Brown, "We Burned Detroit Down and Put America on Notice," *Open City* (Los Angeles), August 17, 1967.

32. Siegel, *The Future Once Happened Here*, pp. 5-10; Seigel credits David Sears with coining the term "riot ideology."

33. For a glimpse of post-1967 riot fears in Detroit, see Jacoby, *Someone Else's House*, pp. 239-52.

34. Tom Wolfe, *Radical Chic and Mau-Mauing the Flak Catchers* (New York: Farrar, Straus and Giroux, 1970); Siegel, *The Future Once Happened Here*, p. 15.

35. David Stoltoff, "The Short Unhappy History of Community Action Programs," in *The Great Society Reader*, eds. Marvin E. Gettleman and David Mermelstein (New York: Vintage Books, 1967), p. 234.

36.　Sargent Shriver, "The War on Poverty Is a Movement of Conscience," in *The Great Society Reader*, pp. 204-12.

37.　Jack Minnis, "How the Great Society Solves the Servant Problem," in *The Great Society Reader*, pp. 168-70.

38.　"Sketches of Some Black Panthers," Associated Press, August 23, 1989; Michelle Locke, "Black Panthers ride again, this time in a campaign bus," Associated Press, January 25, 1999; Richard A. Walker, "Oakland: Dark Star in an Expanding Universe," unpublished paper, 1997, online at http://geography.berkeley.edu/PeopleHistory/faculty/R_Walker/OaklandDar kStar.pdf.

39.　P. J. O'Rourke, *Parliament of Whores: A Lone Humorist Attempts to Explain the Entire U.S. Government* (New York: Atlantic Monthly Press, 1991), p. 128.

40.　Sowell, *Applied Economics*, pp. 116-20; Thomas Sowell, *The Quest for Cosmic Justice* (New York: Free Press, 1999), pp. 126-30.

41.　O'Rourke, *Parliament of Whores*, p. 124. In 1996 alone, thirty-two public housing projects were scheduled for demolition (Siegel, *The Future Once Happened Here*, p. 282).

42.　Siegel, *The Future Once Happened Here*, pp. 59-62.

43.　Ibid, p. 243.

44.　Ibid, p. 34.

45.　Steven Malanga, "The Conspiracy Against the Taxpayers," *City Journal*, Autumn 2005.

46.　Vitullo-Martin, "Detroit Fights Back."

47.　This account of Coleman Young's career is based largely on Bill McGraw, "Always a Fighter: Coleman Young's Search for Justice Led Him on a Hard Road to Power," *Detroit Free Press*, December 5, 1996. See also Jacoby, *Someone Else's House*, pp. 302-310, as well as Martin McLaughlin, "From Stalinist fellow traveler to servant of big business: The political career of Coleman Young," International Workers Bulletin, December 29, 1997, online at http://www.wsws.org/public_html/iwb12-29/young.htm.

48.　McGraw, "Always a Fighter: Coleman Young's Search for Justice Led Him on a Hard Road to Power."

49.　U.S. Census Bureau, "Population of the 100 Largest Cities and Other Urban Places in the United States: 1790 to 1990," online at http://www.census.gov/population/www/documentation/twps0027.html.

50.　Desirce Cooper, "Incinerator lit a fuse for Detroit artists," *Metro Times Detroit*, December 3, 1997; Jenny Nolan, "Auto plant vs. neighborhood: The Poletown battle," *Detroit News*, online at (http://info.detnews.com/history/story/index.cfm?id=18&category=business).

51.　Jacoby, *Someone Else's House*, pp. 323-32.

52.　Ibid.

53.　Ibid.

54.　"Coleman Young," Wikipedia, http://en.wikipedia.org/ wiki/Coleman_Young.

55.　Ibid.

56. Mackinac Center, "Binding Arbitration in Detroit," online at http://www.mackinac.org/4784; James Q. Wilson, "The Closing of the American City," *The New Republic*, May 11, 1998.
57. Vitullo-Martin, "Detroit Fights Back."
58. Ibid.
59. Cameron McWhirter, "3-day arson spree hurt city's image," *Detroit News*, June 20, 2001.
60. McLaughlin, "From Stalinist fellow traveler to servant of big business."
61. Ibid.
62. Bill McGraw, "Young's presence felt in Detroit mayor's race," *Detroit Free Press*, October 19, 2005. Kilpatrick was reelected with 53 percent of the vote, even as the FBI announced it was investigating allegations of vote fraud (David Josar and Lisa M. Collins, "FBI will examine absentee ballots," *The Detroit News*, November 8, 2005.)

Chapter 9: Fat Cats and Democrats

1. Edmund Burke, *Reflections on the Revolution in France*, in *Harvard Classics: Edmund Burke* (New York: P.F. Collier & Sons, 1969), p. 185. The elision includes Burke's famed "little platoons" passage, in which he was speaking principally of social class and not—as some neoconservatives would have it—of the family.
2. "Enron: The Global Gospel of Gas," *Project Underground*, November 27, 1997, online at http://www.moles.org/ProjectUnderground/motherlode/enron.html; Pratap Chatterjee, "Enron in India: The Dabhol Disaster," CorpWatch, July 20, 2000, online at http://www.corpwatch.org/article.php?id=467.
3. Jerry Seper, "Enron sought Clinton's help for project in India," *Washington Times*, January 12, 2002; Jerry Seper, "Enron gave cash to Democrats, sought pact help," *Washington Times*, January 16, 2002; Charles R. Smith, "Enron and Bill Clinton," NewsMax.com, February 28, 2002; Patrice Hill, "Two administrations listened to Lay," *Washington Times*, May 7, 2002; Patrice Hill, "Clinton helped Enron finance projects abroad," *Washington Times*, February 21, 2002; Michael Weisskopf, "Enron's Democrat pals," Time.com, August 26, 2002.
4. Center for Responsive Politics, "The Fall of a Giant," OpenSecrets.org, November 21, 2001. "Enron makes Whitewater looks like peanuts," Bill Press said on CNN, while the Boston Globe enthusiastically reported: "Enron's dealings are fast becoming the biggest potential embarrassment the Bush administration has faced." (Ellen Sorokin, "Enron collapse likened to Whitewater for Bush," *Washington Times*, January 12, 2002.)
5. Rich Noyes, "Dancing Around Bill Clinton's Enron Deals," Media Research Center (www.media research.org), March 5, 2002.
6. Daniel Kadlec, "Who's Accountable?" *Time*, January 21, 2002. *Time*'s Michael Weisskopf had reported in a previous "notebook" item that Enron was "a bipartisan debacle" ("Democrats: Don't gloat about Enron," January 14,

2002), but this aspect of the scandal seems to have been ignored by the magazine for the next seven months, until it published Weisskopf's "Enron's Democrat Pals" in August.

7. "About Halliburton," online at http://www.halliburton.com/about/index.jsp.

8. Greg McDonald, "Clinton takes real vacation," *Houston Chronicle*, August 16, 1993.

9. Weisskopf, "Enron's Democrat Pals."

10 Ibid.

11. Ibid.

12. Center for Responsive Politics, "Top House Recipients of Enron PAC & Individual Contributions, 1989-2001," and "Enron Contributions to Current Senators, 1989-2001," OpenSecrets.org.

13. John Fleming, "U.S. Foreign Aid was Lever that Moved Enron Deal," *Houston Chronicle*, November 1, 1995; Human Rights Watch, "The Enron Corporation: Corporate Complicity in Human Rights Violations," online at http://www.hrw.org/reports/1999/enron/enron8-2.htm.

14. Robert Wright, "Enron's curious Croatian client," *Financial Times*, February 1, 2002; Jack Cashill, *Ron Brown's Body: How One Man's Death Saved the Clinton Presidency and Hillary's Future* (Nashville, Tenn.: WND Books, 2004), pp. 284-85; Sustainable Energy & Economy Network, "Project Profile: Jertovec 240MW gas-fired power plant," online at http://www.seen.org/db/Dispatch?action-ProjectWidget:624-detail=1.

15. Smith, "Enron and Bill Clinton."

16. Patrice Hill, "Clinton agencies assisted Enron rise," *Washington Times*, April 8, 2002.

17. Michael Weisskopf, "The White House: That invisible Mack sure can leave his mark," *Time*, September 1, 1997; Patrice Hill, "Clinton helped Enron finance projects abroad"; "Enron: The global gospel of gas"; Arvind Padmanabhan and Lola Nayar, "Enron's Indian saga," *News India-Times*, online at http://www.newsindia-times.com/2002/02/22/tow-22-top.html.

18. Pratap Chatterjee, "Enron: Pulling the Plug on the Global Power Broker," CorpWatch, December 13, 2001, online at http://www.corpwatch.org/article.php?id=1016; Patrice Hill, "Panel exonerates Rubin, not Citigroup," *Washington Times*, January 4, 2003; Seper, "Colossal Collapse," *Washington Times*, January 13, 2002.

19. Donald Lambro, "The Enron-around," *Washington Times*, January 17, 2002.

20. Donald Lambro, "GOP scoffs at bid to tie Bush, Enron," *Washington Times*, January 14, 2002.

21. Ibid.

22. Center for Responsive Politics, "The Fall of a Giant."

23. Federal Election Commission, "Top 50 Senate Campaigns by Receipts: January 1, 2005 through Sept. 30, 2005," online at http://www.fec.gov/press/press2005/20051110sen/sen50rec.pdf.

24. "Top Corporate PACs Giving To Candidates," online at http://www.fecinfo.com (retrieved Dec. 26, 2005).

25. Federal Election Commision records online at http://www.fecinfo.com.

26. Federal Election Commission, "Bipartisan Campaign Reform Act of 2002," online at http://www.fec.gov/pages/bcra/bcra_update.shtml; for one example of how Enron was seen as demonstrating the necessity for reform, see Sen. Russell Feingold, "Campaign-Finance Reform? Think Enron," CounterPunch, January 27, 2002, online at http://www.counterpunch.org/feingoldenron.html.

27. "Top Individual Contributors to 527 Committees, 2004 Election Cycle," OpenSecrets.org.

28. Jerry Bowyer, "Rich Republicans?" National Review Online (www.nationalreview.com), July 11, 2005.

29. "2004 cycle Presidential Only—Total Receipts," http://www.fecinfo.com.

30. "2004 cycle Senate Only—Total Receipts," http://www.fecinfo.com.

31. Peter Schweizer, Do As I Say (Not As I Do), Profiles in Liberal Hypocrisy (New York: Doubleday, 2005).

32. Ibid., p. 11.

33. Ibid., pp. 135-52.

34. Ibid., pp. 78-93.

35. Ibid., p. 96.

36. Ibid., p. 100.

37. Ibid., p. 110.

38. Gary Shaw, "So Many Inzunzas, So Few Mayors," San Diego Metropolitan, March 2003.

39. Caitlin Rother, "Strip club donors often hid ties," San Diego News-Tribune, June 22, 2003; Caitlin Rother, "Councilmen met with strip club lobbyist," San Diego News-Tribune, June 24, 2003; "Chronology of events," San Diego News-Tribune, Sept. 9, 2003; Daniel Strumpf, "Lawyers, Sex & Money," San Diego City Beat, May 4, 2005; Seth Hettena, "Ex-Councilman Sentenced in Strip Club Scam," Associated Press, November 11, 2005.

40. Leslie Wolf Branscomb and Tanya Sierra, "Landlord of opportunity," San Diego News-Tribune, December 15, 2005; Shaw, "So Many Inzunzas, So Few Mayors."

41. Branscomb and Sierra, "Landlord of opportunity."

42. Ibid.; Leslie Wolf Branscomb and Tanya Sierra, "Inzunza transfers ownership in 9 sites," San Diego News-Tribune, December 17, 2005. In January 2006, Nick Inzunza announced he was abandoning his political career to concentrate on his real estate business. Caitlin Rother, "Inzunza quits assembly campaign," San Diego Union Tribune, January 11, 2006.

43. Al Gore, acceptance speech, Democratic National Convention, Los Angeles, August 17, 2000.

44. "On the record: Marion and Herb Sandler," San Francisco Chronicle, January 18, 2004; "Top Individual Contributors to 527 Committees, 2004 Election Cycle," OpenSecrets.org.

45. Jerry Seper, "Prosecutors say Clinton on his own in Rivers deal," Washington Times, March 8, 2001.

46. Ibid.

47. Ibid.; also see Barbara Olson, *The Final Days: The Last, Desperate Abuses of Power by the Clinton White House* (Washington, DC: Regnery Publishing, 2001), pp. 157-58.

48. Jake Tapper, "Anatomy of a pardon," Salon.com, February 13, 2001.

49. Viveca Novak, "Doyenne of the Dollars," *Time*, June 14, 1999.

50. Ibid.

51. Martin Huxley, "Denise Rich Writes From Her Heart," BMI MusicWorld, March 1, 2000, online at http://www.bmi.com/musicworld/features/200003/drich.asp.

52. Michael Weisskopf, "Denise & Bill & Beth," Time.com, February 12, 2001, online at http://time-proxy.yaga.com/time/nation/article/0,8599,99072,00.html.

53. Olson, *The Final Days*, pp. 131-32; Jerry Seper, "Financier focus of inquiry," *Washington Times*, December 14, 2004; Marcia Vickers, "The Rich Boys," *Business Week*, July 18, 2005.

54. Olson, *The Final Days*, pp. 129-31, 141; Tapper, "Anatomy of a pardon."

55. Olson, *The Final Days*, p. 128; Tapper, "Anatomy of a pardon."

56. Transcript, House Government Reform Committee, March 1, 2001, online at http://www.washingtonpost.com/wp-srv/onpolitics/transcripts/pardonshearingtext030101.htm.

57. Tapper, "Anatomy of a pardon"; Weisskopf, "Denise & Bill & Beth."

58. Transcript, House Government Reform Committee, March 1, 2001.

59. Ibid.

60. Ibid.

61. Ibid.; Paul Sperry, "Prez: 'Take Jack's Word,'" WorldNetDaily.com, March 3, 2001.

62. Olson, *The Final Days*, pp. 170-75.

63. Ibid, pp. 186-87; Transcript, House Government Reform Committee, March 1, 2001.

64. Ibid.

65. Federal Election Commission records online at http://www.fecinfo.com.

66. Brian Ross and Rhonda Schwartz, "Americans' Role Eyed in U.N. Oil Scandal," ABCNews.com, December 1, 2004; Jerry Seper, "Financier focus of inquiry," *Washington Times*, December 14, 2004; Jerry Seper, "Grand jury probes Rich-Saddam link," *Washington Times*, December 17, 2004.

67. Federal Election Commission records online at http://www.fecinfo.com,

Chapter 10: Presidential Predators

1. Joe Eszterhas, *American Rhapsody* (New York: Alfred Knopf, 2000), p. 29.

2. Robert Dallek, *An Unfinished Life: John F. Kennedy* (Boston: Little, Brown, and Company, 2003), p. 257; Seymour M. Hersh, *The Dark Side of Camelot* (Boston: Little, Brown, and Company, 1997), pp. 90, 95-96.

3. Hersh, *Camelot*, p. 226-227; private telephone interviews between author Vincent and Larry Newman on December 30 and 31, 2005.

4. Hersh, *Camelot*, p. 226-227; interviews with Newman.

5. Ibid.

6. Ibid.

7. Interviews with Newman.

8. Jacob Weisberg, "Seymour Hersh's book is better than the critics say it is," *Slate*, November 14, 1997. Private telephone interviews with Newman, and also with Joseph Paolella on January 2, 2006.

9. Interview with Newman, December 30, 2005.

10. Mary F. Lynn Jones, "Lewinsky scandal isn't playing in Peoria," *The Hill*, August 12, 1998.

11. Ibid.

12. "Kitty Kelley Bush-bashing book publisher seeks damages from Newsweek," www.newsmax.com, September 10, 2004, online at http://www.newsmax.com/archives/ic/2004/9/10/153237.shtml; George Gordon, "George, why don't you ever call me? Bush's aide is 'suicidal' at affair gossip," *Daily Mail* (London), September 10, 1992. In fine British fashion, this story titillates for several paragraphs before revealing that Bush 41's rumored paramour, Jennifer Fitzgerald, is aghast at being called the president's mistress; Eisenhower affair is taken from eHistory, "First Ladies: Mamie Geneva Doud Eisenhower," online at http://ehistory.osu.edu/world/amit/display.cfm?amit_id=2333.

13. Dallek, *An Unfinished Life: John F. Kennedy*, p. 476.

14. Robert A. Caro, *The Years of Lyndon Johnson: Means of Ascent* (New York: Alfred A. Knopf, 1990), pp. 25-27; Elaine Thompson, "Fabulous monster revealed," *The Australian*, July 3,1 1998. This article reviewed Robert Dallek's Johnson biography, *Flawed Giant: Lyndon Johnson and His Times*.

15. Lance Morrow, "The Reckless and the Stupid," *Time*, February 3, 1998, online at www.cnn.com/allpolitics/1998/01/26/time/morrow.html.

16. Stephen Dinan "John Kerry says social justice should guide presidency," *Washington Times*, October 25, 2004.

17. Howard Fineman and Debra Rosenberg, with Matthew Cooper, Daniel Klaidman, Mark Hosenball, and Matt Bai, "Washington at War," *Newsweek*, January 4, 1999; "The President on Trial: The Players, anti-Clinton," *Time*, online at http://www.time.com/time/daily/scandal/players_anti.html.

18. Doris Kearns Goodwin, *No Ordinary Time: Franklin and Eleanor Roosevelt: The Home Front in World War II* (New York: Simon & Schuster, 1994), p. 518.

19. Anthony Lewis, "Abroad at home; Sex and Leadership," *New York Times*, February 23, 1998.

20. Ibid.

21. Ibid; Dan Thomasson, "Exner death closes bizarre chapter," Scripps Howard News Service, October 1, 1999; "Access and Alienation," *Dissent in Wichita: The Civil Rights Movement in the Midwest 1954-1972*, University of Illinois Press, online at http://www.press.uillinois.edu/epub/books/eick/ch8.html.

22. Thomasson, "Exner death closes bizarre chapter"; "Judith Exner: From the outfit to the Oval Office," Crime Library, online at http://www.crimelibrary.com/gangsters_outlaws/mob_bosses/women/4.html.

23. Ibid; Dallek, *An Unfinished Life*, p. 476; Hersh, *The Dark Side of Camelot*, pp. 226-44.

24. "Judith Exner: From the outfit to the Oval Office."

25. Thomasson, "Exner death closes bizarre chapter."
26. Douglas Brinkley, *American Heritage History of the United States* (New York: Viking Penguin, 1998), p. 501.
27. Private telephone interview with Joseph Paolella on January 2, 2006.
28. The Rometsch account is based largely on Dallek, *An Unfinished Life*, pp. 634-38, who himself footnotes Hersh's *The Dark Side of Camelot* as well as other sources.
29. Ibid.
30. Ibid.
31. Ibid.
32. Dallek, *An Unfinished Life*, pp. 475-76. On page 706, Dallek called Kennedy's womanizing "a dangerous indulgence" that made Kennedy vulnerable to national security breaches and "charges of mob influence." But Kennedy was not only vulnerable to such charges, he was in fact, *under* mob influence. Still, Dallek concludes on page 707, that Kennedy's affairs did not diminish his effectiveness as president.
33. Eszterhas, *American Rhapsody*, p. 13.
34. Ibid.
35. Ibid.

Chapter 11: Logical Legacy

1. Private telephone interview between author Vincent and Tommy Osborne, speaking from Stetson's on December 21, 2005.
2. Lloyd Grove, "The Reliable Source," *Washington Post*, March 6, 2001; "GOP lawyer: Facts 'misconstrued' in Rich case," CNN: Inside Politics, March 2, 2001.
3. Paul Sperry, "Task force still sparing big fish," *WorldNetDaily*, July 13, 2001.
4. Elizabeth Drew, *The Corruption of American Politics* (Seacaucus, New Jersey: Birch Lane Press/Carol Publishing Group, 1999), p. 16.
5. Ibid., p. 18.
6. Paula Dwyer, "'A second set of books' for Democrats?" *Business Week*, April 21, 1997; Christopher Caldwell, "A Democratic scandal," *The Weekly Standard*, November 18, 1996; Larry Klayman, "Criminals in the White House?" *Insight on the News*, April 17, 2000.
7. Jennifer Hickey, "Money troubles for Democrats," *Insight on the News*, November 9, 1998.
8. Ibid; James Ring Adams, "John Huang's bamboo network," *The American Spectator*, December 1996.
9. Hickey, "Money troubles for Democrats."
10. Bob Woodward and Brian Duffy, "Chinese Embassy Role In Contributions Probed," *Washington Post*, February 13, 1997.
11. Drew, *The Corruption of American Politics*, p. 1 and see generally Drew's characterizations of Thompson.
12. Larry Klayman, "Reno subverts probe of Clinton scandals," *Insight on the News*, June 23, 1997.
13. "A Chronology: Key Moments In The Clinton-Lewinsky Saga," CNN: All

Politics, online at http://www.cnn.com/ALLPOLITICS/1998/resources/lewinsky/timeline.

14. William Norman Grigg, "Red star over the White House," *The New American,* February 15, 1999.

15. Ibid.

16. Drew, *The Corruption of American Politics,* pp. 97, 106; Jeff Gerth and David E. Sanger, "How Chinese won rights to launch satellites for U.S.," *New York Times,* May 17, 1998.

17. Editorial Desk, "The New China Connection," *New York Times,* May 17, 1998; Gerth and Sanger, "How Chinese won rights to launch satellites for U.S."; Byron York, "Come fly with me," *The American Spectator,* March 1997.

18. Grigg, *The New American,* citing *The Year of the Rat,* an exposé of the Chinagate scandal written by congressional investigators Edward Timperlake and William C. Triplett II; Larry Klayman, "Berger key figure in Chinagate," *WorldNetDaily,* July 21, 2004.

19. Grigg, "Red star over the White House"; Jean Pearce, "How Chinagate led to 9/11," *FrontPageMagazine,* May 25, 2004.

20. Drew, *The Corruption of American Politics,* pp. 105, 125-26.

21. Ibid.

22. Klayman, "Criminals in the White House?"

23. Drew, *The Corruption of American Politics,* p. 13.

24. Ibid.; Caldwell, "A Democratic scandal."

25. Adams, "John Huang's bamboo network."

26. Ibid.

27. Ibid.

28. Drew, *The Corruption of American Politics,* p. 87; Hickey, "Money troubles for Democrats."

29. Paul Sperry, "FBI agents claim DOJ fixed probe," *WorldNetDaily,* July 17, 2001.

30. Ibid.

31. Ibid.

32. Paul Sperry, "Bush FBI pick tied to Reno cohort," *WorldNetDaily,* July 20, 2001. Sperry, "FBI agents claim DOJ fixed probe."

33. Sperry, "Task force still sparing big fish."

34. Ibid.

35. George Stephanopolous, *All Too Human* (Boston: Little, Brown, and Company, 1999), p. 64; Joe Eszterhas, *American Rhapsody* (New York: Alfred A. Knopf, 2000), p. 6.

36. Eszterhas, p. 11.

37. Eszterhas, pp. 162-68.

38. Ibid., p. 11.

39. David D. Kirkpatrick, "Hillary Clinton Book Advance, at $8 Million, Is Nearly a Record," *New York Times,* December 16, 2000.

40. Barbara Olson, *The Final Days: The Last, Desperate Abuses of Power by the Clinton White House* (Washington, D.C.: Regnery Publishing, Inc., 2001). On

September 11, 2001, two days before *The Final Days* was to be printed, Mrs. Olson was killed when the airplane she had just boarded was hijacked by terrorists and crashed into the Pentagon. Mrs. Olson was an attorney, New York Times best-selling author, and the wife of Ted Olson, Solicitor General under President George W. Bush. Her publisher, Alfred Regnery, called her "passionate and courageous . . . a champion of freedom."

41.   Lisa Anderson, "Democrats call him a 'Zellout,' but Georgia senator is unrepentant," *Chicago Tribune*, September 1, 2004.

42.   Ibid.

43.   Sam Smith, "What you won't find in the Clinton Library," *The Progressive Review*, online at http://prorev.com/missingclinton.htm.

44.   Martin Kettle, "Clinton accused of 1978 hotel rape," *Guardian Unlimited*, February 20, 1999.

45.   Smith, "What you won't find in the Clinton Library," *The Progressive Review*, online at http://prorev.com/missingclinton.htm.

46.   "Hillary Rodham Clinton testimony played at McDougal trial," CNN: All Politics, March 16, 1999.

47.   Olson, *The Final Days*, p. 160.

48.   Byron York, "Hillary's false testimony," *National Review Online*, June 13, 2003.

49.   Pete Yost, "File-getter pleads the Fifth," *Associated Press*, June 29, 1996.

50.   Unbylined, Periscope: White House, "Blame the Dead Guy," *Newsweek*, July 15, 1996.

51.   "Filegate: Case closed," BBC News, March 17, 2000.

52.   Olson, *the Final Days*, pp. 9, 99-103.

53.   Ibid.

54.   Ibid.

55.   Ibid.

56.   The Clinton/Coia account was taken from Byron York, "Mob Rules: Bill and Arthur's beautiful friendship," *The American Spectator*, April 1997; John E. Mulligan, "Union probe renews interest in Coia's ties to Clinton," *Providence Journal*, October 26, 1997; Linda Chavez, "Clinton friendship with corrupt union boss," *Human Events*, June 17, 2004.

57.   Draft RICO complaint, United States of America v. Laborers International Union of North America, AFL-CIO, online at http://www.thelaborers.net/documents/draftricocomplaint.htm.

58.   Byron York, "'Mob Rules'" Bill and Arthur's beautiful friendship," American Spectator, April 1997.

59.   Ibid.

60.   Dick Morris and Eileen McGann, *Because He Could*, (New York: HarperCollins, 2004), p. 5.

61.   Kenneth R. Timmerman, "Clinton Mischief," *Insight on the News*, February 26, 2001, p. 10.

62.   Olson, *The Final Days*, pp. 7, 123, 143-57.

63.   Ibid.

64. Ibid.
65. Bob Herbert, "Cut him loose," *New York Times,* February 26, 2001.
66. Sam Smith, "Clinton timeline," *The Progressive Review,* online at http://prorev.com/connex.htm, 1998.
67. Unbylined, "Special Report: Clinton Accused—Bill Clinton and Gennifer Flowers, 1992." *Washington Post,* online at http://www.washingtonpost.com/wp-srv/politics/special/clinton/frenzy/clinton.htm.
68. Sam Smith, "Clinton timeline."
69. Stephanopoulos, *All Too Human,* pp. 64, 67–68.
70. Ibid.
71. Ibid.
72. Gwen Gibson Maturity News Service, "His humor gets better with age," *St. Louis Post-Dispatch,* July 1, 1992.
73. James W. Brosnan, "Solicited funds, Gore admits no crime, he says, but won't use White House again," *The Commercial Appeal,* May 4, 1997.
74. Klayman, "Berger key figure in Chinagate."
75. Private telephone interview with Colette Wilson of the U.S. Justice Foundation, December 20, 2005. USJF represents Peter Paul.
76. Lawsuit: *Paul v. Clinton et al,* online at http://www.hillcap.org/pp_complaint_022504_njw.pdf.
77. Josh Gerstein, "Senator Clinton seeks way out of nettlesome case," *New York Sun,* October 17, 2005.
78. FEC December 12, 2005 Conciliation Agreement signed by Andrew Grossman, online at http://www.hillcap.org/default.php?page_id= 53.
79. Paul demand letter, online at http://www.hillcap.org/default.php/page_id.

Chapter 12: Honor among Thieves

1. Ann Coulter, *How to Talk to a Liberal (If You Must)* (New York: Three Rivers Press, 2004), p. 252.
2. Laurie Kellman, "DeLay Smile May Foil Democrat Campaign Ads," Associated Press, October 20, 2005.
3. Susan Jones, "Dems Complain About DeLay's Smiling Mug Shot," CNSNews.com, October 21, 2005.
4. Ibid.; John McCaslin, "Inside the Beltway," *Washington Times,* October 21, 2005.
5. Hugh Aynesworth, "Wrath of Earle feared in Texas," *Washington Times,* October 10, 2005; "The D.A. And Tom DeLay," CBSNews.com, March 6, 2005.
6. Matthew Continetti, "Money, Mobsters, Murder," *Weekly Standard,* November 28, 2005.
7. Ibid.
8. John Burstein, Tonya Alanez, and Sean Gardiner, "Man held in Boulis slaying incriminates fellow suspects," *Ft. Lauderdale Sun-Sentinel,* November 24, 2005.
9. Continetti, "Money, Mobsters, Murder."

10. Ibid.

11. Terry Frieden, "DeLay ex-aide pleads guilty in Abramoff case," CNN.com, November 21, 2005.

12. Frieden, "DeLay ex-aide pleads guilty in Abramoff case"; Continetti, "Money, Mobsters, Murder."

13. "Moral Values: A Decisive Issue?" CBSNews.com, November 4, 2004.

14. Janet Elliott, "DeLay's request for speedy trial denied," *Houston Chronicle*, December 22, 2005; Silla Brush, "Running for cover," *U.S. News & World Report*, January 9, 2006.

15. National Republican Senatorial Committee, "Democrats Don't Know Jack?" online at http://www.nrsc.org/newsdesk/document.aspx?ID=1362; Center for Responsive Politics, "Jack Abramoff Lobbying and Political Contributions, 1999–2006," online at http://www.capitaleye.org/abramoff_recips.asp.

16. "Democrats Don't Know Jack?"

17. Center for Responsive Politics, "Jack Abramoff Lobbying and Political Contributions, 1999–2006."

18. "Democrats Don't Know Jack?"

19. Center for Responsive Politics, "Jack Abramoff Lobbying and Political Contributions, 1999 – 2006," online at http://www.capitaleye.org/abramoff_recips.asp.

20. George F. Hoar, "Are Republicans in to Stay," online at http://cdl.library.cornell.edu/cgi-bin/moa/moa-cgi?notisid=ABQ7578-0149-74

21. Jerry Seper and Audrey Hudson, "Abramoff-linked probe focuses on 5 lawmakers," *Washington Times*, January 11, 2006.

22. Continetti, "Money, Mobsters, Murder."

23. Free Republic, online at http://www.freerepublic.com/focus/f-news/1551702/posts?page=49#49.

24. Stephen Dinan, "DeLay ends bid to regain leader's post," *Washington Times*, January 7, 2006; Stephen Dinan and Amy Fagan, "House GOP asks leader candidates for platforms," *Washington Times*, January 10, 2006; Stephen Dinan, "Immigration vote stirs concern about Boehner," *Washington Times*, January 11, 2006; Dinan and Fagan, "Boehner, Blunt urge reforms," *Washington Times*, January 12, 2006.

25. Stephen Dinan, "2 Hill lawmakers seek to rally GOP," *Washington Times*, January 11, 2006.

26. John McCaslin, "Inside the Beltway," *Washington Times*, January 12, 2006.

27. Kristin Jensen and Laurence Viele Davidson, "Abramoff Scandal Threatens to Derail Reed's Political Ambitions," Bloomberg News, January 11, 2006.

28. Hoar, "Are Republicans in to Stay."

INDEX

Abramoff, Jack, 14–15, 218–225
Abu-Jamal, Mumia, 121–124
Accardo, Joe, 61
Acheson, Dean, 99
Adams, John, 49
Adler, Solomon, 101
Affetto, Anthony, 80
Ansara, Michael, 85–86
Atlanta, GA (*see also* Mayor Bill
    Campbell), 5, 138
Aurelio, Thomas, 64
Ayers, Billy, 1–3, 8, 12

Baker, Bobby, 189–190, 193
Battle of Gettysburg, 57–58
Baxter, James Odell II, 81–82
Becnel, Barbara, 126–127
Bipartisan Campaign Reform Act
    (BCRA), 165
Bishop, Maurice (*see also* Grenada),
    91–94
Black Panthers, 9–12, 23–24, 121, 148
    New Haven Nine, 10
Blennerhassett, Harman, 52
Blue States, 166
Borders, William Jr., 17–18
Boulis, Konstantinos "Gus", 218–219,
    223
bribery & kickbacks, 3, 6, 17–19, 21,
    24–25, 27–28, 30–31, 35, 80–81,
    137–141, 177, 181, 194, 200, 210,
    219
Brown, H. Rap, 146–147
Brown, Ron, 160–162, 197–198
Brucia, Carlie, 109–115, 118
Buchalter, Louis "Lepke", 67–68
Bullock, Barbara, 82–84
Burr, Aaron, x–xiii, 4, 49–55, 225

Bush, George H. W., 43, 184, 185, 225
Bush, George W., 12, 88, 104–107,
    131, 159, 164–166, 168, 174, 176,
    185, 193, 206, 208
    administration, 7, 105, 159,
    163–164, 224

Calhoun, John C., 54
Campaign Contributions, 5, 21,
    27–33, 35, 75–77, 81, 84–89, 120,
    150, 159, 164–166, 169, 179,
    194–195, 197–201, 206, 210, 216,
    218, 221, 224
Campaign Finance Reform, 165, 194
Capone, Alphonse, 61–62, 68–70
Carey, Ron (*see also* Labor Unions,
    International Brotherhood of
    Teamsters), 84–88
Carmichael, Stokely, 146–147
Cart, Charles, 79
Carter, Jimmy, 184, 186, 212, 225
Castro, Fidel (*see also* Cuba), 91
Central Intelligence Agency (CIA),
    107, 198–199
Chambers, Whittaker, 99–102
Chang, David, 28
Chavez, Caesar (*see also* Labor Unions,
    United Farm Workers), 168
Chavez, Linda, 73, 76–77, 83
Cheney, Richard, 159
Chicago, IL, 4–5, 11, 23–24, 34,
    45–48, 61–63, 68–71, 80,
    137–138, 141, 168, 171, 211
China and Chinese influence (*see also*
    Chinagate), 14, 102, 158,
    160–161, 194–205, 222, 224
Chung, Johnny, 197, 203
Citizen Action, 86, 88

civil rights, 8–10, 143, 146, 187–188, 211
Civil Rights Act, 143
Civil War, xi, 35, 59, 132, 161
Clark, Gen. Wesley, 166, 179
Clark, Mark, 23
Clark, Ramsey, 122
Clark, Tom, 69
Clay, Henry, 53–54
Cleveland, Grover, 62
Cleveland, OH, 28, 46, 74, 138–139
Clinton, Hillary Rodham, 8, 10–13, 75, 82, 133, 160, 164–165, 168–169, 173, 179, 197, 205–208, 210, 212–216, 222
    Living History, 205
Clinton, William (Bill), 6–7, 12–14, 27, 106, 158–162, 172–179, 183–186, 191, 193–216
    administration, 4–5, 12, 28, 84–85, 88, 101, 107, 158–163
    impeachment, 6–7, 186, 196, 205, 207
    My Life, 205
    presidential pardons, 172, 174–179, 193–194, 207, 211–212
    sexual affairs, 6, 12–14, 183–184, 187, 194–197, 199, 204–209, 212–214
    Team Clinton, 13, 14
Clinton–Gore '96, 14, 87, 194–195, 198, 200, 203
Coard, Bernard, 92–93
Coia, Arthur E., 74–75, 209–210
Cold War (*see also* USSR), 94, 98, 101
Community Action Programs (CAPs), 147–148
Conboy, Ken, 86–88
Congress, members of
    Rep. Bob Barr (D-GA), 6–7, 13–14
    Rep. Mario Biaggi (D-NY), 25
    Sen. William Blount (TN), 51
    Rep. William H. Boner (D-TN), 30
    Rep. David Bonior (D-MI), 98, 103–104

Sen. Erskine Bowles (D-NC), 167
Sen. Barbara Boxer (D-CA), 93, 133, 222
Rep. Corinne Brown (D-FL), 19–21
Rep. Dan Burton (R-IN), 13–14, 22, 195
Rep. Albert Bustamante (D-TX), 34
Sen. Robert Byrd (D-VA), 105
Rep. Brad Carson (D-OK), 221
Rep. Tony Coelho (D-CA), 26
Rep. Wes Cooley (R-OR), 32
Rep. Gary Condit (D-CA), 135–136
Rep. John Conyers (D-MI), 122–123
Rep. Dan Crane (R-IL), 36
Sen. Alan Cranston (D-CA), 35
Rep. Randall "Duke" Cunningham (R-CA), 6, 22, 33
Sen. Tom Daschle (D-SD), 106, 167, 179, 221
Sen. Dennis DeConcini (D-AZ), 35
Rep. Peter DeFazio (D-OR), 95
Rep. Tom DeLay (R-TX), 20, 33, 196, 217–220, 222, 224–225
Rep. Ron Dellums (D-CA), 93–95, 97
Sen. Everett Dirksen (R-IL), 190
Sen. Christopher Dodd (D-CT), 106, 179, 201
Sen. Robert Dole (R-KS), 201
Sen. Byron Dorgan (D-ND), 221
Sen. Richard Durbin (D-IL), 133, 194–195
Sen. David Durenberger (R-MN), 32
Sen. Jonathan Edwards (D-NC), 7, 49, 107, 166
Rep. Joshua Eilberg (D-PA), 29
Rep. Lane Evans (D-IL), 95
Rep. Sam Farr (D-CA), 103
Rep. Chaka Fattah (D-PA), 122
Rep. Walter Fauntroy (D-D.C.), 30–34
Rep. Daniel J. Flood (D-PA), 29
Rep. Barney Frank (D-MA), 7, 19, 21–22
Rep. Dick Gephardt (D–MO), 166, 179

Sen. John Glenn (D-OH), 35
Sen. Barry Goldwater (R-AZ), 7
Sen. Bob Graham (D-FL), 113
Sen. Richard T. Hanna (D-CA), 36
Sen. Tom Harkin (D-OH), 97, 128, 221
Rep. Wayne L. Hays (D-OH), 24
Sen. Jesse Helms (R-NC), 31–32
Rep. Earl Hilliard (D-AL), 30
Rep. Andres Hinshaw (R-CA), 31
Rep. John Clifton Hinson (R-MS), 31
Sen. George F. Hoar (R-ME), 45, 59–60, 223, 225–226
Rep. Steny Hoyer (D-MD), 221
Rep. Carroll Hubbard Jr. (D-KY), 30
Sen. Kay Bailey Hutchison (R-TX), 218
Rep. Henry Hyde (R-IL), 13–14
Rep. Bill Janklow (R-SD), 7
Rep. William Jefferson (D-LA), 140–141
Rep. John Jenrette (D-SC), 35
Rep. Chris John (D-LA), 221
Rep. Richard Kelly (R-FL), 35
Sen. Edward Kennedy (D-MA) (see Kennedy, Sen. Edward)
Rep. Patrick Kennedy (D-RI), 221
Sen. John Kerry (D-MA), 14, 52, 97, 106, 133, 164, 166–167, 179, 185, 215, 222
Rep. Dale Kildee (D-MI), 221
Rep. Jay C. Kim (R-CA), 32–33
Rep. Gerald Kleczka (D-WI), 25
Rep. Joseph Kolter (D-PA), 34
Rep. Dennis Kucinich (D-OH), 166
Sen. Mary Landrieu (D-LA), 106, 139–140, 179
Sen. Frank Lautenberg (D-NJ), 29, 106
Sen. Patrick Leahy (D-VT), 133
Rep. Raymond Lederer (D-PA), 35
Rep. Barbara Lee (D-PA), 93, 102, 122–123
Rep. Sheila Jackson Lee (D-TX), 160
Sen. Carl Levin (D-MI), 92, 106

Sen. Joe Lieberman (D-CT), 106, 166, 222
Rep. Bob Livingston (R-LA), 7, 13
Rep. Donald Lukens (R-OH), 31
Sen. Mike Mansfield (D-MT), 190
Rep. Nick Mavroules (D-MA), 30
Sen. John McCain (R-AZ), 20, 35
Sen. Joseph McCarthy (R-WI), 101–102
Rep. Bill McCollum (R-FL), 73
Rep. Jim McDermott(D-WA), 103–105, 128
Rep. John F. McFall (D-CA), 29
Rep. Matthew McHugh (D-NY), 97
Rep. Cynthia McKinney (D-GA), 123
Rep. George Miller (D-CA), 128
Sen. Zell Miller (D-GA), 206
Rep. Austin J. Murphy (D-PA), 26
Rep. John M. Murphy (D-NY), 35
Sen. Patty Murray (D-WA), 221
Rep. John Murtha (D-PA), 35
Rep. Michael Myers (D-PA), 35
Rep. Bob Ney (R-OH), 219, 225
Rep. Mary Rose Oakar (D-OH), 34
Rep. Major Owens (D-NY), 95
Sen. Bob Packwood (R-OR), 32
Rep. Carl Perkins (D-KY), 34
Rep. Charles Rangel (D-NY), 221
Sen. Harry Reid (D-NV), 133, 221, 224
Rep. Mel Reynolds (D-IL), 26–27
Rep. Frederick W. Richmond (D-NY), 25
Sen. Don Riegle (D-MI), 35
Rep. Dan Rostenkowski (DvIL), 34
Rep. Edward J. Roybal (D-CA), 29
Rep. Bobby L. Rush (D-IL), 22–24, 172
Rep. Bernie Sanders (D-VT), 95, 97–98
Sen. Charles Schumer (D-NY), 74–76, 170, 175
Rep. Jim Sensenbrenner (R-WI), 27
Rep. Christopher Shays (R–CT), 178

Rep. E. G. "Bud" Shuster (R-PA), 32

Rep. Larry Smith (D-FL), 30

Rep. Nick Smith (R-MI), 33

Rep. Gerry Studds (D-MA), 36

Rep. Pat Swindall (R-GA), 6, 31

Sen. Herman Talmadge (D-GA), 29

Rep. Frank Thompson (D-NJ), 35

Sen. Fred Thompson (R-TN),
    195–197, 200–201

Rep. Mike Thompson (D-CA),
    103–104

Sen. John Thune (R-SD), 167

Sen. Robert Torricelli (D-NJ), 20,
    28, 179

Rep. Jim Traficant (D-OH), 27–28

Rep. Walter Tucker (D-CA), 27

Sen. William Marcy Tweed (NY), 58

Rep. Maxine Waters (D-CA), 95

Rep. Melvin Watt (D-NC), 74

Rep. Henry Waxman (D-CA), 163

Sen. Harrison Williams (D-NJ), 35

Rep. Charles H. Wilson (D-CA), 29

Rep. Lynn Woolsey (D-CA), 98,
    119–121

Rep. Jim Wright (D-TX), 25, 97

Congressional Progressive Caucus
    (CPC), 95, 98, 102–103

conspiracy, ix, 1, 10–13, 18, 25, 28–30,
    34–35, 38, 51–53, 68–69, 71,
    80–82, 94, 122, 127, 137, 139,
    159, 170, 201, 210, 215, 217, 224

Cook, Wesley (see Abu–Jamal, Mumia)

Cook, William, 121, 123

Costello, Frank, 61–64, 70

Coulter, Ann, 98, 100, 217

crime families
  Gambino, 4, 62–63
  Genovese, 74
  Giancana, 4, 69–71, 187–188

Crips, 126–127

Cuba (see also Castro, Fidel), 91–93, 174

Currie, Lauchlin, 100–101

Daley, Mayor Richard (Chicago, IL),
    46–48, 69–71, 137–138

Dallek, Robert, 184, 189

Davis, Martin, 85–87

Dean, Howard, 129, 166

death penalty, 121, 124, 126

Democratic National Committee
    (DNC), xii, 39, 43, 68, 76, 84–88,
    94, 163, 173–174, 178–179,
    194–197, 200–203, 215, 221

Democratic Party
  Founders, x–xii, 4,
  origins and beliefs, xi–xii, 4, 45–60,
    7–8

Detroit, MI, 5, 54, 63, 84, 141–146,
    151–155
  1967 Riots, 141–146
  Devil's Night, 151, 154
  Kerner Commission, 142–143

Dewitt, Deborah, 78

Diamond, Jack "Legs", 28, 62, 67

Diggs, Charles C. Jr., 24–25

Dinyes, Ed, 110–111, 114

Dohrn, Bernardine, 1–2, 8

Dozoretz, Beth, 173–179

drug crime, 112–113, 115, 132–134,
    153, 212–213, 215

Durbin, Dick, 133, 194–195

Dynergy (see also Enron), 162–163

Earle, Ronnie, 33, 217–218

Eastman Gang, 62

Eastman, Monk, 62, 67

El Salvador, 91, 136
  Farabundo Marti National
    Liberation Front (FMLN), 91

election fraud, 3, 22, 26, 27, 32,
    46–48, 59–60, 67

Electoral College, 45, 50

embezzlement, 78–81

Enron, 77, 157–165, 222

Eszterhas, Joe, 191, 204–205

Exner, Judith Campbell, 187–190

extortion, 25, 27, 68, 80, 170

Farrar, John, 39, 41–42

Faulkner, Daniel, 121, 124

Federal Bureau of Investigation (FBI), 2, 18, 23, 28, 35, 38, 69, 72, 74, 80, 82, 100, 137, 140, 151, 170, 174, 176, 187, 189, 199, 202–203, 208
Federal Election Commission (FEC), 21, 76, 164, 179, 201, 210, 216
Federalist Party, xii, 49–50, 53–54
felon voting rights, 5, 128–134,
Fifth Amendment, 116, 177–178, 202, 208
Fino, Ron, 73–75, 209
Flowers, Gennifer, 13, 204, 213–214
Foster, Vince, 207–208
Fourteenth Amendment, 116, 128, 132–133

Gargan, Joseph, 40–42
Garry, Charles, 10, 12
Gaylin, Willard, 118
Giancana, Sam "Mooney", 69, 71, 187–188
Gingrich, Newt, 13, 30–31, 206
Giuliani, Rudolph, 84, 174
Gore, Albert Jr., 7, 26, 105, 131, 171, 174–175, 200, 203, 215
Grant, Ulysses S., 59
  administration, 6, 223
Gray, Daniel, 76–77, 83
Great Society, 147
Grenada (see also Bishop, Maurice), 91–94
  New Jewel Movement, 91
  People's Revolution Army, 92
Guandique, Ingmar, 136
"Guilty as hell, free as a bird", 1–2, 11–12

Hamilton, Alexander, 49–53
Hamilton, William Jr., 85–88
Hampton, Fred, 23–24
Hamza, Khidir, 103, 107
Harding, Warren, 6, 184
Harrison, Benjamin, 62
Hastings, Alcee, 17–20
Hayes, Rutherford B., 58

Hemphill, Gwendolyn, 81–83
Hess, Stephen, 46
Hewitt, Don, 213
Hillman, Sidney, 67–68
Hiss, Alger, 5, 99–102
Ho, Man, 200, 203
Hoffa, Jimmy (see also Labor Unions, International Brotherhood of Teamsters), 84–87
Hoover, J. Edgar, 187–190
House Un–American Activities Committee (HUAC), 100, 152
Hsia, Maria, 199–200, 203
Huang, John, 195, 200–202
Huggins, Ericka, 11
Hughes, Maury, 68–69
Humphreys, Murray "Curley", 71
Hussein, Saddam, 105–106, 122
Hyde, Henry, 13–14

Ickes, Harold Jr., 84–85, 88–89, 101, 204
Ickes, Harold Sr., 67, 101
impeachment
  Samuel Chase, 51
  Bill Clinton, 6–7, 186, 196, 205, 207
  Alcee Hastings, 18–19
Institute for Policy Studies, 95, 97
Inzunza, Ralph Sr., Ralph Jr., and Nick, 169–171

Jackson, Andrew, 53–55
Jackson, Jesse, 122, 128, 212
Jefferson, Thomas, x–xii, 49–54
Johnson, Lyndon B., 48, 142, 146–148, 184, 189, 209
  sexual affairs, 184
Jones, Paula, 13, 196, 209
Judicial Watch, 197, 200–201

Kansas City, MO, 4, 66–69
Kendall, David, 208–209, 215–216
Kennedy, Robert (Bobby), 71, 189–190
Kennedy, John F., 25, 45–48, 64, 70–72, 181–190, 209, 213

1960 election, 4, 37, 45–48, 70–71
Camelot, 46, 182–183, 186, 189
sexual affairs, 183–184, 187–190
Kennedy, Joseph, 4, 70–71, 168,
181–190
Kennedy, Edward (Ted), 3, 7, 14, 19,
38–43, 105–106, 133, 134, 164,
168–169
Chappaquidick/Mary Jo Kopechne,
3, 39–43, 105,
Kennedy Family, 40, 71, 168, 183,
188, 190
Kidan, Adam, 219–220, 223
Kimbro, Warren, 10–11
King, Martin Luther Jr., 143, 146,
187–188, 190
Kyoto Treaty, 161

La Cosa Nostra (*see also* Crime
Families), 75
Labor Unions, 73–90
AFL–CIO, 76, 86, 98
Amalgamated Clothing Workers of
America (ACWA), 67
American Federation of State,
County & Municipal Employee
Unions (AFSCME), 78
Carpenters & Joiners Union, 80
Communication Workers of
America (CWA), 79
Congress of Industrial
Organizations, 67–68
International Brotherhood of
Teamsters (see also Hoffa, Jimmy
and Carey, Ron), 17, 80, 84–88
Hired Truck Program, 80, 137
Laborer's International Union of
North America (LIUNA), 73–75,
80, 209–211
National Education Association
(NEA), 78
Service Employees International
Union (SEIU), 79, 86
United Auto Workers (UAW),
151–152
United Farm Workers (UFW), 168
National Council of Senior Citizens, 86
Washington Teachers Association
(WTU), 81–83
Lansky, Meyer, 61, 63, 70
Lay, Ken, 158–159, 162–163
Lee, Stan, 215
Levy, Chandra, 135–136
Lewinsky, Monica, 6, 12–14, 183,
187, 194–197, 204, 206
Lewis, Anthony, 187–188
Lexis–Nexis, 36, 217
Lincoln, Abraham, xi, 35, 57, 91, 139,
195
Long, Huey, 48, 65–66, 70
Luciano, Lucky, 4, 61–64, 67, 70–71

Manza, Jeff, 131, 134
Marcuse, Herbert, 3, 8
Marxism, 1–2, 9, 12, 91, 94–95, 97,
99, 102–103, 151
mayors
Marion Barry (Washington, D.C.),
3, 37–38, 136
Bill Campbell (Atlanta, GA), 138
Jerome "Jerry" Cavanagh (Detroit,
MI), 143–145
Richard Daley (Chicago, IL), 46–48,
69–71, 137–138
David Dinkins (New York, IL), 122
Saratha Goggins (Cleveland, OH), 139
Kwame Kilpatrick (Detroit, MI), 155
Marc Morial (New Orleans, LA),
139–140
Ray Nagin (New Orleans, LA), 140
Emmanuel Onunwor (Cleveland,
OH), 139
Robert F. Wagner, Jr. (New York,
NY), 150
Jimmy Walker (New York, NY), 63
Michael R. White (Cleveland, OH),
139
Anthony Williams (Washington,
D.C.), 83
Fernando Wood (New York, NY)

(*see also* Tammany Hall), 56–58, 130

Coleman Young (Detroit, MI), 151–155

Mazo, Earl, 46–48

McAuliffe, Terry, 87, 203

McLucas, Lonnie, 10–11

media, bias of, 2–3, 8–9, 12–13, 107, 158, 159, 164, 201, 205

Merry, Anthony, 51

Messerlian, Krikor (*see also* Detroit, MI, 1967 Riots), 141–142, 144–145

Mill, John Stuart, 3, 5

Mills, Cheryl, 176–177

money laundering, 21, 31, 79, 81, 194, 198–200, 212–213, 217

Monroe, Marilyn, 46, 183, 190

Moorer, Adm. Thomas H., 196, 199

Mozart Hall, 57

Murder, xi, 9–12, 23, 37, 51, 55, 67, 91, 97, 99, 102, 106, 111–115, 118, 122–128, 130, 133, 135–136, 145, 219

Myers, Gustavus, 55–57

Nash, Jere, 85, 87

New Deal, xi, 65, 96, 98

New Left, 8, 10

New Orleans, LA, ix, 5, 51–52, 55, 139–140

New York, NY, x, 2, 4, 48–50, 55, 57–58, 62–65, 67, 141, 150, 173, 211, 218–219

Newman, Larry, 181–183, 188–189

Newton, Huey, 93, 148

Nicaragua (*see also* Ortega, Daniel), 91, 93, 97–98

Sandinista Liberation Front, 91, 97

Nitti, Frank (*see also* Capone, Alphonse), 68–69

Nixon, Richard, 6–7, 45–48, 73, 100, 203–204, 209, 225

Nolan, Beth, 175–176

North Korea, 28, 91, 102

November Group, The, 85–86

Olson, Barbara, 206, 209, 211

O'Rourke, P. J., 20, 149

Ortega, Daniel (*see also* Nicaragua), 97–98

Owens, Albert, 124–125

Paolella, Joseph, 183, 189

Patriarca, Raymond, 74, 210

Paul, Peter, 215–216

Pearson, Stewart, 119

Pelosi, Nancy, 14, 167–168, 222

Pendergast, James and Tom, 65–69

Phan, Tina, 119–120

Philadelphia, PA, 5, 121, 123–124, 136–137

Podesta, John, 175–176, 193–194, 204

police corruption, 56, 62, 66, 70, 140, 155, 170

Political Action Committees (PACs), 74, 75, 77, 160, 164, 165, 210, 211

Political Graveyard, 19–20, 33, 36

political machines

Chicago, IL, 4–5, 45–48, 61–63, 68–71, 137–138

Kansas City, MO, 4, 66–69

New Orleans, LA, 139–140

New York, NY, x, 4, 50, 55

Ponte, Lowell, 109, 134

Powers, Dave, 182, 189

pro–criminal policies, 109–134

Prohibition, 62, 70–71

Project Vote, 86

prostitutes, prostitution, 3, 19, 56, 66, 182

Quinn, Jack, 175–177

racketeering, 25, 62, 75, 80, 84–85, 138, 174

Rackley, Alex (*see also* Black Panthers), 9–12, 23

rape and sexual offense, 111, 114–115, 118–120, 126, 132, 136, 141, 168, 207

Rapkin, Judge Harry, 111–118

Reagan, Ronald, 92–93, 97–98, 171, 174, 185, 225
Reconstruction, 58, 132–133
Red States, 166
Reed, Ralph, 219, 225
Reno, Janet, 21, 88, 99, 174, 196, 199, 203, 224
Revolutionary War, 49, 51, 54
Riady, James (*see also* Chinagate), 195, 203
Rich, Denise, 173–179
Rich, Marc, 173–179, 194, 212, 223
Rivers, Dorothy, 171–172
Romano, Frank and Tom, 17–18
Rometsch, Ellen, 189–190
Roosevelt, Eleanor, 67, 186
Roosevelt, Franklin Delano, xi, 4, 61–68, 98–101, 186–187, 209
Rothstein, Arnold, 62–63
Rutherford, Lucy Mercer, 186

Sams, George Jr. (*see also* Black Panthers), 10
San Diego, CA, 169–170, 203
Sandinista (*see also* Ortega, Daniel), 91, 97
Sandler, Herb and Marion, 165, 171–172
scandals
  ABSCAM, 34–35
  Chinagate, 14, 194–204, 222, 224
    Thompson Hearings, 195–202
    Loral Corporation, 198
  Enron, 151–165
  Filegate, 208
  House Bank, 34
  House Page, 36
  House Post Office, 34
  Keating Five, 35
  Koreagate, 35–36
  Monigate, 6, 12–14, 183, 187, 194–197, 204, 206
  Pardongate, 172–179, 193–194, 207, 212
  Teapot Dome, 6

Travelgate, 194, 207–208
Watergate, 6
Whiskey Ring, 6
Whitewater, 168–169, 194, 195, 207
Scanlon, Michael, 219, 223
Scott, Carlottia, 194
Seabury, Samuel, 63–64
Seale, Bobby (*see also* Black Panthers), 9–11, 148
Secret Service, 181–183, 188, 201
segregation, 49, 66, 132, 146
sexual misconduct, 13–14, 19, 22, 24, 27, 31–32, 36, 37, 184
Seymour, Horatio, 57–58
Shriver, Sargent (*see also* Kennedy Family), 46, 148
Sinatra, Frank, 71, 188
Smith, Bettye (*see also* Barry, Marion), 38
Smith, Gov. Al (D–NY), 61–64
Smith, Joseph P., 110–118
socialism, 95–99, 102–103
Socialist Organizations
  Communisty Party USA, 99
  Democratic Socialists of America (DSA), 95–98, 103
  National Negro Labor Council (NNLC), 152
Soros, George, 165, 217
Sowell, Thomas, 3, 118, 143
Sparer, Edward, 150
Starr, Kenneth (*see also* Whitewatergate), 196, 204–205
Stephanopolous, George, 213–214
Suicide, 25, 114, 135, 187, 207
Sullivan, "Big Tim" (*see also* Tammany Hall), 62

Talmadge, Eugene, 49, 66
Tammany Hall, 4, 48–50, 55–58, 62–64, 130
tax law violation, 21, 25, 27, 30, 34, 56, 66–67, 81, 137, 168, 171–172, 174, 179, 212
Thompson, Mike, 103–104

Tomczak, Donald, 81, 137–138
Treason, 4–5, 49, 52–55, 91–108
Trie, Yah Lin "Charlie" (*see also* Chinagate), 198, 202–203
Tripp, Linda, 13, 181, 204
Truman, Harry, 4, 64, 67–69, 72, 98, 100, 151, 209
Tweed, Boss (*see also* Tammany Hall), 48, 58
Two Americas, 5, 7

Uggen, Christopher, 130–131, 134
United Nations, 103, 104, 120, 179
USSR (*see also* Cold War), 91, 93

Vietnam War, 1, 3, 33, 185, 215
Vilsack, Gov. Tom (D-IA), 129–130
Vitullo-Martin, Julia, 151, 154
vote peddling, 22, 48
voter amnesia, 14, 38, 43

Voting Rights Act, 32, 143, 146

Walker, Richard Lee, 114
War Hawks, 54
Warner, Gov. Mark (D-VA), 130
Washington, George, xi–xii, 7, 49, 51
Washington, D.C., 37, 54, 133, 135–136, 141, 183, 189, 219, 222
weapons violations, 23–24, 112–113, 116, 198–199, 205
Weather Underground, 1–2, 11
White, U. S. Attorney Mary Jo, 28, 84, 88
Wilkinson, General James, 52–53
Williams, Stanley "Tookie", 124–127
witch hunt, 6, 101, 201
Woodward, Bob, 143, 195

Yang, Robert (*see also* Williams, Stanley "Tookie"), 125